# Christ Alive and at Large

Other titles in the Canterbury Studies in Spiritual Theology series:

*Law and Revelation: Richard Hooker and His Writings*
Edited by Raymond Chapman

*Heaven in Ordinary: George Herbert and His Writings*
Edited by Philip Sheldrake

*Before the King's Majesty: Lancelot Andrewes and His Writings*
Edited by Raymond Chapman

*Happiness and Holiness: Selected Writings by Thomas Traherne*
Edited by Denise Inge

*The Sacramental Life: A Gregory Dix Reader*
Edited and introduced by Simon Jones

*To Build Christ's Kingdom: F. D. Maurice and His Writings*
Edited and introduced by Jeremy Morris

*Firmly I Believe: An Oxford Movement Reader*
Edited by Raymond Chapman

*The Truth-Seeking Heart: An Austin Farrer Reader*
Edited by Ann Loades and Robert MacSwain

*God Truly Worshipped: Thomas Cranmer and His Writings*
Edited by Jonathan Dean

CANTERBURY STUDIES IN SPIRITUAL THEOLOGY

# Christ Alive and at Large

*Unpublished Writings of C. F. D. Moule*

*Edited and Introduced by*
Robert Morgan and Patrick Moule

CANTERBURY
PRESS

Norwich

© Patrick Moule and Robert Morgan 2010

Published in 2010 by Canterbury Press Norwich
Editorial office
13–17 Long Lane,
London, EC1A 9PN, UK

Canterbury Press Norwich is an imprint of Hymns Ancient and Modern Ltd
(a registered charity)
13a Hellesdon Park Road, Norwich, Norfolk, NR6 5DR

www.scm-canterburypress.co.uk

British Library Cataloguing in Publication data

A catalogue record for this book is available
from the British Library

ISBN 978-1-84825-018-5

Originated by The Manila Typesetting Company
Printed and bound by
CPI Antony Rowe, Chippenham, SN14 6LH

# Contents

*Preface*                                                                   ix
PATRICK MOULE

**Part 1 Introduction to the Life and Work**
**of Charles F. D. Moule**                                          1

Sermon for the Life and Work of the
Revd Prof. C. F. D. Moule                                          3
ROWAN WILLIAMS

The Spirituality and New Testament Theology
of Charlie Moule                                                          8
ROBERT MORGAN

**Part 2 Writings of Charles F. D. Moule**                    91

| 1 | **The Energy of God: The Meaning of Holy Week** | 93 |
| 1 | The problem of evil | 93 |
| 2 | The problem of good | 96 |
| 3 | The divine energy | 99 |
| 4 | The upper room | 103 |
| 5 | The Good Friday story | 105 |
| 6 | Holy Saturday | 109 |

| 2 | **Biblical Theology** | 111 |
| 1 | Divine action | 111 |
| 2 | In face of the cross (Hebrews 12.2) | 112 |
| 3 | Propitiation | 113 |
| 4 | The Spirit | 115 |
| 5 | The Son of Man | 116 |
| 6 | The beatitudes | 117 |

7   A difficult parable: Matthew 18.21–35                120
8   Self-interest in sayings attributed to Jesus         121
9   Criticisms of St Paul                                122
10  Mary the Mother of Jesus Christ: A response
    to the Report of the Anglican–Roman Catholic
    International Commission                              131
11  Judas Iscariot                                       134
12  Alleged anti-Semitism in the New Testament           136

**3   Christian Practice and Belief**                    **141**
1   What constitutes a distinctively Christian
    faith and practice?                                  141
2   The Bible and the guidance of God                    143
3   Prayer: a non-interventionist 'miracle'              144
4   Petitionary prayer                                   145
5   The sacraments                                       147
6   The New Testament and Eucharistic thought            148
7   Solitary and collective in the Christian Church      152
8   Sunday                                               153
9   After death, what?                                   155
10  Life after death                                     157
11  Advent                                               159
12  The Great Tribunal                                   161
13  The resurrection of Jesus                            163
14  Easter                                               164
15  The language of Christian experience                 166
16  The incarnation of God in Jesus Christ               168
17  Incarnation – climax of creative love                169
18  The Christian doctrine of the Trinity                175
19  The problem of evil: some tentative thoughts
    of a perplexed Bible-reader                          180
20  Exorcism                                             181
21  Sacrifice and propitiation – do the words belong
    in the proclaiming of the Christian gospel?          183
22  On the cost of reconciliation (2 Corinthians 5.19)   185
23  Greed as wanting more                                187
24  Repentance as against expressions of regret          187
25  The treatment of offenders                           188

26  Christianity among world religions 190
27  Gospel truth 191
28  Religion 197

**4  Sermons** 199
1  The Sunday next before Advent. Yetminster, 1995 199
2  Epiphany. Winchester, 1991 202
3  The Conversion of St Paul. Cambridge, 1998 205
4  The Third Sunday before Lent:
   Septuagesima. Pevensey, 2003 207
5  Palm Sunday.  Chetnole, 2000 210
6  'Songs of Praise'. Chetnole, 1996 212
7  St Jude. Clare College, 2004 215

**Epilogue: Salute to the White Doves** 219

# Preface

## PATRICK MOULE

Charlie Moule lived for most of his life in college, at Cambridge: as a student at Emmanuel and Ridley Hall (1927–33), a further year as tutor at Ridley, and after a curacy in Rugby back at Ridley as Vice-Principal (1936–44), at Clare as Dean (1944–51) and Lady Margaret's Professor (1951–76), and again in Ridley Hall teaching New Testament (1976–81). But a long-standing promise took him on retirement to the East Sussex coast, and from 1981 to 2002 he lived in Pevensey, next door to Bishop Stanley Betts, until 2003. Early in 2003 he underwent in Eastbourne Hospital major surgery for cancer, followed by a full course of radiotherapy at Brighton, 20 miles away. My brother Henry and I visited him at Eastbourne the day after the operation, expecting to find him in a bad way – but found him in a chair by the bed, connected to various tubes, and with, beside him on the table, his Greek Testament and the latest Harry Potter. Characteristically he obtained much enjoyment from his daily trips to Brighton through the flowery lanes of East Sussex with volunteer drivers and a car-load of other patients; but with the death of Stanley and the sheer effort of maintaining himself in his own house he realized by the autumn that the time to move into a care home had come. We were able soon to find a room for him at the Old Vicarage at Leigh, three miles from us at Yetminster, in Dorset, and he drove down with us in September, saying that he had always wanted to live in Dorset and asking several times if we had entered the county yet!

It pleased him greatly that his room had been the Vicar's study, and one faithful visitor pleased him still more by saying that she had been prepared for confirmation in that very room. He could look out of his window, where he spent hours every day at his desk reading, writing letters to friends all over the world, dealing with more post than the Home had ever seen and receiving a steady stream of visitors from near and far; and enjoy the beautifully kept garden, the ever-changing trees and distant hills and all the comings and goings. Until the last week of his life, at the end of September 2007, he went to church every Sunday either in Leigh or in Yetminster; at first hobbling determinedly from car to pew and latterly consenting to ride in a wheelchair. He greatly enjoyed drives through the Dorset countryside, complaining about his failing eyesight but spotting at long range interesting birds which we would either have missed completely or else have seen much later. In the summer he enjoyed our garden and occasional small parties – breakfast after early service, in the garden in warm weather; dinner for his birthdays right up to the 98th; supper round the fire on Christmas Eve. He made many local friends and people he didn't know at all felt uplifted when he was with them in church.

Quite early on, talking to the Rector, he said that he felt that his useful life was over. The Rector disagreed and urged him to decide what useful task he ought now to perform. The first fruits of this challenge were some of the essays included here under the title 'Christian Practice and Belief'. As he went on, becoming physically more dependent on the devoted care at the Home but not at all diminished in mental command, he produced various other little pieces, prompted by questions we asked him, items of news or comment in the paper that caught his eye, a Lent course we were having difficulty with ('Beatitudes'), or conversations with other residents ('Judas Iscariot'). These we found among his papers when he died and I have transcribed them in the confident hope that many beyond those who knew him personally will profit from and enjoy the simply expressed manifestations of the wisdom and knowledge of great age. I have added to them a few self-explanatory unpublished pieces from earlier days, including sermons in our local churches. 'And can it be' (below, p. 212, Songs of Praise) is remembered still, and when we were planning his local Thanksgiving Service, several people said that that great Wesley hymn must certainly be sung, as it was with great gusto.

I am very grateful to Charlie's old and dear friend, the Revd Bob Morgan, who visited him often and preached at that service, for sorting out and preparing these pieces for publication, and to Charlie's pupil and successor, the late Professor Graham Stanton, for supporting the project so wholeheartedly in his own last months, sharing our hope that it would contribute to the scholarship fund in Charlie's memory. I hope that these last reflections of Charlie will give insight into some of his teaching and questions, sometimes quite robustly expressed at the end of that remarkable life.

*Yetminster*

# PART I

# Introduction to the Life and Work of Charles F. D. Moule

# Sermon for the Life and Work of the Revd Prof. C. F. D. Moule

## ROWAN WILLIAMS

Saturday, 9 February 2008
*Thanksgiving Service at Great St Mary's, Cambridge*

It's sometimes said that in the Church of England a person's spiritual seriousness can be calculated in inverse proportion to the length of their entry in Crockford's Clerical Directory; it's something to do with the degree to which someone has been able to put down roots and to overcome that restlessness which is part of the curse of Adam's fallen children. And although Charlie Moule's entry in Crockford's is extended somewhat by academic and incidental honours, the bare bones of a biography are very soon related; and we might well think of his life as making the point pretty sharply. Greatness in the Kingdom of Heaven, the kind of greatness spelled out in that luminous passage from Ecclesiasticus (39.1–11) which is so unmistakeable a portrait of our beloved friend, is at least as much to do with patience, the devoting of the soul to a definite place and task and group of people, as it is to do with the volume of business (and, it's tempting to say, the busyness of volumes) or the variegated powers and distinctions achieved in a life.

Charlie's roots lay in Dorset, in a family deeply anchored in the life of the Church of England, a family which had befriended and encouraged the young Thomas Hardy, and which produced several churchmen of distinction, including a deeply loved Bishop of Durham. But Charlie's direct origins were, of course, in China, where his parents were missionaries; if anyone is tempted to think of him as having had a narrow or parochial existence, it's essential to remember that this was a central part of his inheritance. And readers of what is perhaps his greatest work, *The Origin of Christology*, will pick up the echoes of that universal perspective in the reflections, typically both bold and painstaking,

3

on the capacity of Christ to speak to and transform lives in other faiths and cultures that do not name him.

After his first studies at Emmanuel and his immediate post-ordination posting, Charlie left Cambridge only for a brief curacy in Rugby. When he returned in 1936 to Ridley Hall, where he had already both trained for ordination and taught for a year, it was the beginning of a long and unbroken residence. Humphrey Carpenter wrote, in his biography of Tolkien, that after Tolkien's appointment to the Chair of Anglo-Saxon at Oxford in 1925, 'you could say, nothing else really happened'. It would be tempting to say that, especially after Charlie's election as Dean of Clare in 1944, nothing else happened. But that would, of course, be to accept another standard than the 'Crockford's test' with which I began.

What happened in those long Cambridge years – and beyond too, in retirement in Sussex and Dorset – was the shaping of countless lives not only in scholarship but in discipleship. It is impossible to guess how many people's assumptions about the relation of scholarship to discipleship were turned upside down by Charlie – by his quiet insistence on prayer at the beginning of lecture courses, by the utterly engaged and constructive tone of so much of his writing, but above all by his personal example. There was the apparently limitless generosity with his time and attention for students: I am only one of scores who found their way to his rooms in Clare on Tuesday evenings to discuss the sort of issues in New Testament studies that preoccupied us and to discover that so much of what we were struggling and arguing about could be held within a calm and prayerful perspective, within the hugely bigger intellectual and spiritual world that Charlie lived in. And there was the sheer manner of the man: the unforced humility, the shy warmth – and sometimes, at the most unintentionally comic level, the way in which he would make it perfectly clear to you that someone or other's book wasn't really worth bothering with: 'Of course, it's a monument of careful work by a first class scholar, with all kinds of suggestive aspects, and I *so* wish I could persuade myself that it was true . . .'

Because the gentleness did conceal a toughness of theological and exegetical principle that could take you aback on occasion; it appears, classically, in one of the footnotes to the Christology book where Charlie reiterates his allegiance to his particular interpretation of the much contested expression 'Son of Man': 'the fact that I am still in a small minority makes me wonder what is wrong with it. But I can, so far, not find the flaw'. So much of him is in those words: the candid admission that his argument has not carried the day, the real readiness to think he is wrong, but also the equally candid assertion that he can't see that he *is,* failing better arguments against. And he could be no less firm about aspects of liturgy of which he disapproved: his theology was never angular or sectarian (remember his generous support of the liturgical experiments of his successor as Dean of Clare, John Robinson), but there was a clear, eirenic but firm foundation in Protestant principle that made him very uneasy with what he regarded as the drip-feed of some sorts of Catholicizing devotion into Anglican practice. He always insisted (as he did in his beautiful brief work on the Holy Spirit, published not long after his retirement) that you blessed people not things; he was always uncomfortable with the spirituality of the Three Hours on Good Friday, insisting that this was the day above all days when a spirituality of the imitation of Christ was inappropriate, since you were celebrating what Christ alone and unrepeatably had done.

And that takes us back to what happened in those long and apparently quiet years in Clare, in the Margaret Chair, in wonderfully active retirement in Ridley once again. What happened was Christ. Everything Charlie wrote about the New Testament began from the uncompromising and unqualified insistence that we could understand nothing about the text unless we understood that it was rooted in *contact* with Jesus; not memory or inspiration but contact. Paul, he writes, 'speaks of Christian life as lived in an area which is Christ' (*Origin of Christology*, p. 95): what the Spirit does (and he was always cautious about any theology that threatened to define the Spirit in abstraction from Christ) is to 'make manifest' the reality of Christ (p. 104), so that Christ is both the territory Christians inhabit and the one who inhabits it in and with us, still personal yet never just individual, realizing his infinite self in the finite soul and body, in the shared life of believers, 'growing' himself, you could say, towards the infinite and so never-surpassed scope of his eternal relation with the Father.

This is what Charlie taught, consistently and vividly; he taught, more, he communicated, a way of reading the New Testament whole in this perspective – which was why those lectures on New Testament theology were crowded, even (unthinkable now) on Saturday mornings. But it was also what was going on in him. As in every holy person, living in the Spirit, Christ was happening in him. And Christ can happen in his disciples and lovers because he is risen, with utter literalness in the sense that there is no dead body to mark the memory of someone who has gone into the past, only the unqualified and limitless life that now 'contacts' us in the Spirit. No writer in the New Testament speaks of Jesus otherwise than as living; none of them can think of him except as one who is in the fullest sense contemporary. We can't get behind that, Charlie insisted: Jesus belongs in the present and, just as significant, in the future, in the place where God's purposes for creation are consummated. So he belongs wherever any Christian lives in the faith, hope and love that the Spirit gives: what happens where there is faith, hope and love is Jesus.

'Nothing else happened'; nothing but Christ alive and at large (to use the Masefield phrase he loved) in Clare and Ridley and so many other places through the medium of Charlie's discipleship; alive and at large in the brief but luminous books, and in countless sermons and lectures and addresses. He maintained that, in effect, you couldn't understand what the gospel of either the incarnation or the resurrection claimed unless you had been touched by the life of the one who is always and everywhere 'available and accessible' (p. 121). And part of that touch is always going to be in the lives of others who have been touched in the same way. We live because Christ lives, says Saint John; and so one of the many ways in which we know Christ lives is to see his disciples and friends living. And that was why Charlie preached the resurrection so consistently, by being Charlie.

He could preach it verbally in some surprising ways. Again and again in his writing, he will turn to the poets and other imaginative geniuses for help; but not many would have the audacity to take one of Housman's most poignant agnostic poems and turn it on its head. As he concludes his chapter on 'The scope of the death of Christ' in *Origin* (pp. 125–6), he writes: 'Those in every generation from then till now who know [Jesus] alive are able to turn A. E. Housman's bitterly ironical "Easter Hymn" into a genuine invocation:

If in that Syrian garden, ages slain,
You sleep, and know not you are dead in vain,
Nor even in dreams behold how dark and bright
Ascends in smoke and fire by day and night
The hate you died to quench and could but fan,
Sleep well and see no morning, son of man.
But if, the grave rent and the stone rolled by,
At the right hand of majesty on high
You sit, and sitting so remember yet
Your tears, your agony and bloody sweat,
Your cross and passion and the life you gave,
Bow hither out of heaven and see and save.'

Charlie goes on:

If we ask what are the doctrinal implications of this understanding of Christ as making himself available, through his death, to all men, the answer is that they constitute one more factor in a Christology which finds in Christ not just an example but the Mediator between God and Man. It means, if it is justified by the evidence, more than that Jesus Christ *indicates* how a man may become rightly related to other men in an ideal society. It means that Jesus Christ, crucified and raised from among the dead, actually *is*, or *constitutes* that ideal society.

Well, here we are today as very unideal members of that same ideal society; but because we are just that, Christ happens here. And in his happening here, we stand alongside Charlie and all the faithful departed, united in one prayer, one act of turning towards the Father, living 'in an area which is Christ'. And we thank God for the happening of Jesus crucified and risen in the life of our dear friend – in that outwardly even and uneventful life, in which so much happened for the enrichment, the conversion and the joy of all of us, in which the risen Lord made living contact with us. Thanks be to God who gives us the victory in Jesus Christ.

# Introduction

# The Spirituality and New Testament Theology of Charlie Moule

### ROBERT MORGAN

## Youth

Charles Francis Digby Moule was born on 3 December 1908 in the Church Missionary Society compound in Hangchow (Hangzhou), a city on the shores of the famous West Lake, south of Shanghai, in the house where his father Henry William Moule (1871–1953) had been born, and where his grandfather George Evans Moule (1828–1912) had been Bishop in Mid-China from 1880 to 1906. The missionary Moules were part of a larger clerical clan stemming from the Bishop's father, Henry Moule (1801–77), over 50 years evangelical vicar of Fordington in Dorset. Some of the vicar's eight sons distinguished themselves in classical scholarship no less than in evangelical piety, two of them at Cambridge. Charlie senior (1834–1921) was a tutor at Corpus Christi College, and Handley (1841–1920) Fellow of Trinity and first Principal of Ridley Hall, founded in 1879 on 'evangelical principles', then Norissian Professor of Divinity before succeeding Westcott as Bishop of Durham in 1901. Another of the sons was an influence on the young Thomas Hardy in Dorset, and the family apparently provided models for two of Hardy's characters. Bishop George in Hangchow was also scholarly, and translated the Prayer Book into Chinese.

Among the next generation, Charlie's father had been a prize-winning classical scholar of Corpus and became a Hebraist and a Sinologist. Unlike his younger brother, Arthur, he did not publish much, but after his death Charlie saw one of his New Testament exegetical suggestions into print. Arthur (1873–1957), seventh child of Bishop George, returned from China in 1908, became vicar of Trumpington in 1918, and was professor of Chinese at Cambridge from 1933 to 1938.

Charlie's two elder brothers were sent back to England for schooling but he himself was taught at home, initially by his mother, Laura née

Pope, who had come out to China independently, also with the Church Missionary Society. He was then taught classics by his father. His childhood was happy, but cut off from other children. In 1920 the family returned to England, and Charlie followed his brothers to Weymouth College, first as a day boy and then as a boarder, when his father became vicar of Damerham in Hampshire.

In the absence of more than a few lines of autobiography one may perhaps catch the flavour of Charlie's early years from another highly intelligent and sensitive child of CMS missionaries, later a friend and collaborator. Max Warren was four years Charlie's senior, and also had two older brothers at boarding school in Britain while he himself was taught at home by his mother in India before returning to Ireland and England for prep school and public school and Cambridge and becoming briefly a lay missionary in Nigeria. An outstanding church leader, he was vicar of Holy Trinity, Cambridge, while Charlie was Vice-Principal of Ridley Hall (and assisting across the market at the University Church), and an influential General Secretary of CMS (1942–63).

In his autobiography *Crowded Canvas* Max Warren writes:

> It was, I suppose, a lonely childhood, though I was never conscious of loneliness. However, being forced to be somewhat self-contained I developed a shyness which has, in various ways, inhibited me ever since. Yet, at the same time it stimulated my imagination, almost too much so, for I lived largely with my own thoughts . . .[1]

This 'secure and happy childhood . . . never felt strange and alien', and he could mix with local children in British India, unlike Charlie behind barricades in China. Both boys read a lot, and Charlie could have agreed with Max that 'reading has always been for me a form of listening. Good writing has an independent life of its own.'[2] A close friend of them both, Max Warren's biographer, F. W. Dillistone ('Dilly'), wrote of Warren that

> the boy who was often alone in the security of his home . . . gradually built up an interior room of his own, into which he could withdraw with his own thoughts and imaginings at any time. No one in later

---

1 Max Warren, 1974, *Crowded Canvas: Some Experiences of a Lifetime*, London: Hodder & Stoughton, p. 18.

2 *Ibid.*

years could have treated his friends more generously in opening his heart to them in conversation or correspondence. Yet there was always the sanctum, carefully guarded, into which no other human being was allowed to enter . . .[3]

If that is true of the family man in a near ideal Christian marriage, it may be even more true of the friend who probably never contemplated matrimony.

Before Charlie was born, his senior namesake at Corpus had in 1892 been replaced as tutor, and the college began to abandon its evangelical traditions for a more Anglo-catholic ethos. Instead of following their father there, Edward, George and in 1927 Charlie, therefore became instead scholars of Emmanuel College, Cambridge, reading for the Classical Tripos. Charlie obtained his double first with a distinction in Greek verse and special merit in literature (1931) before studying theology mostly on his own while preparing for ordination at Ridley Hall under Paul Gibson, and while starting to teach there in 1933 as a deacon and curate at Saint Mark's. His theological education was partly funded by winning several university prizes, the Evans Prize for knowledge of Greek and Latin patristic texts, the Jeremie Septuagint Prize, and the prestigious Crosse Scholarship, where the runner-up was another serious young evangelical Donald Coggan, who was studying oriental languages at St John's College.

Ridley Hall was to become a large part of Charlie's life. His initial three years there were followed by a curacy at Rugby. This, rather than a Ph.D., was the normal path for future theological teachers in England, pastoral experience and broader reading being thought more useful than research. Even those who went from theological college teaching to become Oxford academic chaplains or Cambridge deans would be combining teaching with pastoral work. In 1936 Charlie returned to Ridley as Vice-Principal, where he remained until in 1944 he was elected to a Fellowship at Clare College and succeeded Telfer as Dean. Ridley students could continue to attend his lectures in the Divinity School. After the usual Cambridge three-year probationary assistant lectureship he became University Lecturer in 1947 and Lady Margaret's Professor in 1951. During these years he was a member of the Council of Ridley (1950–1976), its chairman from March 1972 to December 1976, and a friend and confidant of successive principals. As professor

---

3 F. W. Dillistone, 1980, *Into All the World: A Biography of Max Warren*, London: Hodder & Stougton, p.12.

he remained a Fellow of Clare, living in college. When after 25 years in the chair he retired in 1976, he moved back into Ridley for a further four years' teaching New Testament.

The better documented parallel experience of Max Warren at Ridley throws light on Cambridge religious life around 1930, with its strong interest in overseas missions. (Stephen Neill (1900–84), another rising star of 1920s evangelicalism and later friend of Charlie, had already gone to India as a missionary in 1926, while Charlie was still at school.) Warren won the Lightfoot scholarship and obtained a 'double first' in history and theology (ecclesiastical history) at Jesus College. Then, 'throughout my time at Ridley I got up every morning at 6 a.m. to spend an hour with my Bible. As the guide to my study I took 3 commentaries of Bishop Handley Moule . . .'. These 'taught me in the quiet of those early mornings to listen for the personal voice of God speaking to me as a person and asking for a personal response . . . I listened to the Lord "who called me by my name".'[4]

One advantage in staying at Cambridge for initial theological training was that ordinands heard some excellent lectures. E. C. Hoskyns, a great influence on Warren's contemporary Michael Ramsey at Magdalene, was back in Cambridge with a distinguished war record, and with the then Ridley principal Tait 'taught me to read the Bible as a scholar, though always as a scholar on his knees'.[5] Warren soon came to 'believe there is no substitute for the grounding in the conviction that here is a book out of which at any time and in any circumstance I meet the God who speaks to me and who demands my attention and response'.[6]

Charlie's experience at Ridley after also being drawn to theology while reading (like Warren and Coggan) a different subject was slightly different. Tait had been succeeded as principal by Paul Gibson, lately returned from 18 years as a CMS missionary in Sri Lanka (then still Ceylon). It is also striking that Charlie never attended a lecture by the Anglo-catholic Hoskyns, whose course on Theology and Ethics of the New Testament he would later (in 1952) inherit from Michael Ramsey. And he was never an admirer of his great uncle Handley, whom he met only once as a boy on his return from China in 1920. But in some respects his experience probably did match Max Warren's. In Gordon Wakefield's *Dictionary of Christian Spirituality* (1983) a later principal of Ridley Hall, Michael Hennell, begins his article 'Evangelical

---

4 Warren, *Crowded Canvas* p., 48.
5 *Ibid.*
6 *Ibid.*

Spirituality' with a claim that its 'main ingredients . . . have always been early rising, prayer and Bible study'. At any rate, early rising to 'read the Bible as a scholar, though always as a scholar on his knees' (below, p. 175) became the most characteristic feature of Charlie's 'spirituality'.

Despite its occurrence in this sense as early as the seventeenth century, the word 'spirituality' is not the word evangelicals around 1930 would use in this context. It was more current among Roman and Anglo-catholics, and subsequently used also with reference to other religions and 'new age' religiosity. But it has become a general term since the 1960s, and there clearly is a distinctive 'evangelical spirituality', which was part of Charlie's formation and remained central to his devotional life. Hennell refers to Wilberforce spending two hours each day before breakfast praying and studying the Bible. Charlie's later practice was to read a chapter of the Old Testament in Hebrew and of the New Testament in Greek early each morning, working right through each Testament. The New Testament part of that programme is not surprising, and he was happy to recommend it to others. The Old Testament part was no doubt good for his Hebrew and might on these grounds be recommended to any New Testament scholar, but it is harder to imagine what religious benefits might accrue from it on some days. While Charlie was enough of a biblical theologian to understand how deeply the New Testament is rooted in the Old, and more than enough of a linguist to appreciate the Semitisms of the Septuagint and the New Testament, he was also enough of a liberal Protestant to be critical of the Old Testament where he thought it fell morally and religiously short when measured by its fulfilment in the gospel. The imprecatory psalms troubled him, and he doubtless agreed with Max Warren that Genesis 38 is a 'horribly sordid story' whose inclusion in Holy Writ is hard to justify.[7] Both these devout ordinands rejected the theory of biblical inerrancy espoused by many of their hardline friends in the Christian Union (CICCU). For Charlie, to read the Bible was never to read it uncritically. He would himself read even the least palatable parts again and again in Hebrew, but could not recommend them being read in church. Years later he could still protest (in an aside to a scholarly discussion) about 'the indiscriminate use in certain branches of Christian worship of the entire Psalter, including the fiercely nationalist and bloodthirsty songs . . . '.[8]

---

7 Dillistone, *Warren*, p. 25.

8 C. F. D. Moule, 1962, *The Birth of the New Testament*, London: Black, p. 17n.

To call him something of a 'liberal Protestant' as well as an evangelical suggests how Ridley in 1931-4 had come to reinterpret the 'evangelical principles' on which it had been founded, and had become a standard-bearer of 'liberal evangelicalism'. The main influence on Charlie at this time, as his vocation deepened, was undoubtedly its Principal (from 1927 to 1945). Paul Gibson's emphasis upon personal categories in theology, with personal relationships providing the foundational analogy for our relationship with God, was to remain the hallmark of Charlie's spirituality, ethics and biblical theology. He was proud to call himself a Protestant, and both his critical sharpness and liberality of spirit make it absurd to deny him the adjective 'liberal', but calling him a 'liberal Protestant' is misleading insofar as it implies doctrinal deviation from orthodox Christianity. That would be further from his intentions than from his conclusions. Though doctrinally and critically liberal, Charlie was far from being a Harnack, the archetypal liberal Protestant scholar who was much translated and widely appreciated in England for his relatively conservative conclusions on the New Testament, but who sat light to the Old Testament and to the patristic doctrinal development which he labelled 'the hellenization of Christianity'. The doctrines of the Trinity and incarnation remained axiomatic for Charlie, even in the 1960s and 1970s when some of his closest friends and colleagues were becoming more liberal, though 'the incarnation' could involve a view of Jesus fairly close to Harnack's 'historical' Jesus drawn from the Synoptic Gospels. It insisted on the presence of God in Jesus, making him more than a prophet or teacher pointing to God, but for liberal evangelicals did not primarily evoke the Johannine portrait crystallized in patristic orthodoxy and 1920s Anglo-catholicism. The older notion of a 'historical biblical' Jesus that covers a wide spectrum of modern portraits is perhaps apposite here.

The Christianity of Harnack's *What is Christianity?* (ET 1901), largely based on the Gospel history and its reception, had influenced Charlie's (from 1935) senior colleague and inspiration, C. H. Dodd, but both shared far more of what Harnack affirmed than what he denied. English (and Welsh) liberalism saw less of a gulf between John and the Synoptic Gospels than German scholars who remained in thrall to Strauss and Baur even when modifying these pioneers' conclusions. Charlie is more appropriately labelled a 'liberal evangelical' than 'liberal Protestant', whether of the pre-First World War German variety or of the more traditional Anglican kind, represented in 1920s England by parts of the Modern Churchmen's Union. Yet, a few weeks before he died, he wrote to the editor of *The Tablet* on 8 July 2007, as follows: 'In the *Tablet* for 30 June, Theo Hobson contrasts Liberal Protestantism with "the tighter, tougher, more assertive alternatives", Evangelicalism and Roman Catholicism. What matters, however, is truth, not merely assertiveness as such. Liberal Protestantism holds that the truth is that neither the Pope nor the Bible is infallible; that authoritarianism is alien to Christian faith; that the Mother of Christ is no more than human; and that a Sacrament is an act of worship, not tangible material. All this is clear in the Thirty-Nine Articles and the rubrics of the 1662 Book. This is undeniably assertive; and whether or not tight and tough, it claims to be true' (unpublished). The mid-century Anglican label 'prayer-book catholic' has disappeared as the Prayer Book itself has become marginal, but one way to register this loyal churchman's intellectual honesty and devotion to the historical truth as it appeared to a traditional Anglican of his time would be to shade the basic category 'liberal evangelical' with something like 'Prayer Book Liberal Protestant'.


## Liberal evangelicalism

Like the cautious 'modernism' of the Modern Churchmen's Union and also the more profound 'catholic modernism', 'liberal evangelicalism' became a feature of the Church of England during the 1920s. It characterized Ridley Hall from that period until the tectonic plates of evangelicalism moved again in the 1980s. It signals a major shift away from the older evangelicalism of Handley Moule's Ridley. When in 1976 Charlie returned, on retirement from Lady Margaret's chair, to live and teach for another four years at Ridley, the college was changed, but still liberal evangelical. It now had a bar, which came to be called the 'Moule-hole', and some ordinands with a defective grasp of Anglican history thought the phrase referred to the austere Handley. Conversely, but with better justification, students who around 1960 irreverently referred to Charlie as 'Holy Mouley' did not realize that this honorific title had attached to his great-uncle Handley. As already noted, these two Moules had little in common. The present writer once tried to give Charlie what looked like a rather improving book by the old Durham bishop. It was politely declined.

The differences between the Victorian evangelicalism of Bishop George Evans Moule and his siblings, and the liberal evangelicalism of post-First World War Ridley, Max Warren and Charlie, stemmed mainly from the progressives' acceptance of a moderate liberal Protestant biblical criticism. The more radical German Gospel criticism of Wrede and Bultmann would not make much impression internationally for another 40 years and never persuaded Charlie himself, but in the

1920s many evangelicals were catching up with other parts of the Church of England, which in the 1880s had begun to accept more of the modern world, including the 'higher criticism' of the Bible. This resulted in a drastically changed view of biblical authority, a more human picture of Jesus (not untouched by the new interest in psychology), and the repudiation of many (but not all) Calvinistic elements in Victorian evangelicalism. The changes did not come easily. They led to a split in the Church Missionary Society, with the conservatives in 1922 forming BCMS, the Bible Churchman's Missionary Society. But these changes made it possible for progressive thinkers to remain evangelicals and allowed the party back into the mainstream of English Christianity. The pietism of the eighteenth-century evangelical revival or 'awakening' contained seeds of modernity, and the history of evangelicalism in Britain shows how religious practice proved more adaptable than its old dogmatic underpinning in traditional atonement theology.

Two collections of essays, *Liberal Evangelicalism: An Interpretation* by 'Members of the Church of England' (1923) and *The Inner Life: Essays in Liberal Evangelicalism*, edited by T. Guy Rogers (1925), give some impression of Charlie's own emerging position and its distance from the older evangelicalisms. The first volume contained among its 14 essays one on 'Religion Authority' by Guy Rogers, another on 'The Bible and its Values' (Vernon Storr). Standard doctrinal topics (the Person of Jesus Christ, the Work of Christ, Church – Sacraments – Ministry) were discussed in a fresh and open, but still fairly conservative way. A need for restatement was felt, but nothing too radical was envisaged. The soul's direct relationship to God, the freedom of the Spirit, the authority of the Bible, the centrality of the cross, conversion, tradition, church order, are all reaffirmed. Most of the new energy in liberal evangelicalism was evident at the practical rather than the intellectual level.

Newer topics included Evangelism and Personality, the (non-eschatological) Kingdom of God, the Presentation of the Gospel, both at home and abroad. Episcopal contributors wrote on worship (where the hallmark was still simplicity) and on reunion. This corporate dimension was present also in E. S. Woods' essay on 'Rule of Life': 'For all loyal sons [sic] of the Church of England the Holy Communion, it need scarcely be said, will always be one of the most indispensable *media* for the receiving of the Divine life, for the realisation of the Divine love.'[9] The authority of the Bible was seen by all contributors in relation to the revelation of God

---

9 E. S. Wood, 1923, 'The Rule of Life', in T. Guy Rogers (ed.), *Liberal Evangelicalism: An Interpretation*, London: Hodder & Stoughton, p. 243.

in Christ, and the atonement is no longer tied to a primeval fall or to forensic theories of penal substitution. The import of Christ's personality,
understood as the redeeming love of God in Christ, is central, and Galatians 2.20 is prioritized over Romans 3.25: 'I have been crucified with
Christ; yet I live; and yet no longer I, but Christ liveth in me: and the life
which I now live in the flesh I live in faith, the faith which is in the Son of
God, who loved me, and gave himself up for me' (RV), rather than 'whom
God set forth to be a propitiation, through faith, by his blood' (RV).

The atonement is understood as revelation rather than cosmic transaction. The whole of Christ's life of self-giving reveals God. His death
concentrated into one hour what the life had always been revealing.
Divine punishment is seen as God's holy love reacting against sin, as
in George MacDonald's 'love-made-angry God'. Anticipating Charlie
(below, p. 188), R. T. Howard writes: 'More and more the moral consciousness of the State is coming to realize that the object of civil punishment is not retributory but reformatory.'[10] Hosea is quoted with
approval in this rare incursion into social ethics and is chosen for the
prophet's use of the personal analogy for a loving God.

The title of the second collection of essays, *The Inner Life* (1925), reveals
the movement's priorities and its inspiration (beyond the Book of Common Prayer) in seventeenth-century pietism rather than in the theology
of the Reformers. When the editor insists that the related Anglican Evangelical Group Movement with its 53 pamphlets was intending to 'apply
Gospel principles to personal religion, social questions and the problems
of institutional church life',[11] personal religion comes first. The 'inner life'
finds outward expression in prayer, Bible reading, the corporate life of the
Church, and the Sacrament of the Holy Communion. This inclusion of the
sacrament represents an effort to remedy a weakness in much evangelical
theology, which had to be addressed at a time when Anglo-catholicism was
at its most confident, but 'for us the moral struggle dominates the field, and
the call of Christ to take up the Cross and follow Him demands from each
of us an effective, if a varying, answer'.[12]

The secret discipline advocated in the Sermon on the Mount (Matt.
6.2-6, 16-18) has always been a feature of evangelical piety, and its core
beliefs are often expressed in biblical language. These are here interpreted
in modern, especially psychological, terms. Nature and history are not

---

10 *Ibid.*, p. 128.
11 T. Guy Rogers (ed.), 1923, *The Inner Life: Essays in Liberal Evangelicalism*, London: Hodder & Stoughton, p. vi.
12 *Ibid.*, p. ix.

ignored as Guy Rogers considers 'how God works through the evolutionary process which the history of the world reveals', but what matters most is 'how He enters into and co-operates with the spirit of man and brings him into fellowship with Himself'.[13] The essay on 'The Indwelling Christ' by R. T. Howard understands the Pauline and Johannine language in terms of the 'interpenetration of personality'. The historical source of this experience is located in the disciples' contact with Jesus in his ministry. Human and divine, his personality produced an 'invigorating atmosphere and a unifying force'.[14] This can be expressed in parallel terms as the Holy Spirit, the spirit of Christ's own personality come from him in personal forces and moulding their personalities. As the editor had commented, the collection needed no special essay on the Holy Spirit, 'because every essay presupposes His work. Whether in the evolutionary process of creation, or in a newborn soul, or in the corporate life of the church, the Spirit initiates and sustains man's fellowship with God.'[15]

This activity of the Spirit requires of Jesus' disciples, says Howard, the same kinds of moral effort that Christ himself made. John 14 and Romans 8 are said to reflect this sense of close personal contact with Christ, yet without dissolving the doctrine of the Trinity. The 'experience of personal union with Christ Himself through the Holy Spirit' must now be explained in terms of modern (psychological) thought if it is to remain real for us as it was for them.[16] This actual experience of union with Christ, according to Howard, stems from a spiritual interpenetration of our intellectual, emotional and volitional life whereby Christ purifies, enhances and transforms our spirits. Where some contemporary New Testament scholars were trying to illuminate the biblical language by drawing on pagan parallels from the ancient world, these more practical clergy wrote from an experience of prayer nourished by the biblical texts. Not much is explained, but the contributors were writing pastoral, not dogmatic, theology. Their aim was to encourage Christian practice. In contrast to the revolutionary German Protestant theology of the period, the philosophical and critical assumptions of pre-war liberalism and idealism were still sufficiently alive in England to allow these devout and intelligent church leaders to ease the passage from a cold and brittle to a warmer and more flexible evangelical Anglicanism.

---

13 *Ibid.*, p. vi.
14 R. T. Howard, 1925, 'The Indwelling Christ', in Rogers, *Inner Life*, p. 79.
15 Rogers, *Inner Life*, p. ix.
16 Howard, 'Indwelling Christ', p. 80.

Other essays in the second collection maintained the christocentric character of the whole. Charles Raven, later to become Regius Professor in Cambridge and a powerful supporter of the young Charlie, but in 1925 still the charismatic national figure at Liverpool Cathedral, saw no problems in presenting 'the plain teaching of Jesus' about God as Father.[17] It was, however, 'the person of the Incarnate' that allowed Raven to dismiss the views of God found in the 'less developed' parts of the Old Testament. Sin is 'a terrible fact', but the fear of hell has gone. Judgement is understood rather in Johannine terms as a present reality where 'the light is come into the world, and men loved the darkness rather than the light; for their works were evil' (John 3.19, RV). Writing on 'The Devotional Use of the Bible', M. I. Rogers emphasized its historical dimension and the place of 'comparative study'. He insisted on the need for a concordance and preferred a Greek New Testament to be used if possible. The Holy Communion is the subject of an essay by G. H. Harris. It understands 'real presence' as 'spiritual presence', denies that John 6.51–8 is eucharistic, or at least that it represents Jesus' view of the sacrament, and like others appeals to Galatians 2.20 in speaking of 'mystical' union with Christ. This emphasis on the sacrament contrasted with that of some Anglo-catholicism where Cranmer's having (in a much-quoted phrase repeated on p. 291) 'turned the Mass into a Communion' was overturned. Equally, the 'weaker aspects of Protestant individualism must not be allowed to enter the sphere of eucharistic Fellowship'.[18] There is also a strong reaction here against 'the cold, unlovely "Low Church" setting of the Communion Service'[19] and a recognition of the place of symbolism and the importance of beauty in worship, corresponding to the beauty of God, together with God's truth and goodness. Some ceremonial was compatible with evangelical simplicity and preferable to the careless attitude which had too often accompanied a one-sided emphasis on the sermon.

## Clergyman, scholar, teacher

Liberal evangelicalism became a vibrant element in the Church of England between the wars. It provided the context in which Charlie's theology took shape and his spirituality developed, and also supplied many

---

17 Charles Raven, 1925, 'God as Father', in Rogers, *Inner Life*, p. 59.
18 *Inner Life*, p. 296.
19 *Ibid.*

of the themes of his later teaching and writing. After 'discipleship' it is more natural to speak of his 'churchmanship' than of his 'spirituality', meaning by that not so much where he stood on the Anglican ecclesiastical spectrum as his total loyalty to the institution in which, like many of his forebears, he held office. To be a clergyman of the Church of England meant (in those days) to be saturated in the Bible (Authorized Version) and Prayer Book, to dress in a distinctive manner, and to behave in a conventional way. Charlie was never as conventional as some, and he lived long enough to see many of the conventions disappear. Walking in the Cotswolds one day in the 1950s he chanced upon his opposite number from Oxford, F. L. Cross. Only one of the two Lady Margaret professors was wearing a dark suit and clerical collar. But he was and remained a clergyman, even though his evangelical pattern of prayer and Bible study substituted (as Cranmer had in 1552 allowed) for the daily office of morning and evening prayer appointed to be read in churches (and college chapels) and therefore expected of the clergy.

The new attention to the Eucharist in liberal evangelicalism pointed towards its new centrality throughout the Church of England in the 1950s. By then Charlie had become professor and handed over the deanship of Clare College to John Robinson, while himself continuing to live and worship in college. Robinson was not yet famous as the Bishop of Woolwich and author of *Honest to God* (1963), but as well as being a creative New Testament theologian he was already becoming a prophetic voice in the Church and advocate of the liturgical movement. His account of the 'Clare experiment' at the college Eucharist in *Liturgy Coming to Life* (1960) shows how 'the intelligent use of action, such as the offertory procession – with specially baked loaves and wine from the College cellars' could make it 'genuinely congregational'. The quotation is from Charlie's contribution to his friend Eric James' *Life of Bishop John A. T. Robinson* (1987). Behind John's drastic re-ordering of the Clare chapel furnishings, including 'what I hadn't the courage to do – throw the eagle out', stood 'a clear theology, and out of it arose what can only be called a genuinely theological revival of worship. John translated into an idiom appropriate to the context the main thrust of the Parish and People movement.'[20] Although it is hard to imagine Charlie inaugurating such a daring venture, he was an enthusiastic supporter of his successor in all these developments, as well as an encouraging co-worker in the field of New Testament studies. Both sides of

---

20 Eric James, 1987, *A Life of Bishop John A. T. Robinson: Scholar, Pastor, Prophet*, London: Collins, p. 47.

that deep friendship and fruitful collaboration are recalled in this affectionate memoir. John had died in December 1983, and his Bampton
Lecture-Sermons, on *The Priority of John*, prepared for publication by
J. F. Coakley, were abbreviated and delivered by Charlie in Oxford the
following spring. Charlie's own views of the Fourth Gospel were very
different, but none of his hearers would have guessed.

His own early writings on the Eucharist and on worship in the New
Testament, with their strong christological and ecclesiological emphasis,
were no doubt influenced by this proximity in Clare to John Robinson
as well as by his liberal evangelical background. Living in college most
of his life, over 50 years between 1927 and 1980, a few yards away
from his colleges' chapels with their regular pattern of worship during
term-time, left its mark on the man and his work. Some scholars' regularity of attendance was legendary. In *My Cambridge Classical Teachers*
(1913), p. 13, Handley Moule famously reminisced on J. B. Lightfoot at
Trinity, how 'no man ever loitered so late in the Great Court that he did
not see Lightfoot's lamp burning in his study window; though no man
either was so regularly present in morning Chapel at seven o'clock that
he did not find Lightfoot always there with him.'[21] Evidently Handley
himself was among the early risers present at Trinity and Ridley chapels, as later Charlie was at Ridley and Clare, if free. Regular preaching
also belonged as much to Charlie's ministry as it did to that of other
members of his family. He was neither a Billy Graham nor a Charles
Raven in the pulpit, but the later sermons included in this volume testify
to the care he took in preparation.

The quiet and studious young Charlie was soon recognized as a
promising scholar through the usual evidences of an individual tutorial system ('supervisions'), undergraduate examinations ('Tripos'), and
university prizes, most of these too by examination. But his degree was
in classics, and when he turned to theology it was as a linguist that his
promise was first nurtured by the divinity professors. The return of
Raven to Cambridge in 1932 added sparkle, but in general the professors were less inclined than Hoskyns at Corpus to allow their religious
faith to shine through their lectures. Bethune-Baker and J. M. Creed
were very considerable scholars, but rather dry. They persuaded Charlie
to build on his linguistic expertise in the hope of producing a new gram-
mar of New Testament Greek. This was never his own priority and the
resulting *Idiom Book of New Testament Greek* (1953) never entirely

---

21 Handley C. G. Moule, 1913, *My Cambridge Classical Teachers*, Newcas-
tle upon Tyne, p. 13.

satisfied him, but it provided a good foundation for the short commentaries and many exegetical articles that gradually began to flow from his pen. He was initially slow to publish, and was elected to Lady Margaret's chair in 1951 on the basis of promise rather than achievement, though perhaps a shortage of suitable candidates was a factor in days when Cambridge rarely looked far afield. The promise was more than fulfilled as Charlie became 'probably the most influential British New Testament scholar of his time', according to William Horbury in the British Academy obituary.

The obituary did not call him the greatest British New Testament scholar of his time. That accolade surely belongs to C. K. Barrett. 'The most influential' is a subtle assessment, saying much more than how far his critical judgements were accepted. The phrase resonates with the evangelical impulse to 'influence' people and so bring them to Christ. Yet that was not the way in which Charlie visibly exercised his influence. Like Max Warren who would speak of 'influence' more readily, Charlie was entirely free of any tendency to pressurize people or bring students to his own point of view. Bringing colleagues to his own points of view, or otherwise achieving a desired outcome in an academic committee, was a different matter, but what made him such an outstanding teacher was in part the space he made for his pupils to develop along their own lines. Some of his cleverest research students, such as Margaret Thrall and Sandy Wedderburn, could therefore seem to him (they might disagree) to have learned nothing from him, whereas others owed him more than can easily be measured. This had as much to do with his genius for friendship and a 'ministry of encouragement' (to borrow Graham Stanton's phrase), maintained through personal contact and a huge stream of letters, in some cases over several decades, as with his gentle but sharp cross-questioning of his pupils' work. His willingness to take seriously even the most improbable suggestions of his less judicious students is now best remembered by those who attended his Tuesday evenings' informal groups in his rooms at Clare, as well as from countless individual conversations and letters. Always keen to hear disagreements with his suggestions he was rarely persuaded to change his mind. Research students learned to recognize weaknesses in their ideas through his sharp eye softened by a friendly quizzical interrogation. Gentle and unyielding, 'soft as granite' was one graduate student's phrase.

In Cambridge and Oxford, lecturing was usually a rather formal business, and because professors did not undertake undergraduate supervision they could know personally only a few of their audience.

Their lectures were judged by their clarity and content, but something of Charlie's gentle and modest personality came through, together with the piety evident in a seriousness of style and in his beginning each lecture-course with a prayer – a custom otherwise mostly abandoned by the 1960s. The sobriquet 'Holy Mouley' was no doubt a comment on the solemn aura that surrounded his three lectures a week on New Testament theology in the Divinity School, and public lectures to clergy and conferences and other extra-mural occasions. This sense of the dignity of his subject matter contrasted with the humour and even impishness evident on informal occasions and in personal encounters.

Biblical scholars have usually been teachers and sometimes leaders in the Church. Beyond their influence on research students and contributions to the development of their specialist discipline, some have influenced wider circles, through lecturing (especially when audiences were largely ordination candidates), popular writing, and sometimes broadcasting. While Charlie contributed more than most theologians of his generation to specialist journals, his books, apart from the *Idiom Book* and a small commentary on the Greek text of Colossians and Philemon (1957), were intended for, and are accessible to the wide range of educated Christian Bible readers. Most of his academic writing, like his lecturing, was on New Testament theology, which is by its nature directed at a wider readership than most scholarship. It mediates between its biblical research and the religious communities for which that is only a small part of a larger project. While using historical and exegetical methods shared by secular disciplines it usually aims to serve the churches' mission by helping believers to communicate the religious message of their Scriptures. Although most of its work can be done as well by unbelievers and believers, and gives few explicit signs of the scholar's personal standpoint, it is typically scholars with an interest (positive or negative) in the religious dimensions of these texts who are drawn into this field, and theologians rarely attempt to conceal their own position.

One could argue that this is what makes their work Christian 'theology' as well as the study of early Christian history and literature. Theology, properly understood, refers to religious talk of God, which is necessarily self-involving. New Testament theology as a historical discipline inevitably speaks of 'God' indirectly, describing and explaining what the biblical writers intend. To make this 'theology properly so-called', that is talk of God which is more existentially engaged than most philosophy or history, some scholars implicitly identify with the convictions of the writers whose language and ideas they are trying to understand. Those ancient authors belong to the same Christian community as most of these modern theologians, linked by the witness of the intervening centuries.

The reverent tone of Charlie's writings on Scripture is appropriate to its subject matter, but not achieved at the expense of intellectual rigour. That needs to be emphasized because 50 years ago the professional guild of biblical scholars had a more obviously religious, and even 'churchly' flavour than it has today, and some of Charlie's conclusions, like those of C. H. Dodd, now seem quite 'conservative', because they are more readily aligned with contemporary Christian faith than is typical of recent historical scholarship. They did not seem conservative in Britain back then. A reviewer of *The Birth of the New Testament* in the journal *New Testament Studies* (1963) found it 'quite provocatively *avant-garde* at various points' as well as enjoyable. But even back then, German Gospel criticism was generally more sceptical than most English scholars found reasonable. Lutherans still found in Paul a biblical witness in tune with their own religious beliefs, but depended less on historical portraits of Jesus. Most English scholars, by contrast, still found the 'historical Jesus' personally inspiring and the main explanation of the early Christianity that followed.

Some continue to defend today historical positions that others have abandoned. If Charlie's work is now less in the English-language mainstream than it was when written, that is due partly to cultural change as well as to progress in biblical scholarship. The study of early Judaism has made great advances since the Second World War, and this is reflected in a fresh emphasis on the Jewishness of Jesus, Paul and John. Charlie's discussions of Second Temple Jewish texts in technical essays such as 'St Paul and Dualism' (1956/6) show how professionally he kept abreast of these developments. He uses the new Qumran material scarcely available to Dodd, who had retired in 1949. But they both found apocalyptic material uncongenial, and despite his view of the importance of Daniel 7 for Jesus, Charlie gave less weight to the Old Testament and subsequent Jewish literature in his picture of Jesus than is normal today. It was the language of the New Testament rather than the history of religions that sparked his scholarship. It is fair to say that his work is less attuned to the historical distance of early Christianity than much of the best current biblical scholarship, and gives more weight to the continuities between past and present that are the proper concern of New Testament theology.

A list of Charlie's publications shows a slow start with rapid acceleration from 1952 when, in his mid-forties and settled into Lady

Margaret's chair, he was relieved of the heavy tutorial load and pastoral priorities that have redirected many promising academic careers. Few English theology professors have taken their duty to publish more seriously, but the first 25 years of Charlie's theological studies (like the last 30) yielded well under a tenth of his published work. The typical pre-1960s career pattern for academic clergy was less research-based than the German system (write two books before you can start teaching), but it kept English university teaching and writing strongly rooted in the church it served mainly by preparing ministerial candidates to articulate the gospel. Much of what Charlie published between 1939 and 1957 was directed to a wider church readership and some of it was elicited by the Church Missionary Society, led by Max Warren. Charlie continued mindful of the rock from whence he was hewed, and remained a devoted supporter of CMS after John Taylor became General Secretary in 1963. As canon theologian of Leicester Cathedral and examining chaplain to six diocesan bishops he was constantly in demand and always available for lecturing to clergy conferences and giving advice when asked.

Much of Charlie's early exegetical work related to the beginnings of Christian worship and ministry, and was written with an eye to the contemporary Church of England, where liturgical change had long been felt necessary, and was finally making progress in the 1950s. The 'Parish and People' movement pioneered by Joost de Blank and Ernie Southcott among others, and led by Trevor Beeson and Eric James, made the Parish Communion central to parish life. Charlie's involvement is on record in his contribution on 'The Sacrifice of the People of God' to its 1962 conference, published in *The Parish Communion Today*. By then he had published *Worship in the New Testament* (1961) and could benefit from having E. C. Ratcliff, the greatest English liturgist of the day, as a professorial colleague from 1947 to 1964. *The Birth of the New Testament* (1962), perhaps Charlie's best book (updated in 1981), gives prominence (chapter 2) to 'The Church at Worship'. The chapter begins with the claim that blocks of the New Testament 'glow with the fervour of worship' and that a special concern with this 'has pervaded all departments of Christian practice and research. In England the liturgical revival and the practical experiments associated with the "Parish and People" movement have gone hand in hand with a new appraisal of the setting of much biblical literature . . .'.[22] However, this strong liturgical

---

22 Moule, *Birth of the New Testament*, p. 11.

interest never led him into 'panliturgism', and his early essay on 1 Peter (*NTS* 1956/7) was a critical response to F. L. Cross, *1 Peter, a Paschal Liturgy* (1954). Sober historical judgement was a marked feature of his scholarship and this led him to take seriously the influence of worship on early Christian language. When in 1959 he explored 'The Influence of Circumstances on the Use of Christological Terms', striking prominence is given to liturgy as affecting selection.

### Eucharist and sacrifice

A characteristic example of New Testament theology built on a secure exegetical base and oriented to the Church's worship and its theology is provided by four Holy Week 1955 lectures given at Cuddesdon and published the following year, *The Sacrifice of Christ* (reprinted in 1964 and again in 1998). Here was an eirenic evangelical scholar invited to speak in a theological and devotional context at what was then a 'Prayer Book catholic' theological college, and choosing a topic where the dividing lines between catholic and evangelical Anglicans were still sharp. He hopes that although 'the merest amateur' in philosophy, (church) history and liturgy, his 'ephemeral tentative' discussion 'may prove to be some small contribution to the healing of our divisions'.[23] In that hey-day of 'biblical theology' it was widely expected that a return to biblical roots would further ecumenical endeavour. This was needed as much within the large tent of Anglicanism as in relation to other denominations. Looking back and introducing the 1998 reprint he hoped it might 'still be of some value as reflections on eucharistic theology' as well as serving 'as a small historical monument to a certain stage of ecumenical relations'.[24]

*The Sacrifice of Christ* is concerned with eucharistic doctrine, in particular the relationship between the Eucharist and the 'one true pure immortal sacrifice' on the cross. Neither the 'sacrifice of praise and thanksgiving' (cf. Heb. 13.15) nor the offering 'of ourselves, our souls and bodies' (cf. Rom. 12.1) was in dispute, and the liturgical movement was converting Protestants to the second-century offering of gifts as a kind of weekly harvest festival, but whether the Eucharist was representing (in some sense) or simply remembering the sacrifice of Christ

---

23 C. F. D. Moule, 1998, *The Sacrifice of Christ*, in *Forgiveness and Reconciliation and Other New Testament Themes* London: SPCK, p. 136.
24 *Ibid.*, p. xi.

on Calvary, remained disputed. Fr Hebert is quoted at the outset as fairly close to what these lectures are trying to say.

> The eucharistic Sacrifice, that storm-centre of controversy, is finding in our day a truly evangelical expression from the 'catholic' side, when it is insisted that the sacrificial action is not any sort of re-immolation of Christ, not a sacrifice additional to His own Sacrifice, but a participation in it. The true celebrant is Christ the High Priest, and the Christian people are assembled as members of His Body to present before God His Sacrifice, and to be themselves offered up in sacrifice through their union with Him . . . We offer it only because He has offered the one Sacrifice, once for all, in which we need to participate.[25]

'The subject', says Charlie, is 'so great and deep a mystery that we can hardly think about it too often. It is the strange paradox which lies at the very heart of our faith, and which arises from the finality and yet constantly repetitive nature of salvation – the finished work of God in Christ, over against his continued work in the Body of Christ which is the Church. It is the tension set up by the distinction, yet union, between Christ as an individual and the Corporate Christ in his Church. It is the restless question of the relation between the sacrifice on Calvary and (as some would put it) "the sacrifice of the Mass".'[26]

As a biblical theologian and an evangelical Charlie has far more to say about the Atonement than about sacramental theology, but what he says about the Atonement extends to its appropriation by subsequent believers, and already here the relationship of Christology to ecclesiology in Charlie's most characteristic emphasis on 'the corporate Christ' is explicit. He wants to do justice to both the Protestant emphasis on the 'once for all' stressed by the Epistle to the Hebrews, 'the precious good news that salvation is complete and Christ's finished work sufficient',[27] and also to the Roman Catholic stress on 'the frequentative and the repetitive aspects of salvation' with its closer attention to 'the Church as the Body of Christ contemporary with every age – the continuation of his presence'.[28] He refers to the evangelical statement in *The Fullness of Christ* (1950) to which he was a signatory, that

---

25 *Ibid.*, pp. 135f.
26 *Ibid.*, p. 136.
27 *Ibid.*, p. 137.
28 *Ibid.*

the Eucharist is the divinely instituted remembrance of Christ's sacrifice, and in it God gives and the Church receives the fruits of that
sacrifice, the Body and Blood of Christ. In virtue of this, and only so,
the Church is enabled to make that offering of praise, thanksgiving,
and self-oblation which (apart from the alms) is the only sacrifice actually offered in the Eucharist. Only as united to Christ in his death
and resurrection through receiving the Body and Blood of Christ is
the Church able to offer itself acceptably to the Father.[29]

He then quotes Alan Richardson's criticism of the statement for 'implying that the bread and wine are *not* offered in the Eucharist', thus
denying 'the primitive (second-century) conception of the Eucharist as a
sacrament of Creation as well as of Redemption' – every Sunday a harvest festival as well as an Easter Sunday. Charlie denies that the report
intended to destroy the symbolism of the people's offering (to which
John Robinson's Clare experiment was giving powerful expression),
but he recognizes the difference of emphasis – one on receiving and the
other on giving. He also notes the extreme anti-sacrificial position of
some evangelicals which he would want to qualify, and also (deferring
comment until later) Roland Walls' criticism of the Clare manual for
not doing justice to the Church's 'joining in and pleading the offering to
the Father of the one perfect sacrifice of the Son of God'.[30]

Roland Walls' quotation of William Bright's 'extremely beautiful'
eucharistic hymn is expanded in Charlie's brief survey of varying viewpoints on p. 140:

And now, O Father, mindful of the love
that bought us, once for all, on Calvary's Tree,
and having with us him that pleads above,
we here present, we spread forth to thee
that only Offering perfect in thine eyes,
the one, true, pure, immortal Sacrifice.

Charlie is not quite comfortable with this account of 'the catholic obla-
tion'. It 'can be justified in terms of that internal dialogue within the
Godhead – God's mercy pleading with his justice. It can be justified
in terms of Christ's obedience being inherent in every act of man's
obedience. But both because of my hesitation in identifying those two

---

29 *Ibid.*, p. 138.
30 *Ibid.*, p. 140.

obediences, and because of my fear of propitiatory language, I feel a reluctance about such phrases.'[31] He was also 'wholly unconvinced by the attempts to make the *anamnesis* ("this do in remembrance of me") mean that God is here reminded of what Christ has wrought: "Do this to remind God of me". Reminding God of man's deserts is indeed a conception not absent from the Old Testament; but I cannot find room for it (or for the adapted form – reminding God of Christ's merits) in the New Testament. Nor do I think the linguistic arguments for doing so are at all persuasive.'[32]

In his already mentioned article on 'The Sacrifice of the People of God' in *The Parish Communion Today* (1962) he would again quote Bright's 'noble paraphrase and adaptation of the *Unde et memores*'.[33] Describing the Christian's 'dependence on Christ in terms of an appeal to him as a heavenly Advocate, and of a presenting before God of Christ's offering and sacrifice' troubles him, however. Being united with Christ as really present does not (in Charlie's view) 'involve also "presenting Christ to God" or "reminding God of Christ": rather it is a being presented to God in Christ, and a being "reminded" of God in him – and so an act of obedience'.[34]

In both these discussions of the eucharistic sacrifice, Charlie is plainly a Protestant. 'If we must use labels, I am proud to call myself an Evangelical.'[35] A footnote added here in 1997 explains that in 1955 'an Evangelical' still meant 'one who, whether conservative or not regarding the authority of the Bible, insisted that the Church of England was not only Catholic but reformed, who recognized the value of the Reformation (much though this is now questioned), and who tended to judge "catholicism" by the norm of the apostolic age reflected in the New Testament'.[36] Some gentle criticism of contemporary evangelicalism is apparent here, and his view of biblical authority would not allow him to be described as a conservative evangelical, but he remained a more traditional Protestant than some more modern evangelicals who show little interest in the Reformation, and even less understanding of its scriptural principle.

---

31 *Ibid.*, p. 165.

32 *Ibid.*

33 C. F. D. Moule, 1962, 'The Sacrifice of the People of God', in Alan Paton (ed.), *The Parish Communion Today*, London: SPCK, p. 79.

34 *Ibid.*, p. 92.

35 Moule, *Forgiveness and Reconciliation*, p. 136.

36 *Ibid.*, p. 175.

If the Protestant emphasis on the once-for-all act of atonement was Charlie's point of reference, he nevertheless strove to appreciate alternative viewpoints.

> Where different branches of the Church advance opposite views or stress opposite ends of a series, there is generally something precious in both insights. And it is not so much the mean between the two that we must seek, as the common root from which these two different growths shoot up . . .[37]

He expected common ground to emerge from further biblical study and shared worship, and that from this mutual understanding God would build a stronger and more united Church. The Christology which he finds in Paul ('the corporate Christ') opens out into ecclesiology in a way that engages Roman Catholic emphases and may lead to greater agreement in eucharistic doctrine.

The final lecture of *The Sacrifice of Christ* takes up Gregory Dix's *The Shape of the Liturgy* (1945), which was at the time very influential. Dix had posted the dilemma of the impasse between Protestants for whom the Eucharist is only a *remembrance* of the sacrifice, and late medieval Catholics for whom it was in some sense a *repetition*, as arising from the limitation of redemption to Calvary, which made that choice between two ways of entering it inescapable. Charlie finds a resolution in 'the mystical union that is betwixt Christ and his Church',[38] as the Prayer Book has it, echoing Ephesians 5.32. By this union of *koinōnia* – fellowship not identity – or being 'with' or 'in Christ', we 'in some way enter into his obedience'. Our derived and dependent obedience thus goes to God 'in the perennial stream of his obedience'.[39] Westcott is quoted insisting that 'our approach to God, our worship, our spiritual harmony, must always be "in Him" in Whom we have been incorporated'.[40] Thus 'whenever we approach God it can only be in Christ or in the Spirit'.[41] Every act of our obedience is joined with Christ's. In the sacrament, a focal point of obedience, both are offered to God together. Paul and other Christians 'are offered as a sacrifice; he does not speak of offering Christ, or even of Christ continually offering Himself'.[42]

---

37 *Ibid.*, p. 141.
38 *Ibid.*, p. 169.
39 *Ibid.*
40 *Ibid.*
41 *Ibid.*, p. 170.
42 *Ibid.*

For Charlie, the Church's sacrifice is derived, but being united with Christ's it becomes *in this sense* a continuation 'of what Christ has wrought'.[43] Careful qualification is needed, but it is 'Christ in us, Christ within humanity, Christ expressing man's obedience to God's loving purposes, Christ's once-and-for-all sacrifice being implemented in us. And every Eucharist is a "focal" point of that; not a mere recalling to the mind, nor yet a re-enactment; but an entering into what Christ has done – just as indeed is every symbol of obedience.'[44] The link between the sacrament and the moral life is again emphasized. The 'repentant person making restitution' is also using a sacramental act as a channel for his or her acceptance of God's gift of forgiveness on 'the rock face of our life's ascent in time and space' as we grasp what God has done.[45] Human merit is excluded,[46] but good works done positively 'for the Lord's sake', or a pleasure 'which appears to hinder the Lord's work' refused – 'a secret transaction of the soul' – are all part of the still flowing 'stream of the sacrifice of Calvary'.[47] William Temple's 'marvellously comprehensive and measured statement'[48] in *Christus Veritas* is quoted, and only the word 'reproduced' said to require qualification or further explanation.

> The sacrifice of Christ is potentially but most really the sacrifice of Humanity. Our task is, by his Spirit, to take our place in that sacrifice. In the strict sense there is only one sacrifice – the obedience of the Son to the Father, and of Humanity to the Father in the Son. This was manifest in actual achievement on Calvary; it is represented in the breaking of the Bread; it is reproduced in our self-dedication and resultant service; it is consummated in the final coming of the Kingdom.[49]

Or again, from the same context:

> The Eucharist is a sacrifice; but we do not offer it; Christ offers it; and we, responding to His act, take our parts or shares in His one sacrifice

---

43 *Ibid.*, p. 171.

44 *Ibid.*

45 *Ibid.*, p. 172.

46 *Ibid.*, p. 171.

47 *Ibid.*, p. 172.

48 *Ibid.*

49 William Temple, 1924, *Christus Veritas: An Essay*, London: Macmillan, pp. 238ff.

as members of His Body . . . Redeeming love so wins our hearts that we offer ourselves to be presented by the Love that redeems to the Love that created and sustains both us and all the universe.[50]

The trinitarian basis of Temple's world-encompassing theology corresponds to Charlie's Second-Adam Christology, where Christ is the New Humanity, 'representative Man offering representative obedience to the Father's will'.[51] The final sentence of the book is a prayer for our incorporation: 'God enlighten us and lead us forward together by his mercy into the mystery of his love as Creator, Redeemer indwelling Spirit of Obedience'.[52]

This small book on a subject (eucharistic doctrine) surely marginal to New Testament theology reveals something of the doctrinal structure of Charlie's biblical theology. Elsewhere its trinitarian and incarnational axioms, and its relating the atonement to the continuing moral life of Christians are less prominent than its focus on Christology. There the New Testament theologian's primary task is (arguably) to relate what can be said about the historical figure of Jesus to the early churches' diverse witness to him so far as this is attested in the New Testament. But introducing Charlie's theology through his early reflections on the sacraments highlights his preoccupation with the contemporary Church and its mission, evangelism and worship.

Most of his subsequent scholarly work provides exegetical support for this traditional pattern of belief, conduct and worship as it became increasingly challenged (and in some circles modified) over the 50-odd years which remained to him following the Cuddesdon lectures. The short essays published here come from the final stages of his pilgrimage. Neither they nor the substantial scholarly oeuvre which preceded them can be said to offer a much more profound theological exploration of Christian faith than what is already germinally present in the popular form of Holy Week lectures (1955) and broadcasts (1976, below pp. 93–110). Their value lies rather in what they offer Christians whose faith depends on an honest and responsible reading of Scripture, but one related to the tradition in which they stand and to their own varied experience.

The Bible gives most Christians enough to chew on without their ever tasting the riches to be found, say, in Barth's *Church Dogmatics*.

---

50 *Ibid.*, p. 241.
51 Moule, *Forgiveness and Reconciliation*, p. 172.
52 *Ibid.*, p. 174.

Fourteen large and well-used volumes of that Christian classic could
be seen on C. K. Barrett's shelves. Charlie does quote them in his
book on *The Holy Spirit* (1978), but his own theology probably owed
more to Dorothy Sayers. He did not aspire to the breadth of learning
he expected in a Regius Professor and recognized in Henry Chadwick
and Geoffrey Lampe. Joachim Jeremias called himself 'a narrow man',
and many biblical scholars could say the same. Charlie was frank
about the limits of his own expertise while modestly claiming 'some
experience . . . in biblical exposition'.[53]

By the time these lectures were twice reprinted that was unduly modest. He knew the importance for the Church, its mission and its theology, of securing its title-deeds and responding to their detractors,
including some scholarly detractors. The exegetical underpinning which
he expected New Testament scholarship to provide for Christian
belief and practice included linguistic clarifications and historical arguments, but New Testament theology cultivates in particular the correspondences that are seen to exist between modern interpreters' own
doctrinal beliefs and what they understand the New Testament writers
to have believed. These presupposed correspondences are apparent in
Charlie's accounts of Paul's theology and in his understanding of the
historical Jesus. The latter are only implied in *The Sacrifice of Christ*
(which is the self-offering of Jesus of Nazareth before it can be anything
else) but are unfolded exegetically elsewhere. Before examining that,
the larger theological topics introduced in this early work deserve some
further consideration.

The final lecture on eucharistic doctrine is based on the preceding
discussion of the uniqueness and finality of the sacrifice of Christ on
the cross (the Protestant emphasis on the atonement), but also on some
discussion of Christology and ecclesiology, 'on the correlative truth
contained in the New Testament phrases of repetition ("I fill up that
which is lacking in the afflictions of Christ")'.[54] This too 'is implicit in
the doctrine of the coinherence of believers and Christ. The doctrine of
the Church as the Body of Christ carries in it the corollary that in some
sense the sufferings of the limbs are the sufferings of the Head, and vice
versa.'[55] How far he has made that intelligible, or was to make it clearer
in subsequent writings, needs investigation. This will supply material
for deciding whether Charlie's biblical theology, unlike Bultmann's or

---

53 *Ibid.*, p. 136, originally in 1956.
54 *Ibid.*, p. 141, quoting Col. 1.24.
55 *Ibid.*

F. C. Baur's, is not closer to 'spirituality' than to philosophical theology or dogmatics.

## New Testament theology

Colossians 1.24 is often quoted by Charlie, and he thinks that this epistle was written by Paul. He recognizes the differences, but has no difficulty in combining its account of Christ the head of the (universal) Church, with the rather different accounts of the (local) church (or 'you', or 'we') as a (or the) body of Christ in 1 Corinthians 12, or 'one body in Christ' at Romans 12.5. Even without Ephesians this appeal to Colossians gives more prominence to ecclesiology than was until recently usual in Protestant theology, and also strengthens its link with Christology. Reviewing John Robinson's *The Body* in *The Journal of Theological Studies* he comments that 'the really great thing about this book is its trenchant presentation of the uncompromising Pauline gospel of the union between Christ and the Church'.[56] He would himself place more emphasis on the believer's response (faith, and thinking in the Spirit) and like Ernest Best in *One Body in Christ* (1955) he recognizes the language is metaphorical. He resists Anglo-catholic talk of the Church as the extension of the incarnation, but together with the element of Ritschlianism common in liberal evangelicalism one can see here a more catholic element in Charlie's Pauline interpretation and, corresponding to this, in his own theology.

In a judicious discussion of these passages many years later he came unusually close to a retraction: 'There was a time when I would have given more weight, for Christological purposes, to Paul's use of *sōma*. I would have said that his allusions to "the body of Christ" did indeed mean that Christ himself *was* this inclusive body: . . . that, antecedently, the risen Christ *was* the body, already complete; and that it was by union with this body and by incorporation in it that Christians became Christians.'[57] He still insisted on his conviction that 'I depend upon the body of Christ: the body of Christ does not depend on me or my fellow Christians', but he had come to 'doubt whether the *sōma* language in itself, lends much support to it, if any'.[58] 1 Corinthians 12.12 ('so also

---

56 C. F. D. Moule, 1953, 'Review of J. A. T. Robinson, *The Body*', *JTS n.s.* 4.1, p. 75.

57 C. F. D. Moule, 1977, *The Origin of Christology*, Cambridge: Cambridge University Press, p. 70.

58 *Ibid.*, p. 71.

is the Christ') might lend support, and even 1 Corinthians 6.15, but 1 Corinthians 12.28 ('You are a body of Christ') could mean simply 'a body belonging to Christ'. As at Romans 12.5 ('we many are one body in Christ'), the point 'appears to be that Christians owe their organic unity with one another to the fact that they are "in Christ" – incorporated in him'.[59] The substance of Charlie's theology has not changed, but some of its exegetical support has gone.

It is self-evident that New Testament theology consists largely in Christology and ecclesiology, and also that the person and work of Christ cannot be separated. However, this way of relating Christology and ecclesiology is far from typically Protestant. It appeals to Paul, but has remarkably little to say about justification by faith. It can find further support now from E. P. Sanders' revival of Albert Schweitzer's emphasis upon 'the realism with which Paul thought of incorporation into the body of Christ' at the heart of his theology.[60] Douglas Campbell's elephantine deconstruction of justification by faith in favour of making Romans 5 to 8 central to Paul's soteriology also invites new attention to Charlie's work.[61]

While stressing incorporation into Christ, Charlie was already in *The Sacrifice of Christ* also placing great weight (more weight than Paul does) on language drawn from human relationships speaking of 'reconciliation'. This emphasis was facilitated by his inclusion of Colossians (not Ephesians) among the Pauline epistles, still the majority view outside Germany at the time.

The Epistle to the Hebrews is usually more prominent in English than in German New Testament theology, and is naturally central to Charlie's biblical theological discussion of salvation set here in the context of eucharistic theology. Hebrews 2 will again become important in his later discussions of the (corporate) 'Son of Man', but the whole epistle is 'one of the key documents' in regard to both the finished work of Christ and 'the work of Christ continuing'.[62] In Hebrews 7.25 'the Great High Priest lives continually to make intercession', but particularly important for Charlie was the application to Jesus of 'the ideal picture of man in Psalm 8', likening Jesus to Adam.[63]

---

59 *Ibid.*

60 E. P. Sanders, 1977, *Paul and Palestinian Judaism*, London: SCM Press, pp. 434–63.

61 Douglas Campbell, 2009, *The Deliverance of God: An Apocalyptic Rereading of Justification in Paul*, Grand Rapids: Eerdmans.

62 Moule, *Sacrifice of Christ*, rp. in *Forgiveness and Reconciliation*, p. 142.

63 *Ibid.*, p. 158.

For his individuality is somehow inclusive: he is representative man; he includes mankind and in fact fulfils the destiny of man . . . therefore Christ's obedience is man's obedience.[64]

Going beyond Hebrews, but perhaps helping to make sense of Hebrews 7.25, he continues: 'And if man, as a result, begins to obey, that may be called Christ's obedience in man. There is, then, a continuity in some sense between Christ and man, and between man's obedience derived from Christ's, and Christ's perfect, underived holiness.'[65] Other New Testament passages (Rom. 8.27, 34; John 14 – 16; 1 John 2.1) and other doctrinal topics, especially baptism, are drawn into the discussion, and a further all-important dimension of New Testament theology, namely ethics, is included here through an emphasis on our obedience corresponding to that of Christ.

In *The Sacrifice of Christ* the lecture on 'The finished work of Christ' is foundational. A masterly survey presents the variety in the New Testament writers' accounts of what God in Christ has done. Some witnesses emphasize the cross, but its unity with the resurrection is always implied. Sometimes the death is understood in sacrificial and sacerdotal terms. This discussion of the Epistle to the Hebrews is prefaced by reference to the two Markan sacrificial texts, 'his life a ransom for many' (Mark 10.45) and the 'blood of the covenant poured out for many' (Mark 14.24), and the surely symbolic story of the temple veil being rent at the death of Jesus. That tells of a new access to God that contrasts with the now superseded 'manipulation by the accredited priests of the blood of animal victims'.[66]

This opening up a new way for Gentiles, described at Ephesians 2.14f. as the wall of legal observance being abolished, is touched on in 1 Peter and unfolded in Hebrews, with special emphasis on the contrast between the daily repeated imperfect sacrifices of the old covenant and the final, perfect, unrepeatable sacrifice of Christ which constitutes the new. Decisive for Charlie, however, is the shift from cultic to personal categories: 'one is transported into the great realm of the dealings of a personal God with his children'.[67] Christ's sacrifice is efficacious because (unlike the Levitical) it is the voluntary surrender made by a human personality, willing obedience offered by the representative man. 'Christ is

---

64 *Ibid.*
65 *Ibid.*
66 *Ibid.*, p. 145.
67 *Ibid.*, p. 147.

the priest of an eternal order offering the eternally valid sacrifice.'[68] The Christology of Hebrews in which 'Christ is both perfect and representative Man and also the eternal Son of God' makes this self-offering 'not only the one perfect response of Humanity to the will of God but also . . . the will of God going out to man in yearning love'.[69] Christ being 'both the Man and the eternal effulgence of God's glory' explains why 'he bridges the gap between man and God' and why 'in him acceptance is complete' and why 'through his torn body, surrendered in obedience to God's love for those who tore it, the way lies open for access'.[70]

What matters most for Charlie is how here 'we have been lifted off the analogical level of ritual acts on to the level of personal dealings' through a Christology that sees 'Jesus as representative man fulfilling that destiny of obedience and harmony with God from which Adam by transgression fell'.[71] The parallel with Philippians 2.6ff. is striking. Hebrews 2 contrasts the ideal for humans, described in Psalm 8, with our present state. But then it identifies One in whom human destiny is 'completely realized – Jesus who because of his obedience in death has been crowned with the glory and honour due to man'.[72] The Christ-hymn in Philippians 2.6ff. included here is read as 'virtually a Son of Man passage', in which the eclipsed and suffering Son of Man is ultimately vindicated and exalted.[73]

This transition to Paul who is also 'capable of viewing the incarnation in terms of a new dispensation – a superseding of the old' moves on 'into a kind of explanation of forgiveness in terms of the unique event'[74] – so far as one can 'explain' such mysteries at all. The Old Testament speaks of forgiveness, and the free graciousness of God was no new idea. But how could the holy and righteous God forgive? In Romans 3.25f. Paul does for once 'step aside from his essentially activist, practical preaching of the fact of salvation, to say a word about its how and why'.[75] 'The holy God himself met the sin, accepted its entail, entered into its costliness, suffered redemptively in his own Son'. Only 'a radical, a drastic, a passionate and absolutely final acceptance of the terrible

---

68 *Ibid.*, p. 148 with a long quotation of Heb. 7.23–8.
69 *Ibid.*, p. 148.
70 *Ibid.*
71 *Ibid.*, p. 148.
72 *Ibid.*, p. 149.
73 *Ibid.*
74 *Ibid.*, p. 149.
75 *Ibid.*, p. 150.

situation, and an absorption by the very God himself of the fatal disease so as to neutralize it effectively' could suffice.[76]

Here the point is 'the finality and uniqueness of Christ', a theme returned to in *Faith, Fact and Fantasy* (1964) and again in the 1970s, but reference to Romans 3.25 touches also on another central emphasis in Charlie's New Testament theology and his own understanding of the Atonement. The New Testament itself uses priestly and sacrificial categories, but he is uneasy with this language and much prefers that of personal relationships. His reservations repeatedly come to a head in his fierce opposition to what he is absolutely clear is a misunderstanding of this New Testament language in terms of 'propitiation'. That translation of *hilasterion* is excluded in Romans 3.25 because God is the subject of the sacrificial verb 'set forth', not its object, and at 1 John 2.2 and Hebrews 2.17 the object of *hilasmos* and *hilaskesthai* is sins, not God. The root should therefore be translated 'expiation' not 'propitiation', and the main point is that God initiated the event. Any atonement language that drives a wedge between God and Christ, as substitutionary language may, is a distortion.

> [T]he sacrifice of Christ was not, according to the New Testament, propitiatory . . . It is a grave misfortune that the misleading word 'propitiation' has got into the English Scriptures at Rom. 3.25 and 1 John 2.2, and so into the Prayer Book.[77]

Christ's sacrifice 'is not propitiatory but it is God's absolutely effective and final meeting of sin'.[78] In sharp opposition to some traditional atonement teaching Charlie took the liberal evangelical position with its element of late nineteenth-century Ritschlianism included, and insisted that 'in the New Testament, then, the idea of a propitiating of God never comes into view . . . still less, then, is there anything propitiatory about any derived or related sacrifice of the Church'.[79] *Hilasterion* and *hilasmos* in secular usage spoke of propitiating an alien deity or person, but

> in the Bible generally, and certainly in the New Testament, the amazing revelation of God's redemptive dealings with man has spun the

---

76 *Ibid.*
77 *Ibid.*, p. 164.
78 *Ibid.*, p. 171.
79 *Ibid.*, p. 164.

word round face-about, and has compelled it to have, as its object, not God but sin. It is not that Christ or man tries to propitiate God, but that God in Christ expiates sin: God – marvel of marvels – suffering in order to neutralize man's sin. The very initiative is God's: how then can God be said to be propitiated? He is the subject of the verb, no longer its object.[80]

The language of intercession and pleading found in the New Testament (for example Romans 8.34 and Hebrews) cannot mean Christ pleading our cause before an alienated Judge. Similarly on 1 John 2.2, 'we simply cannot allow these juridical terms – part of the apparatus of "theodicy" – to drive a wedge between the Persons of the Trinity. If we use the figure, it must be held firmly as an internal dialogue – God's own self-sacrificing meeting his justice'.[81] Westcott is quoted with approval: 'The modern conception of Christ pleading in heaven His Passion, "offering His Blood" on behalf of men, has no foundation in the Epistle (to the Hebrews). His glorified humanity is the eternal pledge of the absolute efficacy of His accomplished work. He pleads, as older writers truly expressed the thought, by His Presence on the Father's Throne.'[82]

The devotional context and style of the Cuddesdon lectures catch the flavour of the biblical theology articulated at a more technical level in his article 'On the Judgment Theme in the Sacraments', written in 1952 to 1953 for the *Studies in Honour of C. H. Dodd, The Background of the New Testament and its Eschatology* (1955). The lectures reveal a devout scholar reading Scripture with close attention and offering other believers some solid and thoughtful biblical exposition. The scholarship in both the technical and the more popular presentations provides intellectual support for a religious system whose plausibility rests on the experience of those who have already accepted it. The biblical theologian can communicate the presupposed belief in relatively simple terms, warning against distortions and clarifying the texts on which it is based, but has less to say about its general credibility in a culture that was about to move further away from its religious roots.

This high degree of loyalty to traditional biblical language, understood differently from much of the tradition but not in a radically revisionist way, contrasts with Bultmann's New Testament theology, which was making an international impact in the 1950s at the same time as his

---

80 *Ibid.*
81 *Ibid.*, p. 165.
82 *Ibid.*

demythologizing proposal was receiving a mixed reception from philosophical and doctrinal theologians. Many English readers at that time were critical of Bultmann's scepticism about the historicity of the Gospels, but more impressed by his powerful New Testament theology. They did not agree that the proclamation of Jesus was only the 'presupposition' of New Testament theology, and they thought history important for the Fourth Evangelist, but Jeremias' continuation of Dodd's work on the parables and especially his interest in *The Eucharistic Words of Jesus* (ET 1955) had reopened communications across the North Sea, and Bornkamm's *Jesus of Nazareth* (1956, ET 1960) and news of 'a new quest of the historical Jesus' persuaded some that even the Bultmann camp was coming to a better mind. The American 'biblical theology movement' was under attack, and even the more scholarly biblical theology of C. H. Dodd's disciples such as Charlie and George Caird began to seem less persuasive in the 1960s as a more radical German New Testament theology and criticism was assimilated. Cullmann was still read and Kümmel appreciated but 'salvation history' was no longer so fashionable.

One may ask how far Charlie's New Testament *theology*, in contrast to his more technical linguistic and exegetical work, bears the marks of that older style of biblical theology, even though most of it was published after 1960. He recognized the vitality and variety of early church life creating new forms and traditions and developing independently of Old Testament prototypes. He was more of a historical scholar than biblical theologians like Hoskyns, Michael Ramsey or Alan Richardson. In Cambridge Donald MacKinnon's strictures against 'biblical theology' showed respect for the scholarship of Dodd and Moule while being sharply critical of Alan Richardson's *Christian Apologetics* (1947), but some of his pupils were less polite.

Charlie was himself quite negative about Richardson's *Introduction to the Theology of the New Testament* (1958) without his *JTS* review being devastating, like L. E. Keck's article in *Novum Testamentum* (1964). However, by the 1960s, his own kind of New Testament theology also seemed 'soft' and lacking in philosophical grit, political engagement and existential *Angst*. He had been attracted to Platonism as a classicist, and one of the reservations about Platonism in the aftermath of two wars was its account of evil as merely the absence of good. The broadcast talk from 1976 that opens this collection provides evidence of Charlie's recognition of the reality of evil. His own experience of serious illness in his thirties and the early loss of an older brother[83]

---

83 On this 'inconsolable grief' see *Theology* 88, March 1975, p. 114.

made him unlikely to underestimate the sheer negativity of sickness and death. In a sentence resonant of MacKinnon he observes that '(t)here is tragedy built into every step of the Christian story' (below, p. 95)

It was perhaps Charlie's reserve which accounted for some of the perceived differences from MacKinnon. His view of the world and human nature was full of hope, but the future transformation to which he looked forward was no more an easy ride for him than for St Paul. He interprets 2 Corinthians 4–5 in terms of a process already begun rather than of a crisis in the future – 'in terms of the painful process of using up one's strength and parting with one's physical health in obedience to the will of God . . .'[84] He was acutely sensitive to the pain involved in forgiveness and reconciliation in inter-personal relations, but conscious of having himself lived 'a pretty sheltered life' (below, p. 93). Neither the trenches nor the Holocaust seem to have dented his idealism and faith in God's future.

Charlie's article on 'The Borderlands of Ontology in the New Testament' was suggested by the MacKinnon occasion for which it was written rather than by any special competence in philosophy, but his passion for natural history was well-informed, though less so (he would say) than that of his surviving elder brother George. He once even surprised the biographer and hero-worshipper of John Ray, Charles Raven, by discovering a species in Grantchester meadows that was not believed to grow in Cambridgeshire, and his Ethel M. Wood lecture on *Man and Nature in the New Testament* (1964) shows an ecological imperative stimulating his biblical research. But his classical education was more literary than philosophical. Those who criticized his New Testament theology for its simplicity might call it 'spirituality' rather than 'theology' without impugning its academic integrity; Charlie did want his writings to be 'edifying' in the Pauline sense of 'building up' the Church, and admitted to being an amateur in some areas of theology, but the learning, professionalism and brilliance of the philological, critical and exegetical work underlying his New Testament theology command respect and admiration.

The main thrust of that New Testament theology and the mid-twentieth-century liberal evangelical standpoint it reflects are both evident in *The Sacrifice of Christ*. Charlie's evangelical emphasis on 'the finished work of Christ' had led him to speak of uniqueness and finality, and so brought him back to Paul who, 'for a different purpose in a quite different context' had spoken of 'the absolute priority of the Son over

---

84 'St Paul and Dualism' (*NTS* 1965/6) rp. *Essays in New Testament Interpretation*, Cambridge: Cambridge University Press.

creation'.[85] The Christ hymn in Colossians (1.15–20) and the new (last) Adam at 1 Corinthians 15.45 make

> the Man Christ Jesus . . . the heart of the mystery. Whatever angle you approach it from, you always reach the centre: in Jesus Christ God is at work uniquely, with incomparable intensity. The incarnation is something absolute and final because of its unique quality: an act of creation only comparable to God's initial creation.[86]

Karl Barth had famously explained his aims in the Preface to the second edition of his epoch-making *The Epistle to the Romans* (1922, ET 1933) in the following sentence among others: 'Intelligent comment means that I am driven on till I stand with nothing before me but the enigma of the matter; till the document seems hardly to exist as a document, till I have almost forgotten that I am not its author; till I know the author so well that I allow him to speak in my name and am even able to speak in his name myself.'[87]

Unlike Bultmann, Hoskyns, Käsemann and Barrett, but like many other historical critical exegetes, Charlie had no enthusiasm for Barth's explicitly theological exegesis, which seemed to him arbitrary. Most New Testament theology speaks of God in indirect speech, describing the authors' discourse rather than speaking of God confessionally. If present at all, its contemporary thought of God is implicit, present in the modern scholars' tacitly identifying with what they think Paul and other biblical authors are saying about God. But sometimes it is clear enough that what is being described or wrestled with corresponds to what the modern writer actually believes. In that sense Charlie's account of Paul's theology comes close to Barth's aim. Even though he was conscious of the historical distance between himself and the biblical texts, his exposition seeks to bridge it, not merely describe it.

Charlie is sensitive to the differences between the New Testament writers but is convinced that they are at one in essentials. 'The Johannine writings, in their own special idiom, tell the same story.'[88] The Johannine Prologue is set alongside Colossians 1, the Gospel's 'only begotten of the Father' corresponding to the Pauline 'first born' – only 'set in an

---

85 Moule, *Forgiveness and Reconciliation*, p. 150.

86 *Ibid.*

87 Karl Barth, 1933, *The Epistle to the Romans*, 2nd edn, trans. Edwyn C. Hoskyns, Oxford: Oxford University Press, p. 8.

88 Moule, *Forgiveness and Reconciliation*, p. 151.

even wider context of thought'.[89] 'And although very broadly it may be true that whereas for St Paul Christ saves by his death, for the Fourth Evangelist it is by his life, yet for the Fourth Evangelist too the death is the decisive thing.'[90] John 10.11, 12.32 and 12.24 are echoed in support of this belief in the essential unity of the New Testament.

The uniqueness and finality of the incarnation, and 'the centrality, for all Christian thinking, of the Jesus of history', are what he wants to emphasize here, rather than any particular theory of atonement.[91] 'The "scandal of particularity" is ruthlessly forced upon us by the New Testament wherever we turn.'[92] That English translation of Kittel's phrase in *Mysterium Christi* (1930) has become almost a technical term for the inescapably unique *historical* reference of the incarnation, against all idealisms. Both Gospel sacraments are sacraments of the death of Christ, but while 'baptism especially represents the finality and unrepeatability of it',[93] the Holy Communion 'represents repetition'.[94] The latter point is the theme of *The Sacrifice of Christ*, but before it is unfolded 'The Work of Christ Continuing' is considered in more general terms as 'the approach of the living God – the personal approach of the living God to man'.[95] For Paul the gospel is 'the power of God leading to salvation – leading, that is, to total soundness, completeness and integrity of personality . . . more than a declaration . . . something which we do not merely know about but experience, essentially God's action to reconcile estranged man to himself'.[96] If this 'is the living God at work, and it is part and parcel of the fellowship which issues from his work and in which it is perpetuated' then 'there can never be an end absolutely to this reconciliation'.[97] And so, as the Fourth Evangelist put it at 2.19, 'Destroy this Temple, and in three days I will raise it up again' – referring to the temple of his body.

> And thus it was that the physical body of Christ, given up to death and raised from death, brought with it that fellowship which we call the Church, the Body of Christ . . . And in a sense, too, the Church

---

89 *Ibid.*
90 *Ibid.*
91 *Ibid.*, p. 152.
92 *Ibid.*, p. 151.
93 *Ibid.*
94 *Ibid.*, p. 161.
95 *Ibid.*, p. 152.
96 *Op. cit.*, p. 153.
97 *Ibid.*

was continuous with the People of God of the old dispensation. The unique incarnation, for all its uniqueness and finality, is found to be the centre of history – not discontinuous; a great flowing stream, not a separate draught of water; the apex of a pyramid, not an unattached point in mid-air. Or, better, it is the point of intersection of the two lines which, narrowing as the faithful remnant showed itself to be a minority, and converging to vanishing point when the remnant came to be one perfect Man, yet diverge again as the one Man becomes the growing point of a new society.[98]

With echoes of Cullmann's theory of 'salvation history', the connection is made here between 'the position of Jesus in history' and ecclesiology – which belongs with 'the universally agreed doctrine of the Person of Christ. If in any sense the incarnation is continuous with the People of God before it, then in some sense redemption must be continued in the Church after it.'[99]

This is saying that salvation cannot be simply an event in the past. It must continue in the present because it is essentially a matter of reconciliation between the personal God and human persons, and reconciliation requires on-going action for ever after the decisive moment. The parable of the prodigal son, drawn out beyond the intentions of the text in Luke 15, implies a continuation and also provides the best account of 'the reciprocal quality of reconciliation'.[100] This human analogy

> provides a salutary touchstone of our soundness. For after all, there are no higher, no profounder categories known to us than the personal; and the most elaborate sub-personal analogies of ransom, bond or sacrifice, or the most abstruse abstracts of metaphysics, however valuable they are as contributory explanation.
>
> The boy could see, as he looked at his father, what suffering had gone into that reconciling love, how costly it had been. But it is done . . . by the father's forthgoing initiative. The son came home, true; but the father it was who alone could initiate the offer of restoration.[101]

However, a reconciliation between persons cannot be one-sided or mechanical. 'It has to be both received and reciprocated. The son

---

98 *Ibid.*
99 *Ibid.*
100 *Ibid.*, p. 154.
101 *Ibid.*

progressively responds'.[102] The hostile older brother has to be forgiven by the prodigal. 'Here is the test: can the younger brother sacrificially enter into his father's conciliatory attitude? Can he align his will with his father's will for the wholeness of the family? . . . In a sense it all depends now on him.'[103] Acceptance and transmission of forgiveness are a necessary part of the expanding picture. The passage in Colossians about the Apostle taking his share in the afflictions of Christ (Col. 1.24) is again brought into the discussion because 'the Christian and Christ are somehow connected. To be in Christ is of course to share Christ's sufferings', and (in line with Jewish apocalyptic doctrine of the messianic woes due to be completed before the end comes) 'there is a quota of sufferings which the whole Church, the corporate Christ, has to exhaust before God's plan of salvation is complete'.[104]

The costly experience of forgiveness and reconciliation implied by the parable connects with his christologically based doctrine of the Church. The messianic community has to suffer, and 'the more mystical conception of (disciples) sharing Christ's cross'[105] is part of that. In a book he greatly admired, *Communion with God in the New Testament* (1953), A. R. George had insisted that Paul's '*own actual sufferings are a real participation in Christ's sufferings, suffered by virtue of his communion with Christ*'.[106] 'The family' implied by the parable becomes the Church which similarly 'has to enter into the realization of the reparation' – and that is the highly qualified sense in which 'Christ's sacrifice can be spoken of as constantly renewed'.[107] And as the Eucharist is in this sense a sacrifice related to Calvary, 'so was the obedience of Abraham. Since Christ is the centre of history and, though a real individual, is yet more than an individual, he gathers up into himself all the God-ward activities of all his people and creatures, past, present and future: he is one with mankind and with creation'.[108] The reciprocal nature of redemption has led Charlie here to speak of Christology and the Trinity, and he develops this in terms of 'the inclusive Christ as the Second Adam, the New Man, the beginning of God's new creation'. Christ is more

---

102 *Ibid.*
103 *Ibid.*
104 *Ibid.*, p. 155.
105 *Ibid.*, p. 156.
106 A. R. George, 1953, *Communion with God in the New Testament*, London: Epworth, quoted in Moule, *Forgiveness and Reconciliation*, p. 156. Italics added by Moule.
107 *Ibid.*
108 *Ibid.*

than an individual, he is representative Man, fulfilling human destiny. 'Therefore Christ's obedience is human obedience. And if humanity, as a result, begins to obey, that may be called Christ's obedience in humanity.'[109]

This 'real element of continuity' between Christ and humanity, between his obedience and ours, which is derived from Christ's 'perfect, underived holiness' is not really explained.[110] Much of what counts as explanation in biblical scholarship consists in providing parallels from the history of religions. As a theologian Barth rightly wanted more. Charlie's precise description and grammatical analysis of Paul's 'in Christ ' texts scarcely provide this. If he is content to inhabit rather than explain them his work is as much spirituality as theological interpretation.

The first task of the biblical theologian is to describe the texts in ways that relate them to each other and to subsequent Christianity before venturing into the deeper and uncertain waters of historical and theological explanation. Any attempt to understand the texts involves interpretation, but theologians are generally aware of the risk of distortion they take in attempting to communicate the gospel in a new world of thought. Bultmann remarked in 1926, 'It is no small matter when we so to speak interpret away *those* ideas of Paul which *at first sight* are the clearest and which were doubtless important to him, such as the whole "end of history" scenario, whether by reinterpretation or through critical sifting.'[111] Charlie did not need to be so bold, because he allowed for fluidity and change in Pauline conceptions of the end, and his historical judgements about New Testament eschatology were closer to Dodd's modernizations than to the apocalyptic emphasis of Bultmann and his teacher, J. Weiss (cf. below, pp. 155–62). His attempt to understand 'The Influence of Circumstances on the Use of Eschatological Terms' (1964, rp. 1982), following a similar exploration of christological terms in the same *Journal of Theological Studies* in 1959, is historical rather than hermeneutical, and his historical description, like that of many British scholars at the time, corresponded sufficiently to his own beliefs to function as New Testament theology. Whether he or Bultmann understood Paul or Christianity better need not be adjudicated here. In the communion of saints there are diverse theological interpretations of Scripture, not all mutually exclusive. Both the gospel and

---

109 *Ibid.*, p. 158, made gender inclusive.

110 *Ibid.*

111 Rudolf Bultmann, 1969, *Faith and Understanding* 1, trans. Louise Pettibone Smith, London: SCM Press, p. 86. Translation modified.

Scripture are illuminated by the interplay of different, and sometimes conflicting, attempts to understand them.

## The Church

In Charlie's account of the atonement, 'the one, final, definitive act of God in Jesus Christ' is also his *continuous* act. The father's act of welcoming his son 'was only the "focal" point of a long-formed character and constant activity . . . The father's character is the real continuum. He is that sort of father: that is why reconciliation can take place. God is a self-incarnating God and that is how man is related to him.'[112] There is no question of Christ offering himself or being offered again.

> Yet, because we are incorporated in Christ, the work of salvation is in a sense actually continuing among us: it is not ours but it is Christ's in us . . . Thus the church is not the source of salvation, but it is the transmitter of salvation and the sphere in which God's saving work continues.[113]

He will not say that the Church is the extension of the incarnation, or even of the atonement, because nothing can infringe the uniqueness of Christ. 'The Church is not co-equal with God as Christ is.'[114] A Christian's act of obedience, including participation in 'the sacrament of obedience', is Christ's obedience in us, but it cannot be fully identified 'with the absolute and perfect act of obedience by God incarnate in Christ'.[115]

A line is drawn, 'but on any showing Christ is closely concerned in the activity of his Church: the Church's sufferings are his. And the Church, if not fully an incarnation, is destined to grow up in all things into Christ's full stature . . .'[116] Charlie goes even further than this language of Ephesians in daring to speculate on the eschatological 'coming Great Church'[117] – a dangerous phrase common in the 1950s. Talk about 'the century of the Church', and church unity in a generation, risked an element of triumphalism, as do all schemes of 'salvation history', with

---

112 Moule, *Forgiveness and Reconciliation*, p. 159.
113 *Ibid.*
114 *Ibid.*, p. 160.
115 *Ibid.*
116 *Ibid.*
117 *Ibid.*

their strong ecclesiological slant. Unlike some more recent Anglican ecclesiology the impulses coming out of the World Council of Churches and the Second Vatican Council 50 years ago were Scripture-based and owed much to the revival of theological interpretation triggered by Barth's exegesis. Charlie's theology and spirituality reflect that earlier period. Their New Testament basis ensured that his ecclesiology remained dependent on and subordinate to Christology and atonement theology. As he continued to probe the exegetical roots of his own theology, and aimed to secure its foundations, it was Christ rather than the Church that was his theme. But his emphasis upon 'the corporate Christ' meant that he was often at the same time talking about life in the Church, as was the Epistle to the Colossians.

The parable of the Prodigal Son does not necessarily invite reflection on the future of the personal relationships within that family, but Charlie's emphasis upon the continuing process of reconciliation is a legitimate application for a Christian preacher. It is not a scriptural argument, but we can see here one way in which biblical interpretation informs and stimulates Christian reflection. Very little, if anything, can today be 'proved' from Scripture, but much can be and is suggested by its authoritative witness. Beyond providing some essential Christian language and an overarching story within which believers live and move and have their being, it contains countless passages that alone or in combination with other passages may at any moment become a *source* of faith for an individual, and are an inexhaustible reservoir nourishing the faith of the Church. The witness of Scripture as a whole, or rather the New Testament together with everything in the Old which is necessary for a correct theological understanding of the New, also provides some control against modern accounts of Christianity that can scarcely claim to be true to Scripture and tradition. It is this role of Scripture as a 'norm' of authentic Christianity which in a historically conscious age calls for a New Testament theology based on historical exegesis. Other forms of biblical interpretation have their place in the life of the Church, and not only in private devotion. But just as Thomas Aquinas insisted on the 'literal sense' as a control in theological argument, so historically responsible exegesis is essential wherever theological arguments appeal to Scripture. New insights often come from elsewhere, including from more imaginative readings of Scripture, but the hard work of testing the spirits requires attention to the original meanings of Scripture as well as to subsequent tradition and contemporary experience.

Charlie expected historical-exegetical New Testament theology to inform and inspire contemporary Christian witness. The parable was used to illuminate what he wanted to say, not as a proof-text. The theological foundations of his position are to be found more in his understanding of the life of Jesus than in his teaching, and especially in the Pauline (and deutero-Pauline) epistles, above all in the phrase 'in Christ'. He interprets this phrase (as Bultmann does) with an ecclesiological emphasis – though the Church for him is the empirical institution as well as Bultmann's eschatological congregation. The prodigal's fellowship with the father, the union of their wills, leads him to share the father's sacrificial love and so (perhaps) win over the elder brother and 'be his true self and make his contribution to the wholeness of the family'.[118] 'Our own obedience is imperfect, but in union with Christ's perfect obedience it is offered to God, and may it not be said ... joined in the stream of Christ's obedient love which flows to the Father?'[119]

That quotation, closely relating sacrament and ethics, indicates how Charlie could say 'we offer' at the Eucharist. We offer our obedience as well as our gifts and our praise and thanksgiving. The exposition also recalls his basic belief in the Triune God. He would later resist the liberal Protestant readiness of his colleague and friend Geoffrey Lampe (1912–80) to jettison the doctrine of the Trinity. He had some sympathy for the former evangelical Lampe's moderate liberalism, but the shape of his own theology kept him within the parameters of patristic and Anglican orthodoxy. In his post-retirement contributions to the debate stimulated by a collection of essays edited by John Hick and provocatively entitled *The Myth of God Incarnate* (1977) he is critical of Hick's 'puerile travesty' of the doctrine of the atonement and repeats (and refers back to) what he had written in *The Sacrifice of Christ*. He argues further that 'on a theistic view, it is impossible not to believe that God's creative work of reconciliation permeates the whole of his creation and all history, so that every act of self-sacrificing service and genuine forgiveness by anyone at any time is a part of it'.[120]

These and other post-retirement writings (including those published here) reflect the same orthodoxy as his earlier work. He had in the 1960s shared a staircase and the chapel at Clare with John Robinson's successor as dean, the former evangelical and increasingly liberal Maurice Wiles, but had seen no reason to change his own position and will have answered 'No' when Wiles followed 'In defence of Arius' (1962) with 'Does Christology Rest on a Mistake?' (1970; both reprinted with

---

118 *Ibid.*, p. 166.
119 *Ibid.*
120 *Ibid.*, p. 86.

similar essays questioning patristic orthodoxy in *Working Papers on Doctrine*, 1976). A similar consistency can be observed in Charlie's New Testament scholarship, but before turning to the historicity of the Gospels and arguments about the resurrection more can be said about the Christology (and related ecclesiology) summed up in the phrase 'the corporate Christ'. This needs to be given priority as a reminder that the emphasis upon the historical Jesus, which Charlie shared with some less orthodox liberal Protestantism, was in his case part of a larger and more catholic picture.

The theological correspondences that he saw between the New Testament and his contemporary Christian belief are explored in *The Phenomenon of the New Testament* (1968) and *The Origin of Christology* (1977). Both have chapters entitled 'The Corporate Christ', discussing Paul's phrase 'in Christ'. The later book does so at greater length and includes a long section on 'the Body' and a short one on 'the Temple'. Charlie's exegesis of the key 'in Christ' texts, sometimes reflected in the New English Bible's paraphrases, accepts that the 'in' is often instrumental, meaning 'through' the salvation wrought by Christ. However, he argues also for some passages (including baptism 'into' Christ) having a strong, incorporative sense. Comparisons with other New Testament writings suggest that the experience that lies behind the phrase was not limited to Paul, and other scholars as different as John Robinson and Ernst Käsemann are marshalled in support. Charlie's interest is not to establish a 'high' doctrine of the Church, but to suggest that here we have 'a christological datum of great significance'.[121] He admits to 'puzzlement' about what it might mean, but insists that here is something new and remarkable. Paul

> does seem to conceive of the living Christ as more than individual, while still knowing him vividly and distinctly as fully personal. He speaks of Christian life as lived in an area which is Christ; he speaks of Christians as incorporated in him. He thinks of the Christian community as (ideally) a harmoniously co-ordinated living organism like a body, and, on occasion, thinks of Christ as himself the living body of which Christians are limbs.[122]

Unlike most New Testament scholars, Charlie does not look for parallels from the history of religion, which might throw light on Paul's

---

121 Moule, *Origin of Christology*, p. 53.
122 *Ibid.*, p. 85.

conception of 'the body of Christ' and being 'in Christ' (closely related at Rom. 12.5). Dodd turned to the religious language of Hellenism to explain the Johannine 'union with God' before concluding that love is 'the only kind of union *between persons* of which we can have any possible experience'.[123] Charlie does little more than 'substitute the Pauline doctrine of the corporate Christ for the Johannine Son of Man doctrine' in which Dodd thought that 'a new insight is revealed into the relation of the individual and the corporate in the realm of the personal'.[124] He is unsure about 'the meaning of incorporation',[125] but sure it is based on Paul's experience of the risen Christ. Rather than invoke general Christian ecclesial experience to make sense of Christology he describes Paul's corporate language which (he infers) must be based on a specific experience of the risen Christ, and draws from that an argument for the truth of the Christian estimate of Jesus.

It is surely right to find in Paul a high ecclesial ideal, even though this was constantly being challenged by empirical realities in Corinth and elsewhere, and has been continually put into question by subsequent Christian history. This history weakens any apologetic argument, but one task of New Testament theology is (arguably) to draw from the texts an ideal by which the empirical Church can be measured, tested, challenged and inspired. That requires making the ideal intelligible, however, and explaining Paul's phrase by reference to his religious experience is likely to illuminate only those who can lay claim to a similar experience. It is hard to doubt that Charlie heard in Paul's language something that corresponded to his own experience. This relates his New Testament theology to his 'spirituality'. He 'inhabited' this biblical language. But it was difficult to communicate to others who did not share his experience of the living Christ. In one discussion following the publication of *The Origin of Christology* a sceptical colleague suggested he ask Jesus how Jim Callaghan's government was getting on. Alternative ways of decoding Paul's language in terms that are both historically plausible and illuminate contemporary Christian practice and belief are surely needed, but Charlie's deriving ecclesiology from Christology contains a warning against reducing the apostle's phrases to meaning membership of God's family or being 'in' the family, true as that also is. Charlie valued the family imagery of Paul, John and

---

123  C. H. Dodd, 1953, *The Interpretation of the Fourth Gospel*, Cambridge: Cambridge University Press, p. 199.

124  Moule, *Origin of Christology*, p. 51.

125  *Ibid.*, p. 49.

Hebrews, but the 'many brothers and sisters' of Romans 8.29 are second to Christ the first-born, as are 'the children God has given me' (Heb. 2.13) and as, too, are the disciples supposedly included in the corporate Son of Man idea.

## Jesus alive

Charlie's early publications from 1944 to 1962 on the New Testament Church, its worship and its ministry, were stimulated by his work as a theological teacher in the mid-twentieth-century Church. At the end of this period, a few years into his tenure of Lady Margaret's chair, Cambridge became noteworthy for what passed as more radical thinking than biblical theology and liturgical renewal. In 1962 Alec Vidler edited a collection of essays entitled *Soundings*, and the following year John Robinson (by then on the South Bank as Bishop of Woolwich) trailed *Honest to God* with an article in *The Observer*, 'Our Image of God Must Go'. Charlie, Robinson and Maurice Wiles who succeeded them as Dean of Clare in 1959, were considered too traditional to be invited into the *Soundings* group, but Charlie contributed to the series of Open Lectures by which the Divinity Faculty enjoyed its new public profile. He also signed the Faculty's public statements opposing exorcism and advocating inter-communion. But he remained more traditional than some of his friends, including Hugh Montefiore and Geoffrey Lampe in *Soundings*, and Lampe in a published dialogue with Donald MacKinnon on *The Resurrection* (1966). Among several contributions to the 1960s debates on the resurrection, both popular (in *The Franciscan*, 1963) and technical ('St Paul and "dualism": The Pauline Conception of Resurrection' in *New Testament Studies*, 1965/6, rp. 1982) was his Introduction to the 1968 English translation (which he edited) of a recent German collection of essays on the resurrection of Jesus.[126]

This volume arose out of disquiet in the German churches about Bultmann's and later Marxsen's understandings of this event, but Charlie took the opportunity to discuss the English debate, and engaged with Lampe (though not with MacKinnon). He notes that 'Professor Lampe rests his faith on the good evidence that Jesus was found to be alive after

---

126 Willi Marxsen (and others), *The Significance of the Message of the Resurrection for Faith in Jesus Christ*, ET ed. and intro. by C. F. D. Moule, London: SCM Press.

his death . . . which cannot have been due to mere hallucination . . .'.[127] Lampe (he says) 'expressly dissociates himself' from the (supposedly) Bultmannian position 'that Jesus "rose" only in the sense that his followers came to understand his true significance'.[128] Lampe maintains 'that there was an encounter, which they hadn't dreamed up for themselves, between the objective presence of Christ "outside" themselves, and their own selves'.[129] But Lampe 'does not believe that the story of the empty tomb is to be taken literally', partly because he thinks the evidence weak, and partly 'because, as a theologian, he repels any inference that the character of Christ's resurrection is different from that which, as Christians believe, belongs to those who are in Christ (whose bodies undoubtedly decay and are destroyed)'.[130] Charlie disagrees. The empty tomb 'is not altogether easy to dismiss as a late, apologetic development. Neither . . . is it easy to see how it can be a symbol of the involvement of the resurrection within time and space unless there is also something literally spatio-temporal about it.'[131] He therefore tries to answer Lampe's theological objection with a theory of total transformation of the entire created order which would be 'congruous with the idea of a God who never creates without a purpose'.[132] He admits his theory may seem 'ludicrous', but resists accepting the empty tomb as a symbol of the space-time involvement without trying to elucidate it. Why the symbol requires the fact, not merely the story, is not made clear.

Charlie's mild disagreements with Lampe illuminate his own creedal orthodoxy, one which did not worry (as MacKinnon did) over the philosophical language of 'substance'. In an appreciative obituary he discusses a 1978 sermon of Lampe, reprinted posthumously in his *Explorations in Theology* (1981), entitled 'What Future for the Trinity?'. Taking that to mean 'What future is there for the traditional classical *doctrine* of the Trinity?' Charlie reports that Lampe's answer was 'Not much.' The patristic language could not 'do justice today to the conviction that God, as Creator, operates from within his creation and not

---

127 *Ibid.*, p. 3.

128 *Ibid.*, p. 4. The *kerygma* into which Bultmann once said Jesus rose spoke more deliberately of God than that reductionist account suggests, bringing his position closer to Lampe's.

129 G. W. H. Lampe and D. M. MacKinnon, *Resurrection*, London: Mowbray, 1966 p. 21, quoted in Marxsen, *Significance*, p. 3.

130 Marxsen, *Significance*, p. 6.

131 *Ibid.*, p. 9.

132 *Ibid.*, p. 10.

by invasion from without, and approaches human beings on a fully personal level'.[133]

In Lampe's view, God's approach to humankind was better understood in terms of inspiration than incarnation. Charlie comments on Lampe's Bampton lectures *God as Spirit* (1977): 'if pressed to its logical conclusion, its argument would lead to some kind of Unitarianism, since essential to the argument are the interpretation of Jesus as an inspired man (albeit supremely and decisively inspired), and the restating of the resurrection of Jesus in terms of a new experience of the Spirit of God in the light of the life and teaching of Jesus. Correspondingly it would mean an "exemplarist" interpretation of how Christ brings new life . . .'[134] Charlie resists this and thinks that 'it is when he comes to the finality of Christ that he has most difficulty in logically defending his own position',[135] but says that Lampe 'had no intention of abandoning the essentials of Christian faith and practice, of which he was a shining and inspiring example'.[136]

Lampe had said in the 1978 sermon that he believed

> we should rethink the use of doctrinal models which led to the formulation of this doctrine [i.e. that of the Trinity] – but not the faith which they are intended to express. If we do substitute unitarianism for trinitarianism it must not be the unitarianism that denies the divinity of Christ. On the contrary, I believe we can assert that God was in Christ, without using the model of 'God the Son'. It must not be a unitarianism which postulates a deistically-conceived God remote from the world, separated from our human hearts and minds; we must acknowledge the present reality of God with us and in us; yet without, I hope, the confusions of the fourth-century theology of the Holy Spirit.[137]

Charlie also held no brief for fourth-century complications. In an article on 'The New Testament and the Doctrine of the Trinity: A Short Report on an Old Theme' he rejects Maurice Wiles' dissatisfaction with Nicene orthodoxy 'so far as the relations between God and Christ go. Here, historical events really did lead on to such an experience of God

---

133 *Proceedings of the British Academy* 67, 1981, p. 404.

134 *Ibid.*

135 *Ibid.*

136 *Ibid.*

137 Geoffrey Lampe, 1981, *Explorations in Theology*, London: SCM Press, p. 36.

as seems to the reason rightly to be described as implying a binitarian conception.'[138] But he is less sure about the Spirit, recognizing that his argument from history and the disciples' experience of Jesus is less strong here. 'It is the place of the Spirit in an "essential" Godhead and the reasons for a trinitarian statement that still seem, on these grounds, less evident.'[139] But he accepts the orthodox doctrine, with a little help from John Robinson, and thinks it possible that 'even if the New Testament scarcely shows this, subsequent reflection, after the New Testament period, rightly recognized that New Testament experience could not ultimately be adequately safeguarded without it'.[140]

His chapter on 'Subsequent Doctrinal Developments' in *The Holy Spirit* (1978) admits that

> 'a fully trinitarian doctrine of God raises difficult questions. It is easier to understand how a doctrine of 'binity' arose. Christ was a vivid personality. He had been known by his contemporaries as a friend and companion. And, if their experience of him, then and subsequently, drove them to see in him not only a historical individual but also an eternal and more than individual reality – 'one with God in his being' – yet this could not obliterate the sense of his distinctness; though one with God he could never be merged in an undifferentiated way in the unity of God. It must be, it seemed, that God's inviolable unity was, somehow and mysteriously, 'plural'. But why include Spirit in this plurality? 'Spirit' is, after all, only one of several terms denoting divine action or divine intention or (especially) divine immanence – that is, God in his activity within his creation . . .'[141]

He notes how 'attempts to define the relation of the Spirit to the Son . . . led to lamentable dissension, constituting one of the most deplorable chapters in the history of hair-splitting theology'[142] and finally suggests 'one ought not to agonize too much over problems of trinity in the description of God'.[143] But he accepts the Church's teaching and appeals to Christian experience. This would lead to binitarianism, when

---

138 C. F. D. Moule, 1976, 'The New Testament and the Doctrine of the Trinity: A Short Report on an Old Theme', *Expository Times* 88.1, p. 19.

139 *Ibid.*

140 *Ibid.*

141 C. F. D. Moule, 1978, *The Holy Spirit*, London: Mowbray, p. 46.

142 *Ibid.*, p. 47.

143 *Ibid.*, p. 50.

'Jesus Christ was found to be not only a historical individual but also a transcendent Being . . .'.[144] But then,

> side by side with but distinguishable from the Christian experience of being 'members of Christ', incorporated in him, was the experience of Christ's character being imparted to each Christian, and Christ's attitude to God being reproduced in each Christian. And this, by common consent, seems to have been best described as the work of the Spirit of God through Christ, or even as the work of the Spirit of Christ. Thus, in addition to the establishing of an intrinsic plurality in the deity, Christian experience led to the recognition of at least two distinguishable 'modes' of God's presence with (humans) . . . .[145]

On the one hand, 'Christ was experienced as Mediator, and Christians found themselves incorporated in him.'[146] On the other, 'the Holy Spirit was found in and among Christians, interpreting Christ and creating his likeness in them. It is thus intelligible that the Church came to speak of God as eternally Father, Son and Spirit.'[147] Charlie's 'conservative liberal' endorsement of the traditional doctrine would not satisfy modern trinitarian theologians. For him the most important aspect of a Christian conception of God is that Jesus lives, the eternal Son. Left to himself he might have been a binitarian, but he was a clergyman of the Church of England, licensed to preach, and therefore committed to its basic doctrines. As a theologian he tried to understand and defend them, but he agreed with Lampe that the divinity of Christ was more defensible by a rational appeal to experience than the post-Nicene debate is.

## History as apologetics

It was in response to the changing theological climate of the 1960s and '70s that Charlie's biblical theological writing became more explicitly apologetic, defending traditional Christology at points where he thought its critics were ignoring or overlooking some of the 'facts' and 'evidence'. Exegetical conclusions published in the 1950s, especially Jesus' apparently corporate Son of Man idea and Paul's 'corporate

---

144 *Ibid.*
145 *Ibid.*, p. 51.
146 *Ibid.*
147 *Ibid.*

Christ', find a new apologetic edge in the face of two challenges: first the revival of reductionist liberal Protestant Christology among English doctrinal theologians; and second the new impact of the radical German tradition on international New Testament scholarship.

Since Wrede's *The Messianic Secret in the Gospels* (1901, ET 1971), and behind that D. F. Strauss and F. C. Baur (most tellingly Strauss' *The Christ of Faith and the Jesus of History*, 1865, ET 1977), the more radical liberal Protestant critics had emphasized the discontinuity between the historical figure of Jesus and the christological faith of the early Church. As this tendency spread, partly through the now international influence of Bultmann, Charlie responded that the historical evidence of the New Testament points in a different direction. The emergence of Christianity suggests that the followers of Jesus were compelled by what they saw of Jesus in his ministry, and shortly after his death, to recognize in him something that transcends ordinary human categories. The truth of their resurrection faith is the best explanation of the evidence.

This argument that the historical evidence for the emergence of Christianity somehow supports its truth was unlikely to persuade many who were not already inclined to accept the New Testament witness. It is, however, surely correct that the historical component of that religious witness should not be ignored. It is relevant to the truth of the message even if it cannot confirm this. Charlie's conclusions about how Jesus saw his mission and ministry may or may not be right. The evidence is insufficient to answer with any confidence some of the historical questions posed by these texts and by the emergence of Christianity. But it is obvious that the origins of Christianity pose a historical question, and that part of any plausible historical answer must lie in the historical reality of Jesus and in what his followers experienced shortly after his death. The main problems with Charlie's proposal lie in his move from a historical effect to a trans-historical cause. Most other historians limit themselves to historical causes, and if these are insufficient to explain what happened they will leave the problem unsolved rather than be driven to accept a kind of explanation that falls outside their naturalist frame of reference.

Even the historical attempt to find much of the post-resurrection belief germinally present in Jesus' own self-understanding is problematic. A picture of Jesus that conveniently corresponds to post-resurrection beliefs can always be suspected of reflecting these beliefs, rather than deriving from the reliable memories of eyewitnesses. There is in any case no reason to choose between an explanation of the origin(s) of

Christology that sees post-resurrection faith developing or unfolding from what was there in Jesus, and one that finds an explanation in the early Church's needs and the resources and pressures of the religious environment. Presumably both played a part and the decisions are about what weight to give to each. However, the attempt to make sense of the continuities that must have existed between Jesus and the Church remains a primary task of both New Testament scholarship and theological reflection, regardless of its apologetic potential. And stripped of its apologetic ambitions Charlie's hypothetical construction of the history remains discussable.

*The Phenomenon of the New Testament* (1967) is explicit about its apologetic intent, and acknowledges that this is unfashionable: 'It is no longer regarded as necessarily desirable to stand up for one's faith . . . Is not Christian faith something that not only does not need to defend itself, but by definition cannot begin to produce evidence without ceasing to be faith?'[148] While not wanting to follow the old 'quest of the historical Jesus' into its earlier cul de sac, Charlie denies that the quest is irrelevant. Both in this book and in the rightly better known *Origin of Christology* (1977) his most distinctive contribution to it may be found in his interpretation of the christological title 'the Son of Man'. He follows T. W. Manson and C. H. Dodd in supposing that it had a corporate sense for Jesus himself, following Daniel 7.22 where the cryptogram represents 'the people of the saints of the Most High'. This provides in Jesus' self-understanding and ministry a root for Paul's 'corporate Christ'.

The hypothesis has not found many advocates outside England, but it was surely a sound instinct to look for anything in Jesus' ministry and teaching that might help explain the Church's post-resurrection faith historically. This need not be reductionist, as though historical intelligibility were incompatible with belief in divine agency. Whether this belief can be prepared for or strengthened by historical hypotheses is more questionable, but making a hypothesis about Jesus' self-understanding part of any attempt to understand historically the emergence of resurrection faith is surely right. What was experienced after the death of Jesus is also important, and this will surely have been influenced by the life and teaching that preceded it. Both are necessary in making historical sense of Christian origins.

An appendix in *The Phenomenon of the New Testament* reprints an essay from 1952 containing part of the ground plan of his New Testa-

---

148 C. F. D. Moule, 1967, *The Phenomenon of the New Testament*, London: SCM Press, pp. 1–2.

ment theology – in which some early Christian theology corresponds to his own. He modestly observes that 'From Defendant to Judge – and Deliverer', which discusses the theme of vindication, reiterates 'what has been said by others – for instance, recently (1950) by Professor T. W. Manson' about the Son of Man. But it challenges the idea of Jeremias and Vincent Taylor that in Jesus' teaching 'the figure of the Suffering Servant of Isaiah 53 is fused with that of the Son of Man'.[149] It was rather (in Charlie's view) Jesus' person and work that led Paul and others to recognize his redemptive significance, more than his words. Already in Daniel 'the Son of Man' means *'the representative of God's chosen people, destined through suffering to be exalted'*.[150] The application of the term to Jesus

> at least represents his expectation of victory through suffering, vindication after defeat. But it means more than being vindicated; it means vindicating; for on any showing the term is to this extent a collective one that the person of Jesus is representative, inclusive, incorporative; and therefore if his cause is vindicated, then with it he becomes the *Vindex* of the body of people whom he represents and sums up.[151]

Other New Testament witnesses are drawn into the discussion, without the variety being underestimated. Some unity in the New Testament is assumed, but it is not forced on the material.

Paul's justification language might be expected to support Charlie's argument, but his exegetical judgement is not tailored to fit the theological case. Or perhaps a different theological interest takes priority. He comments, 'I believe that in some passages these terms have moved so far from a verdict of acquittal or even a triumphant vindication of the oppressed as to be interpretable rather in terms of putting right a spoilt relationship – in short, that *dikaioun* (to justify) is often nearer to *katalassein* (to reconcile) than anything else; and that this use of *dikaioun* to denote a personal relationship restored is probably the most characteristic one in the Paulines.'[152] Romans 8.29–34 and perhaps Romans 4.25 are exceptional in speaking of vindication. Elsewhere Paul's forensic language is assimilated to 'reconciliation'. This term is important in Colossians and Ephesians but exceptional in the undisputed

---

149 *Ibid.*, p. 82.
150 *Ibid.*, p. 89, italics in original.
151 *Ibid.*, p. 90.
152 *Ibid.*, p. 94.

letters, found mainly at Romans 5.10–11 and 2 Corinthians 5.18–19 (see also Rom. 11.15; 1 Cor. 7.11 is not soteriological). The argument about vindication is weakened by this interpretation of justification but Charlie's primary insistence on personal categories when speaking of the divine–human relationship is reinforced.

Second only to suggesting what exactly Jesus may have meant by 'the kingdom of God', the meaning of 'the Son of Man' is the most central, disputed and intractable problem in Gospel study. Charlie's suggestion has the historical and theological merit of making a connection between the Jesus of history behind the Gospel tradition and the faith of the early Church in him as Lord, Messiah, Son of God. This problem was described by Bultmann as 'how the proclaimer became the proclaimed', and in Loisy's remark that 'Jesus proclaimed the kingdom of God; it was the Church that came', and even in Wellhausen's statement of the obvious that 'Jesus was not a Christian; he was a Jew'. When Charlie made his proposal in 1952 this relationship was not the central issue in English theology that it had been for over 50 years in Germany. But as the Second World War receded and normal academic relationships were resumed and developed, and biblical scholarship became more international and interconfessional, the Bultmannian 'new quest of the historical Jesus', triggered by Käsemann's 1953 lecture on 'The Problem of the Historical Jesus'[153] and best represented in Bornkamm's *Jesus of Nazareth* (1956, ET 1960), made an impact. Everyone was talking about the continuity between the Jesus of history and the Christ of faith, or 'kerygmatic Christ', or 'Lord of faith', and *The Phenomenon of the New Testament*, contributed to this discussion, suggesting with Cullmann that 'in a sense, the post-Easter *interpretation* was only a *re-discovery* of what had been there in the teaching of Jesus himself'.[154] Charlie claims that some scholars were 'daring once more, in a sense, to look back to the Jesus of history; but now they are finding, not the Liberal Protestant figure but a figure as challenging, as supernatural, as divine, as is found on the hither side in the apostolic Gospel', and he evidently hoped 'that, one of these days, they might come even to coincide'.[155]

Bultmann's former pupils were introducing a corrective to the view of Barth and their teacher (and, as they perhaps mistakenly thought, Martin

---

153 Published in 1954, ET 1964, *Essays on New Testament Themes*, London: SCM Press. His continuation of the debate with Bultmann may be found in *New Testament Questions of Today*, London: SCM Press, 1969, pp. 35–65.

154 Moule, *Phenomenon*, p. 46.

155 *Ibid.*, p. 47.

Kähler in *The So-called Historical Jesus and the Historic, Biblical Christ*: 1892, 1896²; part ET 1964) that the question of the 'historical Jesus' (so-called) was theologically irrelevant. Bultmann, like the older liberals, had emphasized the discontinuity between Jesus and the Church's faith, but (unlike them) had staked his theology on Kähler's opposite pole. His pupils had now seen some historical and theological continuity in that discontinuity. Charlie emphasized only the continuity. His very different standpoint is evident in his apologetic aim to argue from the existence of the post-resurrection Church to the correctness of the Christian estimate of Christ.[156] The objection to such a jump is recognized and the argument modestly presented. 'All I am trying to do is to present certain undoubted phenomena of the New Testament writings and to ask how the reader proposes to account for them.'[157] He finds himself driven in particular 'to take seriously the "evidence" – if that is the right word – for what Christian belief calls the resurrection'[158] and (unlike Bultmann, but like Pannenberg) allows historical evidence 'a place in the considerations leading up to faith'.[159] He believes that the emergence of the early Church with its belief in Jesus as somehow risen and alive 'rips a great hole in history, a hole of the size and shape of Resurrection' and asks 'what does the secular historian propose to stop it up with?'[160] He thinks 'the Christian interpretation' of 'these indisputable facts' is 'by far the most plausible – almost (I would venture to think) the inescapable – interpretation'.[161]

That will not persuade many biblical scholars today. Historians can offer several hypotheses without bringing God into it and if they are implausible will leave the question open for lack of reliable evidence. Charlie thought naturalistic explanations of the admittedly 'indisputable facts' less persuasive than the Christian answer but does not discuss why most historians think that this goes beyond their remit. It is easy to dismiss his argument as naive, not only because he presupposes a view of the historicity of the Gospels that many today would find optimistic, but more seriously because historians do not usually reckon with divine agency. To say that they should (as Schlatter explicitly does, but Charlie at most seems to imply) is to break off the conversation.

---

156 *Ibid.*, p. 19.
157 *Ibid.*, p. 3.
158 *Ibid.*, p. 2.
159 *Ibid.*, p. 3.
160 *Ibid.*, p. 3.
161 *Ibid.*

One issue here for spirituality as well as for theology is whether historical clarification and arguments can contribute much to religious faith. Charlie's argument for the continuity between Jesus and Christianity could perhaps be stated more strongly, starting from Jesus' possible understanding of the suffering and vindicated Son of Man in Daniel 7, but abandoning the theory that Jesus intended the corporate meaning that the phrase has in Daniel 7. Neither does the case for continuity need the historicity of the empty tomb or of the relatively late appearance traditions in the Gospels. Behind those Gospel appearance stories stand earlier traditions and the emergence of convictions whose character can probably be best grasped from the earlier Pauline (and pre-Pauline) evidence. But even this would only make the emergence of resurrection faith intelligible. It would not say anything about its truth. Charlie says he is 'not so foolish as to be trying to "prove Christianity"',[162] but he did think that his historical argument would help some to see its truth. Perhaps he was right; some may well be helped.

Whether or not they accept the historicity of the empty tomb Christians can agree that their Christian accounts of what happened, accounts that speak of God in Jesus of Nazareth crucified and risen, are more true than alternative accounts that do not speak of God. But they find them plausible because they are looking at the evidence from a standpoint that differs from those of modern historiography. They are unlikely to persuade many who do not share their standpoint. To expect history to support faith so directly is in effect to challenge the historical critical method to expand its scope or range of explanations. Short of that the most apologists can hope to do is to keep the door open for the truth of these historically unverified religious narratives by challenging the plausibility of naturalistic explanations. Some will also argue that a (necessarily speculative) naturalistic historical explanation is compatible with belief in God at work in this historical process.

Charlie's more ambitious line of argument is brilliantly and massively carried through by Tom Wright in *The Resurrection of the Son of God* (2003) – a book he greatly admired. If others find that whole project misconceived they should not underestimate its power to reassure those who (as both scholars recognize) believe on other grounds, but who hope to meet anti-Christian arguments on agreed terms. Apologetics can in any case show that faith is not irrational, whatever the limits of supporting it with rational arguments.

---

162 *Ibid.*, p. 2.

## History and the Gospels

Historical arguments have played a larger role in Christian apologetics in England than in German Protestantism. One reason for this was that scepticism about the historicity of the Gospels, from Reimarus (1694–1768) and D. F. Strauss' *The Life of Jesus Critically Examined* (1835, ET 1846), to William Wrede's *The Messianic Secret in the Gospels* (1901, ET 1971), and Bultmann's *The History of the Synoptic Tradition* (1921, 1931², ET 1963, rev. 1968) made little headway in England despite R. H. Lightfoot's *History and Interpretation in the Gospels* (1935). It was not until the Pelican Commentary on Mark (1963) by Lightfoot's pupil Dennis Nineham became the first book about the New Testament that many English students read, that the critical conservatism learned from B. H. Streeter, Vincent Taylor, Charles Cranfield and H. E. W. Turner met its match.

When Charlie's slim and popular Cambridge commentary on the New English Bible translation of Mark (1965) is compared with Nineham's best-seller, it looks dated in tone as well as content. Readers are brought closer to the Jesus whom they as modern but traditional mid-century Protestant Christians know, rather than to the realities of Second Temple Judaism or to the literary and theological strategies of the evangelist. Charlie's commentary is not remotely influenced by Wrede or Bultmann, but stands rather in the tradition of Sanday and Burkitt, who accepted the truthfulness of the story as reported (and its connection to eyewitnesses) unless there were obstacles in the way of this simple trust.

That 'simple trust', or what some now call a 'hermeneutics of consent', sounds positively pious in comparison with the positivism of some more recent biblical scholarship. This respect was religiously motivated, a 'simple trust like theirs who heard beside the Syrian sea'. J. G. Whittier's hymn refers to 'the gracious calling of the Lord', and so most powerfully does the famous last paragraph of Albert Schweitzer's *The Quest of the Historical Jesus*, '. . . He says the same words, "Follow me!", and sets us to those tasks which he must fulfill in our time'.[163] Charlie's commentary wants to help Christian readers to recognize the Lord that the evangelist wished them to recognize. He does not want the key of historical knowledge to block entry into the kingdom or access to the Lord (cf. Luke 11.52). It is not a devotional commentary,

---

163 Albert Schweitzer, ET 1910, *The Quest of the Historical Jesus*, London: Black, p. 401; expanded 2000 edn, p. 487.

but devout scholarship sometimes sounds closer to spirituality than to modern historiography.

This devout commentator was not uncritical, and he had a few problems with the Markan record. If 'theological criticism' of what Scripture says, based on what the theologian thinks is the essential gospel (*Sachkritik*), is the best indicator of theological liberalism, then Charlie was a respectful liberal. *Sachkritik* resists twisting historical exegesis to support the scholar's own theological convictions, but makes the latter clear, and where possible finds indirect support for them in the text. Thus Charlie does not read his own universalism into 1 Corinthians 15.22 ('in Christ shall all be made alive') because he doubts (regretfully) that Paul shared it, but in an article on 'Punishment and Retribution: An attempt to Delimit their Scope in New Testament Thought' he claims that punishment and retribution have 'no legitimate place in the Christian vocabulary'.[164] He therefore 'would dare to say, the essentially personal character of the Christian gospel is temporarily obscured' when the New Testament makes use of such ideas, as opposed to 'suffering inflicted for disciplinary and deterrent purposes'.[165] Such language is 'not really integrated with the logic of the gospel'.[166] They are 'as I believe, peripheral and alien to a strict exposition of the gospel'.[167] See below, pp. 188-90.

This striking example of *Sachkritik*, or theological criticism of Scripture in the light of the gospel, indicates that what might look like a fudge in a semi-popular commentary is actually a principled theological attempt to communicate the gospel through biblical exposition, not merely 'objective' historical scholarship. Miracles, especially nature miracles, are a stumbling block for many modern Christian readers, not only for critical historians. 'Who can believe that the weather will obey personal commands?'[168] Healings are less of a problem, but the weather? Like other biblical theologians (for example Alan Richardson) Charlie allows his theological reflection to leave open the question of historicity. The Creator can no doubt 'manipulate the very particles . . . and, if Jesus is God's perfect representative, the same may be said of him. But it is another matter to believe that God *will* adjust the weather

---

164 C. F. D. Moule, 1965, reprinted in 1982, *Essays in New Testament Interpretation*, Cambridge: Cambridge University Press, p. 235.

165 *Ibid.*

166 *Ibid.*, p. 237.

167 *Ibid.*, p. 242.

168 C. F. D. Moule, 1965, *The Gospel According to Mark*, Cambridge: Cambridge University Press, p. 41.

to suit the needs of particular individuals. Our attitude to that depends upon on how far we think that this kind of adjustment is in keeping with what we believe to be God's settled purpose, namely, to treat persons as indeed persons with free will and responsibility . . . whatever conclusion is reached about the story, the test ought to be the consistency of God's character.'[169] Not, as Troeltsch would have it, the principle of analogy with our everyday experience, apparently.

His discussion of whether miracles actually happened is clear about the principles that should guide Christian reflection, but non-committal about what can after all never be known with certainty.

> It is right to look for consistency. The mistake is to limit one's view to the world treated as a merely mechanical system, and to ignore the realm of personal relations, and – most important of all – God, as himself personal. The question is not so much: could this happen? as: would God do such a thing? It is difficult not to believe that the evangelist meant the story to be taken quite literally. But if it were not to be accepted literally, it would still be a vigorous picture-language to describe Jesus as Master of the storms of life . . .[170]

The problem of miracle engaged Charlie enough for him to direct his seminar in 1963–4 to the miracle stories of the Gospels, early Church, Josephus and Plutarch, and to invite a philosopher of religion and a philosopher of science to contribute. Most of the papers were published in *Miracles* (1965). His own two excursuses on 'The Vocabulary of Miracle' and 'The Classification of Miracle Stories' are characteristic of his linguistic and form critical scholarship, and his Introduction combines open-mindedness with some of his usual theological emphases. The theist looks for consistency in the character of a personal God.

> It is of his character that the material realm is a manifestation: and what is possible and probable in it is better measured by what is known of the character of God than by what is observed on the much narrower scale of the purely mechanistic. If we have reason to believe that the character of God is best seen in Jesus, and that the consistency of sheer moral perfection is the ultimate consistency, then we may have to revise our ideas of what is and is not 'possible'. And if we have reason to find in Jesus a unique degree of unity with the will

---

169 *Ibid.*
170 *Ibid.*, pp. 41–2.

of God, what is to prevent our believing that where God is perfectly obeyed, there the mechanics of the material world look different from what they do in a situation dislocated by disobedience? . . .[171]

Some who sat in that seminar now find such argumentation far from persuasive. The reason for recalling it is to illustrate how a biblical theologian's historical judgement may be affected by religious beliefs in a way that most New Testament theology has tried to avoid. Such apologetic arguments sound more like C. S. Lewis than C. K. Barrett. They are perhaps effective in assisting believers to appropriate the witness of the Gospels, but belong more in a theological than in a historical seminar. They are closer to spirituality than to the human sciences. Charlie rejects the 'conjuring tricks' of the infancy Gospels and does 'not think that God held the sun still for Joshua', but asks 'why should we not allow that it seems consistent with all we know of God if perfect goodness of character "cannot" be held by death – in other words, that the resurrection of Jesus was inevitable, given his absolute obedience to the will of God?'[172] The boundaries between critical history and devout commentary are sometimes blurred in apologetic arguments and Charlie's repeated insistence on 'the facts' and 'the evidence' did not impress those with harder noses. That does not say who was right; only that different views are possible even in the Church and among close friends.

In the Mark commentary his willingness to trust the Gospel narrative where possible is clear in his discussion of Mark's stories of healings. 'It seems that, wherever Jesus went, surprising things did happen. But the importance of them lay not in their marvellous quality: they were not, like conjuring tricks, merely astonishing; nor were they ever done merely to surprise. They always seem to have been the result, simply of Jesus' concern for people and his perfect and absolute obedience, as Son of God, to the will of his Father.'[173] We may note this easy transition from confident historical judgements, where the sources are far from unproblematic, to an interpretation of the history that coincides with his own religious belief. There is nothing wrong with that in the context of ecclesial discourse, but it is scarcely critical historiography.

Charlie's assumption 'that there is a regularity and consistency about nature, and that effect can always be relied upon to follow cause' is

---

171 C. F. D. Moule, 1965, *Miracles: Cambridge Studies in their Philosophy and History*, London: Mowbray, p. 16.
172 *Ibid.*, p. 17.
173 Moule, *Mark*, p. 15.

qualified by the thought that 'we have never ourselves witnessed a situation in which persons needing help are reached by a man quite perfectly in line with God's will . . . Might it not be that what we call a miracle would be the natural and inevitable effect, given such a cause, and given also enough of what the Gospels call faith – trust in God – on the part of the other persons concerned?'[174] The discussion of the raising of Jairus' daughter similarly resists 'a hasty judgment'.[175] The resurrection of Jesus is recognized to be different 'for it is treated as a final and absolute raising into a new and eternal life', but his mention of both in the same breath suggests that his willingness to entertain the historicity of these biblical stories is driven by a concern to protect the central Christian mystery.[176]

His trust in the Gospel narrative makes a few incidents perplexing. The Gadarene swine, for example: 'The incident of the pigs raises unanswerable questions. Are we to explain the story away by saying that they were really stampeded by the man's wild cries? That is a lame explanation. Or is that bit of the story pure legend? If it is not, did Jesus really allow the owner to be robbed like this of a valuable herd of pigs? No doubt we all agree that the man's sanity was more valuable still: but the owner of the pigs was not consulted.'[177] And no doubt the RSPCA would take a view.

It is the moral dimension that causes him concern, rather than the economic. The cursing of the fig-tree is similarly disturbing: 'very odd'.[178] 'It is easy to find destructive wonders in the late fictions about the life of Jesus known as the apocryphal Gospels. But in the accounts of Jesus in the New Testament there is practically no parallel.'[179] He suggests ('Perhaps we may guess') that 'the evangelist, or the tradition on which he drew, has here put together bits and pieces of scattered incidents and sayings into a shape which does not correspond either with the mind of Jesus or with the actual facts'.[180] Charlie's view of biblical inspiration did not hinder analysis of the texts in ordinary, historical terms, even if his conclusions were reverently cautious. The historicity of the 'paschal privilege' of releasing a prisoner (Mark 15.6) is disputed: 'It seems highly improbable that the people could really demand a release and choose

---

174 *Ibid.*, pp. 15–16.
175 *Ibid.*, pp. 45–6.
176 *Ibid.*, p. 46.
177 *Ibid.*, p. 42.
178 *Ibid.*, pp. 89–90.
179 *Ibid.*, p. 90.
180 *Ibid.*, p. 91.

their man, and there is no external evidence of this custom . . .'.[181] The veil of the Temple being torn is perhaps Mark's 'own dramatic, theological comment', surely not to be taken literally.[182]

A more urgent passage for reflection on the historicity of Mark is 'the little apocalypse' in chapter 13. The diverging opinions are as ever laid out in a fair-minded way, and the question posed: 'Can we really believe that Jesus himself thought in this bizarre and fantastic way about the future? Did he really expect signs and portents in the sky and the sudden winding-up of history by some single, instantaneous, supernatural event (see verses 24–7)?'[183] And in view of the expectation that this would all happen within that very generation (vv. 30–1), 'Are we to think that Jesus made a vast mistake?'[184]

Charlie is clear that 'this kind of picture-language must not be taken literally'.[185] 'In a sense' (a common phrase in his writing), 'such "future" and "above-human" language is the only way in which to explain the tremendous importance of the present and the human'.[186] If Jesus 'was actually mistaken in expecting the end of things so soon . . . it still would not alter all that is implied by the evidence for his unique nearness to God and the unique nearness of God's reign in him' because it is 'clear that Jesus was a real man; and his actual *knowledge* was limited, however unlimited may have been his penetrating wisdom and understanding of people and his perfect harmony with God'.[187] And anyway, 'in a manner of speaking, he might have been absolutely right if he said what verses 30 to 31 say; for there is a sense in which great prophets see so clearly and expect so eagerly that they get the perspective, as it were, foreshortened . . . But we still have to reckon with the possibility that they are the words of some later writer, wrongly attributed to Jesus.'[188]

Despite a later disavowal of the cul de sac into which liberal life-of-Jesus research once led, this is all much closer to that than to Wrede's history of traditions analysis with its consequent scepticism. It is instructive to compare the Pittsburgh lectures (1966) published in *The*

---

181 *Ibid.*, p. 124.
182 *Ibid.*, p. 127.
183 *Ibid.*, p. 101.
184 *Ibid.*, p. 170.
185 *Ibid.*
186 *Ibid.*
187 *Ibid.*
188 *Ibid.*, p. 103. This suggestion of a foreshortened perspective is eloquently developed by A. E. Harvey, in *Jesus and the Constraints of History*, London: Duckworth, 1982, pp. 66–97.

*Phenomenon of the New Testament* (1968) with the lectures given by C. K. Barrett also in North America (Yale) a year earlier, *Jesus and the Gospel Tradition* (1967). Barrett also is writing New Testament theology, and reflects on 'how far is *our* [my italics] present relationship with the exalted Lord Jesus conditioned by or dependent upon historical research into the records of the earthly life of Jesus of Nazareth?'[189]

Barrett thinks (though he expressed himself more cautiously on p. 48) that 'Jesus was mistaken, and since the things he looked for did not happen, he died with the disillusioned avowal that God had forsaken him'.[190] That startling Bultmannian thesis (strongly contested by Heinz Schürmann and others) is not entertained by Charlie, even though he accepted that Jesus may have been 'actually mistaken in expecting the end of things so soon' and, unlike Bultmann and Lightfoot, accepted the historicity of the cry of dereliction, and found it 'difficult to believe that Jesus only quoted these words because they led on to the triumph and confidence with which that Psalm ends'.[191] 'It is more realistic to gain from them an appalling glimpse into the sense of utter defeat and despair which Jesus suffered in obediently accepting that terrible "cup" of trouble alluded to in 14.36.'[192]

The alternative, more sceptical view, which rejects the historicity of this word from the cross is lucidly presented in Nineham's commentary with a quotation from Lightfoot that also encapsulates the two quite different ways of reading the Gospels.[193] Unlike Luke and John, Charlie accepts Mark's account, and (unlike Lightfoot and Nineham) accepts it as evidence of Jesus' 'sense of utter defeat and despair', but unlike Schweitzer, Bultmann and Barrett he does not speculate that Jesus' last cry (15.37) came from realizing that he had been mistaken about God's eschatological plan. Barrett thinks that Jesus' 'errors . . . emerge clearly enough from historical study of the gospels',[194] but insists on 'the difference between Jesus and all deluded enthusiasts . . . They call attention to themselves, and therefore stand or fall with their ability to convince others of the truth of their own claims and the security of their own position. Jesus did not make claims for himself, nor was he in the least interested in his own security. The end of the story was a fulfillment,

---

189 C. K. Barrett, 1967, *Jesus and the Gospel Tradition*, London: SPCK, p. ix.

190 *Ibid.*, p. 105.

191 Moule, *Mark*, p. 102.

192 *Ibid.*, p. 127.

193 Dennis E. Nineham, 1963, *The Gospel According to Saint Mark*, Harmondsworth: Penguin, pp. 427–8.

194 Barrett, *Jesus and the Gospel Tradition*, p. 105.

more precise and radical than he himself had expected, of what he him-self had taught.'[195] This moves smoothly from history into the doctrine of God, paradoxically combining a historical conclusion about Jesus' eschatological belief with a theological judgement that 'again Jesus was mistaken: God had not forsaken him'.[196] Barrett sees God's glory in the negation of natural human expectations and so reclaims a fallible Jesus for Christianity.

Charlie's analysis and evaluation of the Gospel tradition is very dif-ferent. Their basic theological convictions are close, though Barrett's evocation of Luther's theology of the cross to make sense of Jesus' failed eschatology has no parallel in Charlie. For both it was the truth about God rather than historical and apocalyptic timetables that Jesus was concerned to proclaim, and that is what the Gospel tradition is interested in, not 'the niceties of accurate narrative'.[197] But Charlie does not make unnecessary difficulties for their Christian pictures of the historical figure by adding unverifiable speculations about what Jesus was thinking on the cross and why. The traditional view that Jesus felt forsaken by God is as much as the text authorizes. That has not precluded further spiritual and theological reflection, some of it very profound, but this should not be confused with historically grounded claims. The evidence, critically assessed, does not permit a historical judgement about whether, let alone why, Jesus felt forsaken by God. The evangelist's narrative claims that he did, but it does so in a way that is more interested in the fulfilment of Scripture than in psychological states. Bultmann's throw-away remark in 1959 about Jesus probably 'suffering a collapse' was his (unfortunate) way of disowning his pupils' 'new quest' of the historical Jesus.

Barrett generally stood with the new questers. History and historical study of the Gospels are important for Christian theology, he adds, be-cause Jesus 'saw his own ministry as constituting a crisis in God's deal-ing with' humans.[198] It was because 'the God whose final envoy Jesus was . . . was the sort of God Jesus declared him to be', and because God 'desired to be related to men in the sovereignty of grace', that 'Jesus foresaw obedient suffering, followed by vindication, as his own role in the task of making God known, and renewing man's relation with his Creator. He would incorporate in himself the loving initiative of God

---

195 *Ibid.*
196 *Ibid.*
197 *Ibid.*, p. 107.
198 *Ibid.*, p. 108.

in re-establishing his sovereignty, and the loving response of man in accepting it and its implications . . .'[199]

That has much in common with Charlie, and both scholars made Jesus' use of the term 'the Son of Man' a key to his understanding of his ministry – though Charlie added into it T. W. Manson's improbable corporate meaning. Both scholars insist on the theological importance of historical study of Jesus. Barrett's final sentence that 'not least when we study the gospels with the most stringent historical discipline, he speaks to us as the word of God, in our speech'[200] could count on Charlie's strong agreement. But their assessments of the historical reliability of the Gospels differed radically. Barrett had been largely persuaded by Wrede and Bultmann, as Nineham had, and as Charlie had not. One result of this is that when in the Pittsburgh lectures the following year he is drawn into the current language contrasting 'the Jesus of history' with 'the Lord of faith',[201] there is no trace of the liberal Protestant strategy of playing one off against the other in a way that is fatal for orthodox Christology. His model comes close to the traditional christological idea of one and the same person in two 'states', the state of humiliation and the state of exaltation, where the earthly Jesus is already worthy of worship. The radical Wrede, by contrast, saw a gulf between Jesus and Paul, whose Christology is discontinuous with the historical Jesus. Charlie's emphasis is so strongly upon the 'continuity', that he thinks historical Jesus research can provide evidential support for post-resurrection faith. Other theologians are content to find congruence rather than a historically demonstrable theological continuity between Jesus and Christian truth.

This short popular commentary on Mark shows no trace of being influenced by any of the Germans that R. H. Lightfoot had sympathetically introduced to English students 30 years previously, much less by Lightfoot himself – or his brilliant young protégé Nineham. Wrede's *Messianic Secret* was again much discussed following its translation in 1970. Charlie wrote an article 'On Defining the Messianic Secret in Mark' for the collection *Jesus und Paulus* (1975 n. 205) honouring his Marburg friend (Bultmann's successor), W. G. Kümmel. The clarity and precision are typical and the essay contains some shrewd observations. It lacks the polemic of William Sanday (uncharacteristic of one of whom it was said, 'I have long heard of the milk of human kindness; now I've seen the cow!'). Sanday reported that Wrede's book was 'not

---

199 *Ibid.*
200 *Ibid.*
201 Moule, *Phenomenon*, pp. 43–76.

only very wrong, but also distinctly wrong-headed . . . he writes in the style of a Prussian official'.[202] Lightfoot found the 'condemnation . . . regrettable',[203] but T. W. Manson wrote in the 1956 essays in honour of C. H. Dodd that 'the Wredestrasse . . . is the road to nowhere'.[204] Charlie was always courteous towards those with whom he disagreed and was generally keen to see grains of truth in an opponent's position. Behind this essay, however, stands his very different frame of reference, shared with Sanday and Manson. While trying to be scrupulously fair, and succeeding in his accurate presentation of the data, he seems not to get the measure of Wrede's intuition that Mark 9.9 provides the key to the Gospel. Perhaps it doesn't, but this surely calls for close attention when assessing Wrede's hypothesis.

Jesus there tells the three disciples to say nothing about what they have seen 'until the Son of Man has risen from the dead'. It is easy to find fault with the details of Wrede's theory, and even to argue that 'the old-fashioned notion . . . that Jesus allowed that he was the Messiah but reinterpreted the meaning of the title . . .'[205] can explain all the data. The question, however, is which intuition about the character of the Gospel is historically more correct. In this division of opinion most historical critics have sided with Wrede, and historical Jesus research has become a wilderness of conflicting opinions. This has led to some disenchantment about its religious or theological value and to a new interest in literary approaches to the Gospel narratives. Charlie remained optimistic about the historical quest and clear about its theological importance, but his conclusions were so much closer to the Gospel narratives than those of many historical critics that one may ask whether he was engaged on the same enterprise. There seemed to be different kinds of writing about the historical figure of Jesus, some theologically and others historically questionable. Wrede and Schweitzer criticized the nineteenth-century 'lives' on (very different) historical grounds, Martin Kähler and Schweitzer on (very different) theological grounds.

Theological criticisms of 'the quest of the historical Jesus' are not new. Luke Johnson's admirable critique of the Californian 'Jesus seminar', in

---

202 *The Life of Christ in Recent Research*, Oxford: Clarendon Press, 1907, p. 77.

203 *History and Interpretation in the Gospels*, London: Hodder & Stoughton, 1935, p. 17.

204 *The Background of the New Testament and its Eschatology*, ed. W. D. Davies and D. Daube, Cambridge: Cambridge University Press, 1956, p. 216.

205 Moule, *in Jesus and Paulus*, ed. E. Earle Ellis and E. Grasser, Göttingen: Vandenhoeck und Ruprecht, 1975, p. 241.

*The Real Jesus: The Misguided Quest for the Historical Jesus and the Truth of the Traditional Gospels* (1996), echoes Martin Kähler's 1892 contention that 'the real Christ is the preached Christ'. Long before the 1910 English title of Albert Schweitzer's history and critique of the enterprise made the phrase 'historical Jesus' popular, Albrecht Ritschl had criticized the quest. He saw the importance of understanding Jesus historically, but did not think that this should involve 'first divesting oneself' of the 'religious valuation of His Person' that one shared as a member of the community Jesus founded.[206] He was caustic about 'that great untruth which exerts a deceptive and confusing influence under the name of an historical "absence of presuppositions". It is no mere accident that the subversion of Jesus' religious importance has been undertaken under the guise of writing His life, for this very undertaking implies the surrender of the conviction that Jesus, as the Founder of the perfect moral and spiritual religion, belongs to a higher order than all other men.'[207]

Ritschl was equally critical of attempts to 're-establish the importance of Christ by the same biographical expedient. We can discover the full compass of His historical actuality solely from the faith of the Christian community.'[208] This questionable suggestion that a Christian standpoint is the condition for an adequate historical understanding of Jesus occurs in a systematic theology, and is itself a theological judgement. As a Christian he thinks that 'authentic and complete knowledge of Jesus' religious significance'[209] depends on occupying a Christian standpoint, and it is important to recognize that some historical accounts of Jesus subvert religious faith, but Christian apologetics (in contrast to dogmatics) has usually welcomed the way historical study allows historians with different standpoints, believers and unbelievers of various sorts, to discuss the historical figure of Jesus despite their conflicting descriptions and evaluations. Some of these are compatible with Christian faith and others are not. The apologist will argue that some of the former do better justice to the evidence than any of the latter, but rational argument is possible. However, to follow this path and engage with other historians' proposals, Christian historians have to respect the conventions of the discipline. These do not allow for su-

---

206 Albrecht Ritschl, ET 1900, rp. 1966, *The Christian Doctrine of Justification and Reconciliation* (vol. 3, 1874), Edinburgh: T&T Clark, p. 2.

207 *Ibid.*, p. 3.

208 *Ibid.*

209 *Ibid.*, p. 2.

pernatural causality. The believing historian's standpoint is a matter of perspective, rather than access through religious experience to a kind of evidence not available to others.

It would be possible to defend Charlie's historical conclusions about Jesus as one possible reading of the public evidence, persuasive to some who share his Christian standpoint, if not to many others. The least a theologian can do is to show that there are ways of reading the evidence about Jesus that cohere with Christian belief. But to say that his construction is just 'possible' is a weak defence in a critical climate that is more sceptical now than it was 50 years ago. Rather than defend a particular construction it seems more true to his intentions to analyse its character or genre. The issue here is not the necessary task of apologetics, but the more fundamental problem of how Christians might love and hold fast to Jesus their Lord while reading the Gospels in a cold historical critical climate. The family resemblances between Charlie and Ritschl, neither of whom wrote a 'life of Jesus' or 'Jesus book', may be suggestive.

Rather than take flight from history into literary and theological interpretations of the biblical portraits of Jesus, they both assumed that the historical reality of Jesus committed them to modern historical investigation of the man from Nazareth. But they both accepted and wanted to combine with their historical study what they thought was the main thrust of the interpretations of Jesus in post-resurrection Christology. They thus resisted the dichotomy proposed by Strauss between *The Christ of Faith and the Jesus of History* (1865, ET 1977). Some such analytic distinction is inevitable in historical Jesus research as we distinguish between what we think can be reliably attributed to Jesus and what is more obviously the product of subsequent reflection, but this procedural distinction cannot be absolutized by orthodox Christians (who refer both phrases to the one person, Jesus of Nazareth, crucified and risen), or by anyone who understands the limitations of historical research. The historian never possesses 'the Jesus of history', only evidence and reconstructions, and one problem with the phrase 'historical Jesus', which in effect means no more than the Jesus of some historians, is that it wrongly suggests that this 'historical Jesus' is 'the real Jesus'.

Many theologians since Strauss have wanted to construct a historical picture of Jesus without (like him) abandoning their Christian belief that this historical figure somehow transcends all others. They have therefore been uncomfortable with Martin Kähler's famous title which reflected Strauss' dichotomy even though Kähler himself welcomed modern historical Jesus research for liberating modern Christians from the sterile dogma which as a pietist he called 'the Byzantine Christ'. He did not (like Strauss) pit modern historical research against all Christian belief in Christ, but contrasted Christian perceptions learned from Scripture (which insisted on the historical reality of Jesus and included some historical information about him) with the non-Christian constructions preferred by some historians. His rhetorical contrast of 'Jesus' and 'Christ' was misleading, and his use of the German contrast between *historisch* and *geschichtlich* a distraction, despite opening up fruitful consideration of Jesus' impact. His 'historical, biblical' Jesus Christ would be an account of Jesus of Nazareth open to modern historical research but in tune with the whole biblical witness. The best example would be Schlatter's *History of the Christ* (1909, 1920²; ET 1995) were it not ruined by uncritical acceptance of the apostolic authorship and eyewitness testimony of the Gospels of Matthew and John.

Charlie's perception of Jesus combined openness to modern critical historical research with loyalty to the biblical witness. Whether interpreting it as a 'historical, biblical Jesus Christ' and part of his New Testament theology advances the discussion depends on whether the category itself is defensible. Charlie did not publish an overview of Jesus nor of his New Testament theology. Nevertheless, he was a New Testament theologian and said in his inaugural lecture (1952) that he 'would fain be a theologian if I could' (p. 4). As such he had in his head a faith-picture of Jesus refined by historical study, an overall view of the New Testament witness, and a view of what Christianity essentially is. These three factors were for him closely related. His faith-picture of Jesus was, like Kähler's, congruent (a flexible term) with the New Testament witness as a whole. It stemmed from the biblical witness, reflected his own theology and spirituality, and drew on the historical criticism rightly prioritized in most biblical scholarship.

Charlie would resist any defence of his work that denied its validity as history. New Testament theology is a historical discipline, for all its religious aims and standpoint. Instantiations of the category 'historical biblical Jesus Christ' bring modern historical study into faith-images of Jesus. They do not claim to be disinterested historical research. Like Käsemann, Charlie was 'a partisan', his New Testament theology 'engaged'.

Recognizing that his historical Jesus research was part of his New Testament theology does not make his historical judgements any more or less correct. They are of their time, and while still defensible they belong today to the history of the discipline rather than to its cutting edge. If he, like Cullmann, may be said to preserve the Kähler–Schlatter model of a 'historical biblical Jesus Christ' while greatly improving its critical historical components, his most productive student James Dunn may be said to have developed the model further by further refining its historical components in *Jesus Remembered* (2003). One indication that this major contribution to historical Jesus research can, like Charlie's more piece-meal observations, be classified without prejudice as New Testament theology, is their inclusion of the resurrection (not merely resurrection faith) in their accounts of Jesus.

New Testament theology is usually Christian in intention – a form of scriptural interpretation making use of modern historical and exeget-ical methods. Much of it has adopted the history of religion framework suggested by the new methods and by the modern secular definition of the subject matter as 'religion'. An idealist metaphysics of history once made this a vehicle for Christian theology. When that crumbled other frameworks were needed for New Testament theology, whether salvation history patterns, revisions of the older thematic presentations based on dogmatics, or some version of the literary paradigm suggested by the word 'interpretation' (of texts).

Charlie found the 'salvation history' option congenial but did not sep-arate it from general history. He belonged, with Max Warren and other biblical and missionary theologians, to a generation whose parents' historical experience confirmed their religious belief (below, p. 160). Despite its faults and failures the British empire could be thought on the whole a force for good. They did not isolate from the rest of history a special history in which God was active, neither did they theorize much about history, but belief in God's active presence in history was not for them the dangerous ideology it came to appear to those who like Käse-mann, having survived the German church struggle, were alert to the perils of discerning God's hand in contemporary political revivals, and therefore in history generally. Cullmann's 'salvation history' theology, culminating in *Salvation as History* (1965, ET 1967, substitutes 'in' for 'as') was not as popular among German Protestants as it was in Eng-land, the World Council of Churches, and Roman Catholicism.

Bultmann combined the scepticism of Wrede and Wellhausen about historical knowledge of Jesus with the early Barth's distrust of finding God in the historical process. Both sides of this retreat from history were alien to Charlie. He was more at home with continental critics of Bultmann, notably Dodd's admirer Jeremias, the moderate Kümmel, the slightly older biblical theologian Cullmann, and even (with reserva-tions) Stauffer. Friendships within the new and mainly European Society of New Testament Studies were important as the churches contributed to reconciliation in Europe after the Second World War. Fundamental theological disagreements rarely surfaced in the friendly discussion of exegetical details. He found much to admire in Bornkamm's *Jesus of Nazareth* (1956, ET 1960) and engaged with the so-called 'new quest' of the historical Jesus, but his 'maximalist' approach to the Synoptic Gospels, accepting their historical reliability where there seemed no obvious reason to doubt it, was very different from that of critics who accepted nothing until it had passed the most stringent criteria of authenticity. Both starting-points have their place in the process of sifting the sources, but on its own the one is insufficiently critical and the other tends to exclude too much relevant data. Charlie's conclusions were perhaps too easily aligned with subsequent Christian belief and practice, but the minimalist 'new quest of the historical Jesus' did not lead far before being overtaken by a less theologically motivated phase of the enterprise. In retirement Charlie did not show much enthusiasm, even for the contributions of the friends whose other work he admired, E. P. Sanders and Tom Wright. In conversation he shared Henry Chadwick's view that Sanders' initial proposal in *Jesus and Judaism* (1985) did not account for the emergence of early Christianity, and he wondered what light Wright's construction threw on contemporary Christianity. That question itself confirms that he expected theologians' historical Jesus research to be part of their New Testament theology.

The prevailing winds of mid-century English theology supported the religious conservatism of that time. In the 1960s, and more so today, the wind was blowing in other directions. Even when Charlie's account of Jesus and Christian origins is relieved of the burden of providing an apologetic, it seems to offer fewer foundations for theology than he had hoped. His view of Jesus can still be entertained as a reasonable working hypothesis, but with its critical assumptions challenged, and lacking a classic presentation like that of Bornkamm or (from a very different standpoint) E. P. Sanders, it is no longer influential in contemporary historical Jesus research. Its value today resides less in its historical details than in its theological genre.

The suggestion to see it as part of his New Testament theology, and therefore closely related to his own theology and spirituality, is scarcely controversial. It merely distinguishes his work from some recent historical Jesus research that is emphatically not New Testament theology, and relates it to other work in the field that is also (by some definitions) New Testament theology, whether or not this is recognized. A more controversial suggestion, that New Testament theology, rightly understood, is the only appropriate framework for Christian theologians engaging constructively in historical Jesus research, would require more argument than can be provided here. Some theologians choose to meet critics of Christianity on their own positivistic ground, and therefore (for apologetic purposes) bracket their own beliefs, but if they are orthodox Christians they are committed to saying more about Jesus than they can say as historians. They will therefore surely judge all positivistic, 'purely historical' accounts of him ultimately inadequate and, insofar as they claim to tell the whole truth about him, untrue. In that case Charlie can still teach Christian scholars who write about Jesus that doing so might involve their own theology, ethics and spirituality, not merely historical criticism and the history of religions.

Charlie wanted to be a historian and a theologian as well as an exegete, but like many New Testament theologians he sometimes wondered whether his history or his theology could match the professional standards of his exegesis.

Some accounts of New Testament theology might press that question. Wrede and his successors wanted New Testament scholarship to conform to the norms of secular historiography. By that standard Charlie was not a great historian any more than he was a significant philosophical or dogmatic theologian. But on another understanding of the task New Testament theology only draws on those disciplines to enable it to communicate the witness of these texts in the interpreter's own day. Its practitioners normally adopt a standpoint in accord with the biblical witness, whether or not they are themselves actually believers. How far Charlie's New Testament theology still communicates the witness of these texts 60 years after he took over Michael Ramsey's revival of Hoskyns' lectures on the subject (as Kingsley Barrett had earlier taken it over in Durham) will be answered differently by different readers.

Interpreting his historical Jesus research as New Testament theology (even though he did not write a Jesus book or a complete New Testament theology) shows one way a devoted Christian with a distinctive liberal evangelical spirituality integrated his faith and his scholarship. As a believing biblical theologian he had in his heart and mind a faith-picture of Jesus that included the results of his careful but not iconoclastic historical study of the Gospels, and also a construction of Christianity that continued to let itself be informed and challenged by close attention to the whole biblical witness. He had been accustomed over many decades to relating this witness to the rest of his knowledge and experience. The resulting New Testament theology is itself a large part of his spirituality – the part most nearly available to inspection, though hardly to assessment. It is not the aim of this Introduction to evaluate, much less to criticize his 'spirituality', even if a discussion of his New Testament theology inevitably touches on points where others may think and pray differently. Aspects of his spirituality, including his love of nature and enjoyment of poetry (preferably the poetry he could understand) have barely been mentioned, and the cast of his mind has been only indirectly implied. He knew his spirituality was more 'cerebral' than that of many believers, and even when believing more than some of his friends he wanted to see 'evidence', and had a taste for 'facts' that some approved and others found unpauline.

The argument that has led conservative New Testament theologians like Schlatter (with whom Charlie, unlike Hoskyns, felt no affinity) to enlarge the scope of historical investigation sufficiently to explore theological terrain has some force. The Christian truth about Jesus seems to demand that kind of interrogation. Charlie felt the attraction of this argument without surrendering to it in a way that would break off the discussion with other historians. Like most contemporary theologians he wanted a faith-picture to fit both the historical evidence and his own provisional convictions. Such constructions are unlikely to persuade those who occupy a different standpoint or whose aims are different. Theologians cannot expect, either, their faith-pictures of Jesus to include the whole of their Christian understanding of God, the world and themselves, any more than (in Charlie's opinion) the evangelists packed their whole theologies into their narratives. But orthodox Christian belief does imply a degree of congruence between the historical truth about Jesus and subsequent Christian belief, and it can expect New Testament theologians to clarify this. Without sharing Schlatter's uncritically biblical picture of 'the history of the Christ' Charlie firmly maintained his own 1950s historical judgements about Jesus and the Gospels long after they had become (as he recognized) unfashionable. He did not think that necessarily discredited them.

## A Christian scholar reads his Bible

The place of Scripture within the religious community and in the individual's religious practice exercised Charlie right to the end of his 90-odd years' engagement with the Bible. At his mother's knee and in his father's study in pre-1920 China, on his own knees and in his own study from Weymouth in 1920, to Cambridge in 1927, Rugby in 1934, back to Cambridge in 1936, to Pevensey in 1981 and back to Dorset in 2003, he read the Bible and thought about what he read, and lived a life that became visibly gifted with St Paul's fruit of the Spirit: love, joy, peace, patience, kindness, goodness, fidelity, gentleness and self-control (Gal. 5.22 NEB). As the Spirit was the source of his life the Spirit directed his course. In retrospect St Paul's conditional indicative and hortatory imperative can safely be mutated into a confident judgement without claiming to be a 'fact'.

In the late summer of 2007 he was still scribbling away at his desk (only the upright seat suited his arthritis), writing letters and some of these last reflections, but first and foremost every day reading his Bible thoughtfully and prayerfully, sometimes jotting down a reflection or an arrow prayer in a notebook. His early writings on biblical authority continued the liberal evangelical critique of literalism and biblicism. The Bible is essential as witness to Christ, but cannot be absolutized or made into an authority independent of God in Christ. It is not so much a map as instruction for finding the pilot (also below, pp. 111, 144, 197). But the Pilot is knowable because he was a historical figure in early first-century Palestine before he was the risen Lord of anyone's faith, and that fact not only gives licence to historical study but also gives to the New Testament a centrality and authority not shared equally by the Old, indispensable though the Old Testament is for a correct theological understanding of the New. C. H. Dodd's *According to the Scriptures* (1952) was significantly sub-titled 'The Sub-structure of New Testament Theology'. The faith of Israel is foundational, but the fulfilment of the Old in the New, another basic theme of Charlie's biblical theology, leads to something new. It is this firm hold on the christological centre which makes him remarkably free in his theological criticism of Scripture (*Sachkritik*). Always reverent, he is prepared to extend it to parts of the New Testament witness, notably the book of Revelation. But hearing and preaching the gospel remains dependent on the witness of both testaments, even though that requires a bold theological criticism of parts of the Old Testament. The New Testament by contrast contains a normative cloud of witnesses to the gospel of Christ crucified and risen.

The need to rebalance the authority of Scripture, tradition and reason in the light of the christological centre of Christian faith became clear to intellectual evangelicals such as Max Warren, Donald Coggan and Charlie himself from their experience of the divisions in 1920s evangelical Christianity. The collapse of Christendom in the scandal and horror of the Great European War seems not to have dimmed their vision of the world-wide Church in which some of them had been children of missionary parents. Their perception of a need for theological renewal was matched by an impressive confidence and energy in undertaking it. If English culture was decadent in the 'low decade', these students, like their Anglo-catholic competitors, had an alternative to offer.

English theology was not greatly affected by the new stir in Switzerland and Germany, even though, as not only Hoskyns, but C. H. Dodd's 1936 inaugural lecture at Cambridge shows, its desire for a more theological study of the New Testament was widely felt. English scholars (including Hoskyns) were distrustful of a theology that repudiated any search for God in nature or history, and never really learned the 'German Christian' lesson of how perilous the supposed sight of God's hand in contemporary history and politics can be. As Charlie matured into one of the most influential English biblical scholars of his day he continued, like Dodd, to think in terms of 'history and the gospel', a history whose centre was the incarnation.

Much of his influence was personal, stemming from example and dialogue as well as from his own independent and sometimes original published exegetical suggestions. One can ask how long it will last as personal memories fade, but his writing retains the freshness of his lucid and attractive literary style. His more practical and devotional writings are simple and direct. They reflect a culture that was more Christian, and a Church that was more confident, than what he lived to see, but may offer thoughtful Christians today insights that correspond sufficiently to their own religious standpoint to be able to inform and challenge it. If so they will continue to build up and nourish Christian community, and so serve the wider human community. Even those who live in the biblical world post-critically, not sharing his confidence in matters of historicity but expecting the biblical narrative to inform and shape their religious responses, may find his clarifications of the biblical language helpful.

Matters that were disputed 50 years ago are still disputed, and while the specialist debates must continue this permits readers of Scripture some latitude in choosing interpretations that make sense to them religiously while being also historically and exegetically more or less persuasive. It is essential for historians to emphasize the cultural distance between the first and the twenty-first centuries. It is also of the essence for New Testament theologians to clarify the continuities between the Jesus identified by historical study and the diverse witness of the New Testament, and how both may contribute to how the witness of Scripture is heard in the churches today. Biblical literacy has disappeared from the public arena but remains a priority for the Church. That calls for a descriptive biblical theology that does not try to replace systematic or philosophical theology but which shares with those constructive disciplines a desire to develop and deepen contemporary religious faith. Modern study of Jesus from a variety of religious and secular standpoints offers a welcome resource and fuels interest.

Charlie was clear that Christian scholarship could include an apologetic dimension, and the wisdom of this has been confirmed as some recent writing on the New Testament has again used historical and quasi-historical argument to attack Christian faith and institutions. Tendentious arguments from either side have to be answered. Whether his more constructive apologetic efforts were successful is another matter. It may be thought that in trying to establish too much by historical argument he obscured what his apologetic was actually achieving. Beyond the modest task of removing some of the obscurities facing Christian readers of Scripture, biblical theology has provided the framework of some Christians' relationship to God in Christ. The Reformation generated this expectation and it flowered in pietism. New Testament theology did not provide the institutional framework of Charlie's churchmanship, but Scripture was a living reality for him and its critical reception guided his doctrinal and moral thinking and his liturgical and spiritual practice. His personal demeanour when lecturing may have concealed how independent his thinking was. Whatever his affinities with pietism they did not extend to its hostility to philosophy or dogmatics, sometimes echoed in the 'biblical theology movement'.

Many theologians would deny that 'biblical theology' should attempt to provide believers with an overarching framework for their own theology, or even a pocket catechism, because (they say) that is not how the Bible works in most Christian belief and practice. It was an unfortunate historical accident when Protestantism needed the Bible to provide confidence about its foundations and a new authority to replace that of the Catholic Church. The creeds offer a simpler catechetical framework, and textbooks of dogmatics were found necessary in Protestant orthodoxy.

The pietist reaction against Protestant scholasticism, like the Reformers' reaction against late medieval scholasticism, illustrates the perennial tension between a life of discipleship inspired by Scripture and the necessary thinking that relates Christian faith and practice to all human knowledge and experience. New Testament theology combines the modern rationalism of historical criticism with the religious appropriation of Scripture evident in patristic, monastic and Reformation exegesis. Its modern study of the Bible sets aside older views of inspiration and authority, but retains or reclaims for the Bible its capacity, as source and norm of Christian faith, to challenge false developments and existing hierarchies. The danger of replacing one hierarchy with a 'papacy of professors' is avoided because New Testament theology provides no fixed and final results, but an interplay and on-going conversation between conflicting theological interpretations of these texts. The tendency of professors to disagree with one another preserves the openness of the texts, but the minimal degree of consensus in excluding some accounts of what Christian Scripture as a whole is getting at provides guidance on the range of theologies that can justly claim to be biblical and therefore orthodox.

Charlie was aware that New Testament theology seemed never to fulfil the role in the Church of England that its rational methods and gospel subject matter demands. Unlike Barth he did not need to say,

> I myself know what it means year in year out to mount the steps of the pulpit, conscious of the responsibility to understand and to interpret, and longing to fulfil it; and yet, utterly incapable, because at the University I had never been brought beyond that well-known 'Awe in the presence of history' which means in the end no more than that all hope of engaging in the dignity of understanding and interpretation has been surrendered.[210]

Himself secure in the sense that history bore the revelation of God and that historical criticism had not rendered this kind of theology incredible, he did not fully analyse why many of his students failed to make the connection that he himself had made between biblical scholarship and the task of preaching; why some felt disabled by their critical biblical studies, and set them aside, returning to a pre-critical use of the Bible, or denying it any central place in their preaching and teaching.

In his youth the connection between scripture and discipleship was axiomatic for evangelicals, and strong enough to allow a moderate critical thinking a valued place within it. By the time he stopped regular teaching after nearly 50 years' involvement in ministerial education (the Cambridge Divinity Faculty serves Methodist and URC as well as Anglican institutions) the world was changing, and ordination training with it. The connection with universities that had been a strength did not become a liability (far from it), but in biblical studies it acquired a few ambiguities. As biblical scholarship became further secularized

---

210 Barth, *Romans*, p. 9.

the discipline that held it together with theological reflection became weaker. Instead of recognizing the need to strengthen New Testament theology in ordination and lay training, church authorities responded to the irrelevance of most biblical research to their own religious and theological concerns by acquiescing in the reduction of theological biblical study in their syllabuses. Everything Charlie stood for was thus weakened. It was natural that this discipline, which generates theological reflection on the classic texts of Christianity, should not remain the priority in a more secular academy, but surprising that those responsible for ministerial education should be slow to discern the Church's most urgent requirements.

When Christian identity is challenged, a retreat from classic texts and themes is one possible apologetic strategy; retrieval of them is another. New experiments in biblical interpretation are essential, but Christian identity is so bound up with these texts and the gospel they proclaim that their rational investigation by both believers and critics is inescapable. A rational investigation guided by attempts to express their still powerful religious message is as indispensable today as it has been throughout Christian history. Whether it leads to persuasive biblical frameworks for Christian living and thinking as some biblical theologians have hoped, or only to frameworks that clarify the witness of particular texts, as other historians and exegetes have assumed, some organization of biblical material in larger syntheses is needed for the witness of these texts to be heard, and appropriate responses encouraged.

The collapse of older views of biblical authority and inspiration has not rendered these larger schemes redundant. It is not only conservatives who have found in New Testament theology a guide to Christian living and thinking and praying. The open-minded and (within the limits of a generous orthodoxy) moderately liberal biblical theologian Charlie, and the altogether more radical Bultmann, shared an expectation that New Testament theology will determine the essential shape of their Christian belief, not merely clarify details. They both saw a need for more or less theological adjustment and restatement, and both combined their very different critical conclusions with a theological reading of Scripture that has roots in patristic, medieval and Reformation exegesis.

The discipline has a conservative bias because it aims to maintain continuity with, and conserve the faith of the biblical writers. But it is a rational activity, and this open-mindedness sometimes led to alliances with philosophy, as with F. C. Baur and Bultmann. Even where it did not, as with Charlie and most English New Testament theology, the ancillary disciplines of philology, history, literature and the social sciences were drawn on, with mixed results. The enlargements brought to the understanding of Scripture have been both theologically productive and also distracting; both illuminating the religious witness of the texts and also suggesting other reasons for reading them; sometimes introducing new clarity, sometimes obfuscation.

When Catholic or Protestant scholasticism obscured the biblical witness by paying excessive dues to Aristotle, Reformers and pietists returned to Scripture and a more biblical theology. The new scholasticisms in biblical scholarship, including positivistic historiography and other hermeneutical strategies, may be expected to provoke similar reactions. These texts have revolutionary potential and this has occasionally been realized even by readers whose instincts and training led them to err on the side of caution. It would be rash to expect the end of biblical theology, even when historical critical New Testament theology is being challenged (or complemented) by more explicit forms of theological interpretation of Scripture. The latter are a welcome resource when the Bible is being read as a source of faith, but only historical exegesis can garner sufficient consensus to enable the New Testament to be heard as a norm of Christian faith, challenging developments at odds with the witness of Scripture as a whole and arbitrary interpretations of individual texts.

The relationship between biblical study and believing scholars' own spiritualities has taken many forms. It would best be illustrated by a series of biographies. The few hints provided in this Introduction from areas of Charlie's scholarship where the relationship is clearest are intended as background to the occasional writings gathered for this collection. Section 1, 'The Energy of God', broadcast talks for Holy Week 1976, is the only section written before the 1990s, but a consistency can be seen from 'Revelation and the Bible' in *The Churchman* 1944, to the final writings published here from July 2007, a few weeks before his death on Saint Jerome's Day. That scholar, remembered on 30 September, gained through the Vulgate an influence the translators of the NEB could scarcely dream of. But as a biblical expositor he depended more on Origen than Charlie depended on any one of his many predecessors. It would also be hard to think of any personality more different from Charlie than that irascible polemicist. Of all the Christian virtues that attach to Charlie one that readily springs to mind is the 'sweet reasonableness' once proposed to translate *epieikes*, at Philippians 4.5; AV moderation; RV forbearance; NRSV gentleness; NEB magnanimity; REB consideration of others; JB tolerance; the English editions of Bauer's lexicon add for *epieikeia* clemency, graciousness.

Another applicable Christian virtue is modesty. Given his many and obvious gifts, one might think this was overdone, but it leads to a third: humility – only genuine when unselfconscious, as his most surely was. It is not an easy one to attribute because it too easily invites the riposte about having much to be humble about, and even of using it as a secret weapon. But it is prominent enough in the Gospels and epistles to provide a box to be ticked. The *tapeino* root occurs 31 times in the New Testament. And yet it is an ambiguous virtue, perhaps best approached obliquely by quoting a better writer's judgement on a more profound theologian who has already been cited (above, p. 38).

In a biographical essay on Westcott in *The Leaves of the Tree* (1911), A. C. Benson commented that

> his humility, sincere as it was, is not a very easy quality to define. A friend who knew him well said that he was humble to God but not exactly humble to man. He did not undervalue his own work, nor did he over-estimate the wisdom, sagacity, clear-sightedness, or disinterestedness of others. While he had a very high personal ideal, and was deeply conscious how far short of it he fell, he was very hard to persuade or to convince, and did not modify his opinions in deference to the opinions of others.[211]

But comparisons with the greatest of Cambridge biblical theologians risk diminishing the diminutive scholar who would not for a moment expect to be measured by the trio of J. B. Lightfoot, Westcott and Hort. It is in any case only a small part of his work that concerns us here: theological and pastoral rather than technical philological or even historical. A broader review of Charlie's New Testament scholarship would have much more to say about *The Birth of the New Testament* (1962, rev. 1981) and the essays reprinted in *Essays in New Testament Interpretation* (1982), and several other articles contributed to journals and to the *Festschriften* or celebratory volumes presented to a range of mostly continental scholars, Roman Catholic as well as Protestant. Even these tended, once he had turned 50, to be more on theological topics than historical problems, though the theology never loses its basis in the history, nor its dependence on exegesis.

The new introduction to the later collection, *Forgiveness and Reconciliation* (1998), organized by the then Lady Margaret's Professor,

---

211 A. C. Benson, 1911, *The Leaves of the Tree: Studies in Biography*, London: Smith, Elder, p. 24.

Graham Stanton, to celebrate Charlie's 90th birthday, indicates that Charlie understands New Testament theology to be concerned with 'the bearing on Christian doctrine of the convictions reflected in the New Testament'.[212] One may add 'and practice' to 'doctrine', since ethics and worship are included. Those essays are more germane to this posthumous collection, though the four on 'the theology of forgiveness' are anticipated by three in the 1982 volume. Much of the earlier work anticipates these communications from his final staging-post written when the shades were lengthening and the evening come, the busy world hushed in the quiet of Leigh, the fever of life nearly over, and most of his work long done. Some of them hint at his final preparations. His prayer for a safe lodging, a holy rest and peace at the last through Jesus Christ our Lord was apparently answered.

The 1998 collection's emphasis on the theology of forgiveness is characteristic of Charlie's spirituality. He calls it 'one of my almost life-long concerns'[213] and refers to his reflections on the parable of the Prodigal Son 40-odd years earlier (above, p. 43). The point he emphasizes 'is that to offer forgiveness is possible only for one sensitive enough to feel pain at being wronged. Equally, if one is genuinely to repent, one must begin to suffer in sympathy with the person whom one has wronged. Forgiveness and the acceptance of forgiveness are both painful and costly and emotionally demanding.'[214]

So central is this to Charlie's theology and spirituality and to the New Testament theology that fuelled both, that one may find an epitome of his thinking and praying and writing and teaching at the end of a lecture he gave when at the height of his powers, on 'The Christian Understanding of Forgiveness' (1968).[215] It shows what this Christian scholar reads in the Bible and why he shared Geoffrey Lampe's emphasis on 'Christlikeness'. In the discussion that followed the lecture Charlie was challenged for selecting texts to suit his theory. He disagreed, claiming to have given the gist of New Testament teaching. But of course all biblical interpretation is selective, making some statements central, others peripheral or perhaps even subject to theological criticism. The passage is quoted at length because its emphasis upon the human obedient response to God, which includes worship and ethics, refers to spirituality. It also refers to the theology that explicates both the spirituality and

---

212 Moule, *Forgiveness and Reconciliation*, p. ix.
213 *Ibid.*
214 *Ibid.*
215 Published in *Theology* 71, pp. 435–43.

the gospel that elicits it. The passage is also quoted in order to let the master have the last word.*

He insists

that true repentance means outgoing self-giving love in response to the generous love of (in) forgiveness, and that reconciliation is not complete until there is a *two-way* traffic. Jesus Christ is man as well as God; and as man we believe he did offer to God the devotion and obedient delight in doing the will of God which is the mark of man at his full stature. This is in no way an offering to propitiate an alienated God; but it is the worshipful response of man to God's overtures; and, in a sinful world, it will take the form of pain and costly suffering in alignment with the pain and costly suffering of the Creator. This is indispensable to the achieving of reconciliation. Man's 'offering', man's 'sacrifice', is to put his own love and energy at God's disposal in the work of repairing the lesions of sin and aliena-tion; and even though there is no sin of his own, Christ offers his 'sacrifice' as he identifies himself with man in a situation made pain-ful and crooked by the collective sin of fallen humanity.

In Christ, therefore – such is the Good News – it is possible for us not only to encounter God's generous approach to us with his free, unconditional forgiveness, but also to find ourselves caught up in per-fect man's response of unconditional self-surrender. The Incarnation is a mighty circuit – a circuit in which, like a powerful electric cur-rent, love runs from God to man and back from man to God. And the Gospel is that man is involved in the proper Man, Christ Jesus. And this is how atonement happens. It starts from what God in Man has done, from his gracious approach and the response he has already

* My thanks are due to David Catchpole, Kenneth Cragg, Jimmy Dunn, Christo-pher Evans, Graham Kings, Carl Holladay, William Horbury above all, Christopher Jones, Gene Lemcio, Patrick Moule, Christopher Rowland, Mark Santer, Graham Stanton, Christopher Tuckett and Peter Walker for the conversations and corre-spondence that lie behind these reflections. They are not implicated in my errors. To that list should be added another teacher and friend to most of us: Charlie's learned and affectionate and sometimes infuriating colleague, the late lamented Dr Ernst Bammel, who initiated and edited the first *Festschrift* for Charlie, *The Trial of Jesus*, London: SCM Press, 1970, and also the scribe discipled to bring the New Testament seminar into an orderly narrative over more than 30 years, Geoffrey Styler. Charlie's Cambridge New Testament world would not have been so rich without them and John Sweet and John O'Neill, also recently departed. Acknowledgement is due in addition to Brian Wren, who permitted the quotation on p. 178–9 from *Piecing Together Praise*, London: Stainer & Bell, 1996.

evoked from Man in Christ Jesus. It is by incorporation in Christ, by baptism into his death, that real repentance begins to become possible. Christ, and, in Christ, the Church, is the locus of reconciliation: and, through it, the rest of mankind and, indeed, the whole universe is to be brought into the harmony of God's design.

## Bibliographical Note

A fairly complete list of Professor Moule's publications up to 1972, excluding reviews and some popular items, and missing 'Sanctuary and Sacrifice in the Church of the New Testament' (*Journal of Theological Studies* n.s. 1.1, 1950, pp. 29–41) was included in *Christ and Spirit in the New Testament* (eds Barnabas Lindars and S. S. Smalley, Cambridge: Cambridge University Press, 1973). 1973–83 was a very productive decade and a few further articles followed it, between 1984 and 1997, in addition to more reviews, especially in *JTS*, and *Jesus and the Politics of his Day,* co-edited with E. Bammel (Cambridge: Cambridge University Press, 1984). Eighteen of the academic articles listed in *Christ and Spirit* and three others were reprinted in his *Essays in New Testament Interpretation* (Cambridge: Cambridge University Press, 1982) and some others, including *The Sacrifice of Christ* (1956) and later essays on the theology of forgiveness, Christology, the Holy Spirit, Jesus traditions, and the authority of Scripture, in his collection *Forgiveness and Reconciliation* (London: SPCK, 1998). *The Birth of the New Testament* (London: A. & C. Black, 1962) was enlarged and revised in the 3rd (1981) edition. *The Phenomenon of the New Testament* (London: SCM Press, 1968) was reissued in 1981, and *The Origin of Christology* (Cambridge: Cambridge University Press 1977) has been reprinted several times. Among the writings indicative of his biblical spirituality see especially two Bible readings for a CMS convention at Swanwick and published by CMS in *What Saith the Spirit?* (1948); *The Meaning of Hope* (London: Highway Press, 1953, rp. 1963) was also written for CMS. *Christ's Messengers* (London: Lutterworth, 1957) and *A Chosen Vessel* (London: Lutterworth, 1961) appeared in the missionary series World Christian Books. A popular *Commentary on the Acts of the Apostles* was published in Columbo in 1962. *Expository Times* and *Theology* were repositories of many of his pastoral theological writings on the New Testament and doctrine. In addition to Professor Horbury's memoir in the *Proceedings of the British Academy* (vol. 161, 2009, pp. 281–310), John H. Hayes (ed.), *Dictionary of Biblical Interpretation* (Nashville: Abingdon, 1999), vol. 2, p. 165, and Donald K. McKim (ed.) *Dictionary of Major Biblical Interpreters* (Downers Grove and Nottingham: IVP, 2nd edn 2007), pp. 755–7, contain entries on C. F. D. Moule by F. Thielman and R. Morgan respectively. His own account of the Cambridge New Testament seminar in *Suffering and Martyrdom in the New Testament,* edited by William Horbury and Brian McNeil (Cambridge: Cambridge University Press, 1981), is autobiographically relevant.

# PART 2

# Writings of Charles F. D. Moule

# The Energy of God: The Meaning of Holy Week

## 1 The problem of evil

A friend of mine said to me the other day, 'Don't you think it's a dreadful thing that, the longer you live, the sadder you grow?' I knew exactly what she meant. There's no denying it: nobody can retain the carefree gaiety of youth for long, because life simply forces its tragedies on our attention, even if we escape them ourselves. If a person is the least bit thoughtful and sensitive, it isn't many years before he or she begins to wear that expression we know so well – the expression of one who has looked into the eyes of suffering – perhaps of death. For myself, I happen to have lived a pretty sheltered life. I was born and brought up in China; but that was after the Boxer Rising, and long before the Communist revolution; and it was a quiet and uneventful boyhood. And then, almost for the whole of my working life, I have been an academic – very busy but seldom in physical danger or discomfort. As a clergyman, I escaped military service. As a bachelor, I have missed the joys, but also escaped the anxieties and sacrifices, of family life. So I haven't met as much trouble in my own life as many of my contemporaries. But even I have been very close to the troubles of others. People close to me have died of cancer in the prime of life; five have suffered brain damage, in two cases fatal. You can't avoid seeing disease and death. And – perhaps even worse – how few of our friends escape personal disasters: the break down of marriage, bitterness between children and parents, incompatibilities in the office, the wrecking of some happy relationship, the going bad of a friendship. Life is cruel. And I don't think I'm going to offer the predictable, platitudinous solution which preachers are supposed to come up with, either. For I do not believe there is any *solution* for the problem of evil; and the last thing we must do is to pretend that Easter Day somehow reverses the cross, or lets us off the agony. The Christian faith has no such easy solution.

But I do not agree with that friend of mine that the longer you live, the sadder you grow. I don't think that is necessarily true. I believe it is possible to put trouble to a constructive, creative purpose: and that brings joy. I fully agree that as you grow older you do lose a lot of carefree gaiety. Nobody can see tragedy at close quarters and remain the same. But I deny that this invariably or necessarily makes you sadder. I can think of people who have lost the comparatively carefree attitude of youth, but have gained a very deep joy. It is true that anybody who is at all thoughtful or sensitive soon comes to wear the expression of one who has looked into the eyes of death. But that doesn't necessarily prevent them also reflecting something else – something that I can only call beauty. This, too, you can read in their faces. Some people, certainly, are embittered by grief, and you can often see it in the set of their mouths. When they are not concentrating and don't think they're being watched, in their 'off-duty' expression, you can often read their sadness or bitterness. But some people, on the other hand, are ennobled, and you can see a mature confidence and a tender serenity in their expression, which you know has not been lightly come by. They have gained it the hard way. They haven't run away from pain and distress. But neither have they let it sour them. They have somehow used their tragedy to create something of a deeper, more lasting beauty than could have been created any other way. It's like a sculptor making something beautiful out of a hard, cold, resistant slab of marble.

I'm afraid I am putting this very lamely; but I hope there are many of you who can come to my rescue and fill out my meaning from your own experience. The deep people somehow manage to turn tragedy into material for finer living. Phyllis Bottome – a writer perhaps not read much today – wrote a wonderful novel, *The Mortal Storm*, round just this theme: cruelty, from which a man emerged ennobled. The world-famous doctor who has been put in a concentration camp is visited by his daughter, Freya. When he comes into the room where she is waiting, 'his eyes shone at her with their old clear delight, and when his arms closed round her, she felt safe. His back was bowed, but something she had not dared to hope could still be there was present in his face. His spirit was free and without fear.' People like that, going through anguish 'free and without fear', have a great fund of sympathy. They feel things as keenly as anyone: they don't protect themselves from being hurt; but instead of it becoming a negative factor in their lives, embittering and souring them, it makes them more than ever available to help and support people who are in need. The doctor in *The Mortal Storm* even finds excuses for the young Nazis who had done terrible things to him; after all, he says, the poor boys hadn't enough understanding to see the implications of what they were doing: they were just obeying orders. Such people come through the pain as great healers. It's a healing experience to be with them: you can lean on them and find support.

And that, I insist, is to admit that they have gained joy. They have lost carefree gaiety and faced sorrow in plenty, but gained, not sadness, but a sort of deep, outgoing serenity: the capacity to help others to find stamina for life – and what deeper joy and satisfaction can there be than that? This is strange, but I think it's true; and it's something with which Holy Week has an intimate concern. It's something that is built into the whole of the Christian story. We have had it already at Christmas. In T. S. Eliot's *Murder in the Cathedral*, Thomas Becket's Christmas sermon dwells on the remarkable fact that Christians celebrate Christ's birth with the sacrament of his death – Holy Communion – and shortly before their celebrating the first martyr's death (for the Feast of Stephen is Boxing Day). As Becket says in T. S. Eliot's words, '. . . we celebrate at once the birth of Our Lord and His passion and death upon the cross. Beloved, as the world sees, this is to behave in a strange fashion. For who in the world will both mourn and rejoice at once and for the same reason?' Well, in the same way, in Holy Week we celebrate something that brings the two together: tragedy and deep, outgoing joy.

There is tragedy built into every step of the Christian story. Take an example at random. In St Luke's Gospel comes the story of Peter's denial – the story of a confident person's downfall. Peter had evidently believed that he had discovered in Jesus one who could lead his nation to freedom and success. He also believed that he could himself help this great Leader, as his right-hand man. He enthusiastically supported him, followed him ardently, declared himself ready to lay down his life for him. But when the crisis came, his hero let himself be arrested without protest, and Peter's own courage crumpled up, and he ran away. Lost! Can you imagine a person more completely lost than that? Everything had gone dark. There wasn't a familiar feature left in his landscape. What had seemed a dangerous but glittering line of action – journey to Jerusalem, success for Jesus, triumph for them all to share – had turned to dust. Jesus, a prisoner, Peter a proven coward. Peter was lost. For him, life seemed finished. Alone, shattered, without purpose or direction. Actually Jesus was there though Peter felt as though he had gone beyond recall. In Luke's version of the story, Jesus was actually in sight, and he turned and looked at Peter – a look, one imagines, of mingled reproach and sympathy. The one on whom Peter had pinned his hopes was at that moment pursuing the only way to reconstruction. Peter didn't realize it then – how could he? But what he imagined the end of his hopes was actually a new beginning. And Holy Week is like that – a weave of cross threads: out of despair and tragedy a pattern is emerging. I heard it said, recently, that the Christian faith has a unique way with suffering. The message of Holy Week is that humans can reckon with tragedy and emerge unembittered and undefeated.

## 2 The problem of good

When I say that I am prepared to deny the rule 'older means sadder' don't misunderstand me. Don't think that I'm saying this out of a shallow optimism, or shutting my eyes to the realities. I have in front of me the typescript of an unpublished German poem. It's attributed to an anonymous sufferer in the infamous concentration camp at Buchenwald. It is addressed to God, and the poet, the sufferer who wrote it, bitterly reproaches God – and yet, somehow, goes on owning him. The poem says, in effect, 'If you were not my God, I'd never forgive you! I'd hate you! I'd spit at you! We try to take refuge with you, but you leave us in the lurch. We shriek out for help, and you are silent. When we try to be disciplined and obedient, you just conceal yourself behind your blinding glory. I only wish you were not my God. If only you were a tyrant over a gang of slaves; if only you were just the Church's picture of God, or just a plaything for the stupid, then I wouldn't bother to regard myself as belonging to you any more. But you *are* my God, in spite of everything; and there's nothing for it but to go on accusing, doubting, taunting – yes, and trusting, in silence!' I can't convey the poignancy of the original; but perhaps you can hear in it the agony of one who feels as though God had given him up, and yet can't shake off a loyalty that still goes on.

And certainly this experience is real enough, and not only inside Buchenwald. It is in the Gospels themselves that we find the best known instance of all. Not in St Luke's Gospel, indeed, nor in St John's; but in the accounts of the crucifixion in Matthew and Mark, there is that terrible cry: 'My God, my God, why hast thou forsaken me?' For Jesus, God is still '*my* God', even when it feels as though he had deserted him. So, what I am trying to say is that it *is* possible to go through the valley of the shadow of death, through despair, and yet discover that, somehow, God remains your God. And this means that, in the end, strange though it may seem, the sufferer may be actually more sure of God than before: and that means that sadness does not always or necessarily bring increasing gloom.

It is true that the older we grow, the better acquainted we become with grief. There may even be a time when God simply seems to disappear. Michel Quoist, that well-known man of prayer, calls out, in one of his *Prayers of Life*, 'Lord, Lord, do you hear me?' – and there seems, at first, to be nothing but silence. And yet we all know people who are, somehow, only deepened by sorrow, and who seem to grow in a deep-down, unshakeable joy. Carefree gaiety is lost (you can't keep that in Buchenwald) but it is exchanged for this source of deep contentment. And it's not a contentment arising from resignation either. It isn't because such people just fortify themselves against over-much caring and withdraw into a hard shell, so as to escape being hurt. There *are* those, I know, who encase themselves in a cynical indifference. But the people I have in mind, those deep people who are somehow refined and made serene by suffering, are the very ones who are not wrapped away from others, but are forever expending sympathy and opening their hearts so as to share the troubles of others. Their deep contentment is precisely in sharing others' burdens. It's an extraordinary thing that suffering can bring this compensation: if we will let it, it opens our hearts to others. We go on being hurt, but it is constructive, it is to good purpose.

What has this to do with Holy Week? A great deal, I believe. There is that terrible cry from the cross 'Why hast thou forsaken me?', and yet '*My God*' still. And there's that strange observation that I quoted from Becket's Christmas sermon in T. S. Eliot's *Murder in the Cathedral*, when he says, '. . . we celebrate at once the birth of Our Lord and His passion and death upon the cross. Beloved, as the world sees, this is to behave in a strange fashion.' It is, indeed. But it is exactly what Christians do do, and it is because 'Jesus is there'. Just when we're at the end of ourselves – like Peter who found life intolerable because he suddenly discovered himself a coward, morally bankrupt, all his self-regard shattered – at just such a time, Jesus is there.

And I don't mean that only Christians have this sort of experience. It isn't only those who know that Jesus is there. Many Jews in concentration camps found God – and they did not confess Jesus Christ. So it is, also, with other religions. In all sorts of different religious traditions, God is found in the darkness. But I believe that it is in Jesus most decisively that the God of grace shows himself to us; and it is in Jesus, I believe, that 'the problem of good' becomes most insistent. We all know about the problem of evil. We live with it, it is always filling the headlines: senseless, devilish, random evil. And people say, 'How can there be a God?' But don't forget, goodness is equally difficult to explain. It is not a 'problem' in the same sense in which evil is. If you believe in a good God, then evil is a problem and good is not. But what I mean is that the goodness that springs up in the middle of evil has got to be accounted for; and if we're honest, we have to admit that this presents a serious problem. Where does it come from? What is its source?

I was deeply impressed and touched by the widow of a distinguished medical man, who was killed by a bomb just when he was at the height of his powers as a leader of research into cancer. When she was interviewed shortly after the outrage, she said she felt no bitterness. That was a marvellous moment for me. Another was when I heard the story of the bereaved mother of a boy who had fallen a victim to another of those senseless acts of brutality. When a Minister of Religion was calling on her to try to comfort her, he began to express indignation. But she rebuked him by quietly reminding him of how much the criminal and his mother were to be pitied. That is the sort of thing I mean when I speak of the problem of good. Where does this moral stamina spring from? Where do people like that get this power to forgive, this healing compassion? It seems to me quite as bewildering, quite as problematic, in its own way, as evil. If you say, 'There can't be a God, because how could he allow this evil?' I say, 'There must be a God, because where else does this irrepressible goodness spring from?'

And there is the story of Holy Week. Jesus, in St Luke's version, is a prisoner. He's been betrayed and trapped. It is only a matter of time before he will be pinioned outside the city gate – hung up in public to die in an anguish of thirst and pain. The dreary routine of sham justice is pursuing its course. He has been condemned for confessing to a special closeness to God. He has been taken to the Roman governor Pilate, who tries to get him let off; but there are people clamouring for his blood, so Pilate passes him to King Herod. But it's all just a bitter charade. Herod makes fun of Jesus and sends him back to Pilate. We know exactly how it's going to end. The whole thing is, for all time, the classic miscarriage of justice. But in it and through it all – Jesus! Jesus continues to be himself, his integrity unbreached, steadily, mostly in silence and without a word, going through with God's will. And, in the same way, at the heart of every human wrong there is always, somewhere or other, this ultimate rightness: someone is exhibiting this irrepressible goodness; there's an unaccountable principle of life and constructiveness in the thick of the evil. Why?

So, when I'm tempted to say, life is blind chance, meaningless cruelty, sheer pointlessness, I'm pulled up short by something in the picture that looks purposeful and creative: some sort of redeeming goodness. It's literally true that the crudest of torture-instruments – those two wooden beams, and the nails – have become a universal symbol of life and for-giveness: the instrument of hate and degrading cruelty became the sign of the remaking of character. Hatred and death were turned into love and life. How? By whom? Where did the stamina come from?

## 3  The divine energy

Where does the stamina come from, where do people get the sheer moral force, for turning cruelty and hatred into something new? For this is what certainly happens. It happens in all sorts of circumstances, and has hap-pened throughout history. The late Bishop Wilson of Birmingham was captured by the Japanese during the Second World War, and suffered torture and terrible privations. An appalling, traumatic experience like that – if the victim survives at all – can plunge him into darkness and bitterness for ever. But Wilson somehow found himself able to forgive; and he even lived to baptize one of his Japanese guards into the Christian faith. It does happen, and when it does it deserves as much publicity as the atrocities.

For that reason, I was rather saddened by an account in a paper re-cently of a sentimental visit of some British ex-soldiers to the so-called River Kwai. Many years before, they had been put to forced labour there by the Japanese, on the notorious Burma Road, and now they were revisiting the old scenes. What saddened me was that, in the re-port, there was not the smallest hint of forgiveness or reconciliation; the reporter only alluded to the bad days those people had been through, and spoke of their detestation and recrimination against their captors. Of course, I have never been through horrors like that, and you may say that my attitude is due to having lived a very sheltered life. But to me mention of the River Kwai brings memories of that remarkable book, *Miracle on the River Kwai*, by Ernest Gordon. He was a man who did go through that nightmare and who found a faith in those terrible days. He found a faith which he did not have before and, for the first time, learnt the meaning of forgiveness. Out of that despair, a new hope was born. It does happen and I want to know how. So, the question I would ask is: 'What is the force that is strong enough to work this almost unbelievable transformation?' And I find myself answering 'It must be the power of God'. Even when it is experienced by people who do not consciously believe in God at all, or own him, I still cannot see how anything short of the power of a creator could do this extraordinary thing.

For it is an act of creation. Even the most ordinary and unromantic forgiveness exhibits this power. Think of your own experience. Have you never got over a resentment, and managed to think kindly instead of bitterly of someone who has done you a wrong? We surely must all know something of this experience, even if it's on a comparatively trivial scale. Wouldn't you agree that, when this does happen, it is something to do with a sheer vitality that has to be borrowed from outside? It comes as a gift, perhaps with floods of tears and the unlocking of the door of our emotions. Am I romanticizing or sentimentalizing? I don't think I am.

To draw an analogy to all this from the human body, this experience of reconciliation is not unlike the healing of a wound or the knitting of the bones after a fracture. I think there is a real analogy here, because the metaphorical knitting together of two people when they are reconciled after a quarrel does imply the same sort of life-power, the same sort of vitality, that is necessary for the cure of an injury to your body. Fractures, after all, do not unite in dead bodies. There has to be a fund of life, of vitality, of feeling (usually, with a good deal of pain), if the creative processes of growing together are to be put in motion. I am not sure that even medical men or specialist physiologists completely understand exactly what happens: I certainly don't. But we all know that eventually the fracture can mend. There may be a ridge in the bone, or, if it's a wound, a keel or a scar of some sort: it may never be quite the same again. But it can be positively stronger than before. A new situation has been created by the vitality in the living flesh or bones: damaged tissue is repaired, infection is overcome, normal health is restored.

Every time this sort of process takes place on a personal level – every time a 'wound' or a 'fracture', as we might call it, in human relationship is healed or mended, every time a lesion or a breach is repaired, and an estrangement overcome – I believe it is just plain unsentimental fact that God's life-force goes into it. Bones do not knit without the mysterious thing we call aliveness. Reconciliations do not take place without divine life-force. The parties to the reconciliation may not know or believe this. But I am convinced that the ability to forgive and the ability to repent – the giving and receiving that take place in a reconciliation – are of divine origin. They certainly require life. They certainly require nervous energy. However spontaneous the forgiveness may be, it takes it out of you. However natural the repentance, it means giving oneself away to the other person. And however oblivious of it the two parties to a reconciliation may be, the energy that goes into that repair is – so

Christians are convinced – Christ on the cross. It is Jesus Christ who is God's vitality, God's life-force, in this process.

I mean by this that the events of Jesus Christ's life and death and the sequel lead me to believe that Jesus does not merely show God's character or merely illustrate God's activity. He is not merely an example of long ago. It's more than that. Jesus seems actually to have been God at work. And, if he is alive for evermore, then he continues to be the vitality of the living body that heals the wound or knits the bones. Jesus is the creative power of God the Creator at work.

I am not saying that before Jesus came, there was no healing, and that God could not forgive, whereas after the cross the way of salvation was opened up. Christian preachers do sometimes make it sound rather like that. But that would make nonsense of the Old Testament Scriptures where God's forgiveness is declared. It would also make nonsense of all religious experience outside Christianity, in whatever religion, and we know how profound such experience can be.

We must go back and ask my original question once more. Wherever there is forgiveness, at whatever time, whenever a person has risen superior to bitterness and hate, creating good will and repentance in his or her enemy, how has it happened? Where has the moral force come from? If we say, 'From God' (and I cannot conceive of its being derived simply from inside ourselves), then, as a Christian, I want to go on to say more about this God who supplies the strength to forgive and to repent. This God, from whom the creative, healing vitality of reconciliation is derived – I want to affirm that, to me as a Christian, he is known as the Father of our Lord Jesus Christ. This is the sort of God I believe him to be. He is the source of forgiveness-energy because, eternally and always, he has been the sort of God who, eventually in time and space, actually works out his forgiveness in Jesus of Nazareth. It is because God is permanently like that, that this miracle of creative power which we call forgiveness can take place. It is not (as seems sometimes to be supposed) that God could not forgive until Jesus came and offered him satisfaction. It is because God forgives, and always has forgiven, that Jesus came. God has always been at work as Creator. But eventually, in time and space, at one time and in a particular place, he brings that work to perfection – so far as perfection can be reached in a single individual in a warped society. Jesus is God, pouring his creative energy into the sores and wounds and fractures of human hatred. Jesus is the Creator, exercising his renewing, restorative, growing-power as a man with human society: the Creator's life-force at work within the body of mankind.

The Christian religion often looks like anything but a healing religion. The most terrible deeds of destruction and hatred have been done, and continue to be done, in the name of Christ. In the past, one thinks of the Crusades or the Inquisition. In our own day, inevitably one instantly thinks of the sectarian war in Northern Ireland. But if the abuse of religion leads to these hateful deeds, I believe it's equally true that, without real religion, there is no transcending of hatred. Take away religion, and the life-force is gone. A purely secular society, the humanist may boast, is without that particular type of rivalry that a perverse and persecuting religion sometimes brings. But also it is, in the long run, going to 'run out of steam': there will be no funds of vitality to be drawn on. The situation will be lifeless. Without God, no healing: the organism is dead or dying. And Holy Week means God is at work, wherever we will let him be. His life-force is still available.

Have you brought the realities of Holy Week inside your home? It isn't always easy. It cannot be done without courage and effort. But it has been proved true over and over again that disputes can be settled, antagonisms overcome, estrangements ended by bringing them to God in Jesus Christ and letting him take you through them with him. Jesus went through with the processes of reconciliation. He evaded not a single step in that hard, uphill path. That is precisely what Holy Week is all about. The activity of Jesus is the activity of God the Creator, creating the stuff of forgiveness-making out of the rough edges of life, and the harsh, abrasive situations new growing-points for God's healing vitality: making out of despair and tragedy the new situation that we call Easter Day.

But if this creative power is to come into play, it must be allowed entry. The channels and the ducts must be opened: we have to turn to God. Perhaps we can only do so feebly and hesitantly. Never mind! Only start, only begin to face round to him, and he will meet you half way. And then, others have to be drawn in as well. A reconciliation, a new harmony, is a new creation; and it can no more be created alone than conception can take place in isolation. Two people have to come together, if God's creative work is to begin, if a changed situation is to be born. It can be, because, in Jesus Christ, God has exerted that creative energy and goes on pouring it into our lives. Christ's body given, his blood shed, is God's compassionate life-power being poured into the human situation for healing and repair. It is for us to claim it, to lay hold of it, to appropriate it. And we do this not only by sharing in the sacrament of the body and blood of our Lord in church, but in all sorts of ways outside formal worship. We do it whenever we set about putting an estrangement right; for, in so doing, we discover that we are drawing upon this moral force that comes from beyond ourselves.

That, I believe, is the answer to my question, 'Where does this force of goodness come from?' It is the Creator; it is God himself, in Jesus Christ. And Holy Week is all about Jesus Christ exercising this creative power decisively and, through the cross, coming to live eternally and to be eternally available, pouring his vitality into our homes and our friendships and the environment in which we do our work.


## 4  The upper room

On Maundy Thursday as the Church's calendar calls it, we think of the way in which Jesus deliberately involved his friends in what he was doing, when he sat down to an evening meal with them in the upper room on that Thursday night – the night of his betrayal.

I have been comparing reconciliation to the knitting of fractured bones or the healing of a wound or the cure of an illness. But no cure is ever effected, whether psychological or physical, without the patient's own resources being enlisted, consciously or unconsciously. Healing comes through response to the forces of life. A patient who does not join in the fight for his life will die. And when Jesus sat at table with his friends on the same night on which he was betrayed, he bound them to his cause by the symbols of the food and drink.

I do not know whether you have ever wondered what Jesus meant when – elsewhere in the Gospels – he used the phrase 'the son of man'. A case has been made for believing that, among other things, he was referring to the group of people he was gathering round him. In the seventh chapter of the book of Daniel, there is a vision in which a human figure, 'a Son of Man' as he is called, appears; and this seems to represent the loyal Jews who had refused to compromise and had preferred death to disloyalty. To some extent, therefore, in using this phrase, 'the Son of Man', Jesus seems to have been describing not only his own martyr-vocation but also the vocation to which he called the Twelve and, perhaps, some of his other disciples. He was training them to go to any lengths in the doing of God's will – to be that human figure, that 'Son of Man', whose vindication in heaven is the fact that he gave away his life on earth. If so, then here, in the upper room, Jesus has gathered the inner circle of his band, and he is appealing to them, by the symbols of the shared food and drink, to be united with him in his task.

His appeal was not immediately successful. Later on, that same evening, they all forsook him and fled. They forgot the solemn bond of the bread and wine, forgot their solidarity with him as the 'Son of Man', and behaved like strangers. One of them declared outright that he did not even know him. But the bond was too firm to be broken by that bit of disloyalty. For the time being, Jesus was alone. It is difficult to see exactly what the disciples could have done, even if they had not run away. Jesus had no intention of using force: there was no fighting to be done by his followers. His plan was not to fight, but to enable the kingdom of God to come by sheer obedience. And it is a question what such obedience could have meant for the disciples at that particular juncture. But afterwards, when the ordeal was over and Jesus had been brought to glory, they found that this bond still held – the bond by which Jesus had bound them to himself at that Last Supper. The Lord's Supper, the Holy Communion, the sacramental eating and drinking, turned out to be that same bond by which Jesus had bound his friends to himself. And it was repeatable. 'As often as you eat this bread and drink the cup,' says St Paul, 'you declare the Lord's death, until he comes.' What did he mean by 'declare'? Obviously a mere statement that Jesus died, a mere declaration in that sense, is not going to achieve anything. It must mean – if it's going to be effective – that Christians affirm it by entering with Christ into the healing process of which his own cross is the heart and growing-point. Unless Holy Communion means joining our energy with Christ's in the healing processes that are within our power, we are using it frivolously.

This is of the essence of a sacrament. Sacraments are not magic. They are not a sort of binding spell that works whether or not the object consents. In a sacrament, material things, such as bread and wine, are used in the context of worship. God has promised, in Jesus Christ, to help and redeem us. We respond with our love. And in breaking the bread and pouring the wine and sharing them, we are renewing that original engagement of God with us and of ourselves with God.

It would appear that in the upper room on that original Thursday night, Jesus may have refrained from actually drinking from the cup himself. He passed it to his disciples, but, for himself, he said he would not drink wine again till he drank it new in God's kingdom. What did that mean? It looks like an instance of something that Jews of Jesus' day sometimes did. They would make a vow to refrain from this or that – for instance, from wine or anything made from grapes – until something specified had been achieved for God. It was a way of solemnly binding oneself to a task in the sight of God. So, Jesus seems to have said, 'I vow that I will not drink wine or anything made from grapes again till God's purposes are achieved.' It was a solemn dedication to go through with the task. 'But I shall drink it new with you', he said, 'in God's kingdom.' And Christians, ever since the first Easter, have shared the cup together, believing that Jesus is their unseen Host, feasting with them in God's kingdom.

So, this sacrament means being involved with Jesus Christ in what he is doing. One remembers the stories of Christians in concentration camps in the Far East during the war. Under the strict surveillance of the military guards, not allowed to hold services or get into groups for worship, they would crumble a little bread as they ate their meagre ration, or sprinkle a few grains of rice, and murmur 'I remember . . .'; and the rest would respond, under their breath 'We remember . . .'. And the same with their water or whatever weak drink they had. They were not allowed to say the words of the upper room; but they hinted at them. And they knew that they were, in that secret, unobtrusive way, doing what St Paul called 'declaring Christ's death till he comes'. They were letting themselves be engaged with Christ in his sufferings.

And countless people today derive their strength to keep going from periodically reaffirming their engagement with Christ. There are, perhaps, intolerable frictions in the family. There are burdens to bear that only God knows about. We are just about at the end of our tether. 'Do this, in remembrance of me!' That's what makes life possible: being involved with Christ in the strange work he does – his strange ministry of reconciliation through suffering and death. He doesn't rescue us from the difficulties. But he involves us with himself in them: and that makes all the difference. For Jesus is God the Creator's life-force: Jesus is God at work repairing, healing, giving growth; and he catches us.

## 5  The Good Friday story

I was recently listening to a lecture by an Indian lady, in which she tried to convey something of the atmosphere and outlook of the Hindu way of life. Towards the end, she touched on the subject of guilt, but dismissed it as something that didn't really come into Hinduism. When she had sat down, a Christian theologian who was on the platform spoke next. He expressed great respect and appreciation for what the lady had said, but added that, as a Christian, he had to acknowledge that, for him, sin and guilt were important. 'When you look at Jesus on the cross,' he said, 'and see what we all do to him, it is impossible not to reckon with guilt.'

Now, what did he mean by 'what we all do to him'? Jesus was put to death nearly 2,000 years ago, in first-century Palestine. What have we, today, got to do with that? How can we be said to do anything to Jesus? I answer: 'If we have nothing to do with that, then that has nothing to do with us. If we are not guilty of his death, neither can his death help to bring us life.' But I believe that it does bring us life. There will be some of you who will confirm the truth of this from your own experience of what it means to belong to a Christian group.

So we are brought to consider the Good Friday story. In many ways it is ordinary – as, alas, stories of cruelty tend to be. And, anyway, it is a story of the distant past. Yet, in certain ways, it is contemporary with us.

Viewed as an ordinary historian must view it, the story of Good Friday can be told with a fair measure of plausibility as the story simply of one more execution. On or about the fifteenth day of the month Nisan somewhere about AD 30, a Jewish prisoner was executed outside the old city of Jerusalem by the cruel process of being fastened to a pole and left to die in the sun and the flies. In itself, there was nothing very unusual about that. No doubt it did not happen every day: it was unusual enough to cause a bit of a sensation. But it was no particularly uncommon thing for a Roman governor to sentence a Jew to this cruel form of death, especially if the charge was that he had used violence, or intended to use it, against the Roman army of occupation. There was plenty of unrest among the subject Jewish population. There were freedom-fighters and, especially at Passover time, nationalist feelings ran high. Even after the eventual fall of Jerusalem, which took place about 40 years later than our story, there was still going to be dogged resistance, reaching its climax in an epic stand by the nationalists against the Romans in the desert hill-fortress of Masada. So the Roman authorities dropped on any signs of resistance, trying to nip rebellion in the bud.

But in the case we are considering, it seems not even to have been a concerted effort. It is true, there were two others crucified with Jesus, and they do appear to have been freedom-fighters caught in some incident that had flared up in the Passover crowds. And there are those who suppose that Jesus, too, had, if not attempted a coup himself, at any rate sympathized with the Zealots of the resistance-movement. But I find it difficult to read the evidence like that. The charge nailed up on the cross (no doubt as a salutary warning) was that Jesus was a rebel: 'the King of the Jews', it said. But the evidence shows him as colliding, rather, with the religious authorities of his own people. All through his period of preaching and teaching and healing, he had been too radical, too unorthodox, too disturbing for them to tolerate. It was they, it would seem, who handed Jesus over to Pilate on this allegedly political charge, though they had condemned him themselves on other grounds – on a religious charge. It's a long and complicated story; but that is how I read it.

But why did he ever let himself be caught? Why did he have to go to Jerusalem – putting his head right into the lion's mouth?

It seems to me that he went to Jerusalem to keep the Passover, as a devout Jew within reach of Jerusalem would certainly do. He went also as the great Prophet he was, to make a final bid to call his nation to repentance and godliness in the face of the impending crisis of the Jewish war. If so, it was simply in the course of duty that he was betrayed and arrested. In that sense he was the victim of circumstances. Not that he did not know perfectly well what the outcome would be. But I cannot believe that he deliberately sought death. Historically speaking, he was betrayed and trapped. That is the external story.

But that story is not the whole story. To get the rest of it, one needs to go back to the story of Jesus' life and forward to the story of the sequel to his death. For the man whose whereabouts was betrayed by one of his intimates and who was caught and killed was no ordinary man. During his lifetime, people had found that to meet him was to meet God. I do not know how else to put it. I don't mean that they saw anything but a young man of Galilee. But what they experienced in his presence was a nearness to God which they had never found before. Where Jesus was, God's sovereignty was actually operative. God was being completely obeyed: God's reign had begun. So people found themselves, as it were, stripped bare and convicted of their dishonesty or their censoriousness: they found their conscience searched. Also, in Jesus' presence they found themselves forgiven and they saw their own potentiality. They found a new peace, a new completeness and wholeness to life. Neurotics and sick people found themselves free and well and normal. Not everybody found peace and wholeness. Those who were too proud and too 'religious' to admit their need just became antagonistic and closed up on themselves and left more unhappy than they had come. But they, too, had seen God, and that is how it had taken them.

But meeting Jesus also, in a sense, meant meeting someone fully and truly human. Jesus somehow summed up in himself what really human existence meant. He lived in unaffected honesty and simplicity and openness. To him, people were people. He didn't put them into categories – middle class, respectable, unrespectable, beggars, crooks. He took them as they came, and respected and honoured the real person he saw in each of them. He didn't *condone* their wrongdoing. If he took them as they were, he didn't leave them there. He lifted them up; he took their best selves seriously; he gave them a new sense of what they had it in them to become. Jesus, of all men the most human and humane, was, of all men, the one in whom God and man came together.

So, when this good man, colliding with authority as goodness tends to do, was put to death, it was a special death. Viewed by the historian, it is one more crucifixion – another cypher in the dreary columns. But never before and in no one else had God and man coincided like that. This death was different. Human sin and perversity were brought to a sort of climax. The fear and jealousy and ambition that brought Jesus to the cross were somehow the epitome of all fear and jealousy and ambition in all the long story of humanity before and since. And the resources with which Jesus met them were, somehow, God's resources: his silences, his dignity, his acceptances – all were divine.

And three days later his friends were convinced they saw him alive. Not alive like someone restored to the old, mortal life again; but alive in a permanent, irreversible, inextinguishable way.

Now, this means that what looks to the historian like one more miscarriage of justice in the verdict on a single individual and on an obscure and fairly trivial scale, has something about it that drives us to look beyond the historian's purview. Here is an event in history which achieves something permanent. Necessity and coercion undergone but used with a divinely sovereign freedom; death faced and used so as to create life; defeat handled so as to make it the stuff of a creative new beginning. I've already talked about the stamina that seems to be poured into people when they are under pressure, enabling them to come through creatively. Well, here, in Jesus is the source and fountainhead of this. It is not just a man: it is God's own Son. It is God and man meeting.

And that is why what was done to him was something done by all mankind, including us. And that is why what he did in his circumstances was something done by God, to all mankind, including us. Permanently, we are all present at the crucifixion of this man and we all share in it. It is our sin; and it is God's forgiveness to us. Permanently, he embodies God's response to what we do: judgement and mercy. He condemns us and saves us, because, in him come together human sin and the divine, creative healing.

## 6  Holy Saturday

Many great artists have struggled, on canvas and in marble, with what happened on the Friday evening, after the crucifixion. It is usually called 'the deposition' – that is, the taking of Jesus' dead body down from the cross, or the laying of it in the tomb, with his mother mourning over it. In many cases, an artistic creation of extreme beauty is the result. Michelangelo's *Pietà* – that miracle of tenderness and pathos in St Peter's, Rome – naturally springs to mind.

The imagination shrinks, both in horror and in reverence, from conceiving of the reality. The dead body of one who has been tortured and has died in agony is hardly a thing of beauty. But are the artists right, perhaps, to invest it with a serene beauty? There is a sense in which Holy Saturday, whose keynote is struck by the deposition on the day before, is a day of peace. Cruel fate has done its worst. The suffering is over. The great ordeal is past. The tensity of the drama is relaxed. Tears there may be; but the wringing of the soul is less. All passion spent, the still beauty of the *Pietà* is, perhaps, right.

And this makes one reflect on the aftermath of pain and grief in life in general, as we know it. I have already referred briefly to those people in whose eyes you can read that they have been face to face with death and have come to terms with it. Some of these have come to terms with it in a kind of negative, resigned, enduring way. They have been through searing experiences and have achieved for themselves a way of living with the results. Life holds no more horrors for them, because they have already met the worst: they are initiates, *cognoscenti*; they know. And, by knowing, they have attained to a kind of peace, an equilibrium, a truce with pain.

But there are others who have gone far beyond so negative an answer to life. It seems to me that there is a world of difference between those who have come through and learned to live without hope, and these others who have made out of their sufferings something that belongs to the future. The resigned sufferers are resigned to what is. These others are constantly expecting, and, indeed, actually creating, something new.

Jesus' arrest and death left all sorts in its wake. Two people were in abject distress: Judas, who, too late, came to realize the appalling thing he had done; and Peter, collapsing in grief and self-reproach for having denied Jesus. Judas could face it no longer, and took his life. Something sustained Peter, perhaps, or he was not temperamentally suicidal? I don't know. But what can he have felt like? I don't know whether there is any representation of the deposition with Peter in it, but there is certainly nothing in the Gospels to suggest he was there, and how could he have borne to witness it? Here was the body of Jesus, heroically through with death, leaving the coward behind to live with his cowardice.

Besides Judas and Peter, Jesus' arrest and death left plenty of people in mourning – in particular, his mother. Her heart must have been like a stone. You know how anaesthetized you become for a while. Later on, you come to life again, and the ache comes back, and it is all but intolerable. But at the funeral, something inside you has died. You feel as though you were standing outside yourself! It's all unreal. It's not you at the graveside: it must be someone else! Others, again, who had seen Jesus die, were less closely involved; they were just spectators. They beat their breasts (St Luke's Gospel says) and went back to normal life. On them, the trauma was but slight.

So, the funeral of Jesus projects the usual types: the remorseful, who wish they hadn't treated the departed so badly; the closest mourners, whose grief is silent and frozen; the shallow, who crack jokes with the undertaker. But everything is in a low key. The intense agony is over – at least for the moment.

Holy Saturday is not the end of the story. It closes one chapter; but what of the next? Death is past. What lies ahead? There are people, as I have just said, who have reached a quiet resignation. They have sized up life and taken the measure of it. They know the worst it can bring. They have learnt what to expect, and they don't expect any more. From now onwards, they are going to demand nothing, and so will not be disappointed. Like Ivan Denisovich in Alexander Solzhenitsyn's *One Day*, they accept any spell that is free from acute distress as almost enjoyable: it's a pure bonus, since they are expecting nothing. One better day is more of joy than they expect from life.

But there are others for whom this dead, featureless resignation is not the reaction at all. Because they have been through the worst with God, they are enabled to find in it the promise of new creation. Their faces wear, not the set features of resignation, but the light of hope. They have not achieved the hard shell of a sufferer who can suffer no more. They are alive, with sympathy and tears and laughter still in plenty. They do believe in the living God. And those among such people who are Christians do believe that there was a sequel to Holy Saturday: that somehow, on Easter Day, the friends of Jesus found out the meaning of the death. Not that the death had been cancelled or reversed, but that it was part of God's design of life. He had been raised to life eternal. God had not suffered his Holy One to see corruption. And by him they were shown the path of life.

# 2

# Biblical Theology

## 1 Divine action

Given that one believes that God is a God who acts – a God who does things in the universe – how do we conceive of the manner of such action? Do we believe in an interventionist deity or not? The Bible, though with a wide range of different conceptions, comes down mainly on the interventionist side. In both the Old Testament (as Christians call it) and the New, God is depicted as 'coming' and 'doing things' in this world; intervening, in some crisis, to change the normal course of affairs in this world. The earliest Christians had not yet, of course, any New Testament; and the Old Testament, which was their Bible, is full of divine intervention, from the Garden of Eden onwards: the Exodus from Egypt, the Babylonian Captivity, the restoration and the Second Temple, and so forth.

There is, however, no serious reason for thinking the Bible (either Testament) to be infallible. Indispensable it indeed is, but there is no serious argument to suggest that it never errs; and parts of the Old Testament are, for instance, full of what to a Christian is unacceptable genocide: God is shown as vindicating his chosen people by enabling them to exterminate opponents. That is not a view that a Christian can entertain, once it is accepted that Jesus Christ died because he refused to wield the sword. The Bible, as I suggest elsewhere, is less like a compass or a chart than a guide for finding the Pilot. Precious in the extreme, the Bible is yet not itself the 'Word' of God: that name belongs to Christ.

And how is the action of God in the world revealed to us in Christ? If we believe that Christ is, in a unique way, God revealed in humankind, then, emphatically, he represents the immanence of God. His life and death and resurrection reveal the Creator at work within his creation, overcoming evil by goodness, to the last drop of his own blood, shed because of love for us all, to the very end. God did not rescue his beloved Son by a spectacular intervention. Rather, in that Son, he conquered sin and hatred by absolute compassion, submitting to the worst that wickedness could do, in order to rescue the wicked.

If, then, there is truth in the belief that God makes no promises to snatch us out of disaster, but goes through with it with us, what does that do to our praying? May it be that to offer God our obedience, which is the essence of prayer, is to take an active part in the complex working of the world – to join the Creator within his creation? The model of prayer is 'Let this cup pass! Nevertheless, your will be done.' To utter such a prayer with deep conviction is to know that the one who prays is ready to become an active element in God's design. It is difficult to make a sincere offer of obedience except in a specific prayer; but it is the obedience so exposed that a non-interventionist God can use for his wise purposes, not necessarily the formulation of the prayer. The divine answer is not necessarily in the form of 'rescue from on high'; but the obedience of the one who offers the prayer is certain to be a factor in the working out of God's will within the situation. God raises Jesus from death and makes him the Saviour of the world.

This is a faith that needs to be gradually formed as circumstances allow – if possible, before the moment of stress or extreme suffering. If it is soundly formed, then in the day of agony and stress, it will utter itself creatively, and the obedience of the sufferer will become one of myriad tiny sluice-gates, opening to let through the immanent power of the Creator, to achieve his will; not intervening but indwelling; not in destruction from without, but by creation from within.


## 2 In face of the cross (Hebrews 12.2)

The New Testament writing known as the Epistle to the Hebrews (agreed to be *not* by St Paul) is the most stylish bit of Greek in the New Testament – straining after rhetorical effect sometimes at the expense of clarity. There is a notorious ambiguity in 12.2, where the New English Bible has (with reference to Jesus) '. . . who, for the sake of the joy that lay ahead of him, endured the cross . . .', with the marginal alternative: '. . . who, in place of the joy that was open to him . . .'. At issue is the meaning of the Greek preposition *anti* (by no means the same as the familiar Latin *anti*, 'against'). Does it here mean 'instead of' or 'in exchange for'? Does it mean that Jesus was glad to endure crucifixion for the sake of the joy it would bring, or that, instead of grasping at the relief (of escape) which he might have chosen he went through with the agony?

If it is difficult to decide which was intended, it is possible to recognize that both are true. One of the most remarkable things about the Jesus who emerges from the earliest and best evidence is his disregard of the appalling consequences of sticking through thick and thin to what he believed was right. But it is also true that the ultimate result was the inexpressible glory of implementing, in time and space, the unconditional divine offer of love. It is *there*, '*it is finished*' – if only we are humble enough to receive it.

## 3 Propitiation*

Some Christians speak of Christ as making an alienated God propitious by the offering of himself as a sacrifice on our behalf. This is alien to the startlingly original thought of the New Testament. In the Old Testament the idea of propitiating God by sacrifices and other means is indeed common enough; but in the NT it is almost extinguished.

The root behind Greek words for propitiation (*hilas-*) shows itself eight times in the NT. The verb ('make [someone] propitious' or, without an expressed recipient, 'make propitiation') occurs in Luke 18.13, in the penitent tax-collector's prayer to God: 'be made propitious to me', and in Hebrews 2.17 in a description of an *Old* Testament priest's duty to 'propitiate sins' (presumably there meaning 'to propitiate God regarding sins'). An adjectival form, *hileos*, comes at Matthew 16.22 (Peter's protesting exclamation '[God] have mercy on you!') and at Hebrews 8.12, in a quotation from Jeremiah 31 where God promises that he will be 'propitious to sins' (i.e. sinners?).

The neuter noun, *hilasterion*, is, in the Greek OT, a term for what, in the Authorized Version, comes out as the 'mercy seat' – the throne of God overshadowed by the cherubim, on (or as) the lid of the 'ark' in the Tabernacle or temple sanctuary. In the NT it occurs at Hebrews 9.5, simply as that item in the Tabernacle, but, importantly, also at Romans 3.25, with reference to Jesus Christ, 'whom God set forth [or 'designated beforehand'?] *hilasterion*', i.e. 'as a mercy seat' (if the word is meant as a noun) or (if it is an adjective) 'with propitiatory power' (though, as we shall see, '*expiatory*' power would be preferable).

Finally, *hilasmos*, a noun meaning 'a propitiation' or 'a propitiatory sacrifice' occurs as a description of Christ at 1 John 2.2; 4.10. At 4.10 God is specified as (not receiving but) himself sending Christ as *hilasmos*.

Thus, what, for our purposes, is important is that in the NT God is not spoken of as the recipient of what is referred to, but that, where its

---

*This note was prompted by the words of a 'worship song' which included the words:

'And on that Cross, where Jesus died, the wrath of God was satisfied.'

initiator is mentioned, he is the subject, not the object: Romans 3.25; 1 John 4.10.

If, then, God is the subject or originator, not the object or recipient, of *hilas*-procedures, it is manifestly inappropriate to translate them as propitiatory; one is driven to use a word such as 'expiatory', which has as its object not propitiating a wrathful God but removing a barrier. It is this which is expressed in the famous words of 2 Corinthians 5.19: 'God was, in [or 'by'?] Christ reconciling the world to himself'. So far from being propitiated, God it is who initiates the necessary 'expiation', himself 'one' with his Beloved Son. 'In Christ's name, be reconciled to God' (2 Cor. 5.20) is the Christian exhortation, for 'God made him who knew no sin to be sin [?sin-offering] on our behalf.' Regularly, God is the initiation of the action, not its recipient. The only exception in the NT is at Ephesians 5.2, where 'Christ gave himself up on our behalf as an offering and sacrifice to God for a fragrant perfume' – a virtual quotation from the standard propitiatory language of the OT.

In the Johannine writings a further metaphor is introduced – that of advocacy. John 16 speaks, it seems, of the Holy Spirit as an Advocate, a Paraclete, and 1 John 2 uses the same language of Christ. By itself, such language might suggest a friend to plead our cause before an alienated Judge; but that is hardly compatible with John 16.26f.: 'I do not say that I will ask the Father concerning you, for the father himself loves you. . .'.

I submit, then, that NT usage virtually prohibits the translation 'propitiate', 'propitiation', and necessitates the use of some word with God as subject and sin as object, e.g. 'expiate', in the sense of paying the price for sin's annulment. This is not the only instance of what seems like the centrifugal force of the Christian gospel spinning an OT concept to the circumference, if not beyond, in favour of the astonishing conviction at its centre, classically stated at 2 Corinthians 5.19, 'God was, in Christ, reconciling the world to himself'.

Every reconciliation costs an untold price – the price of forgiveness, the price of repentance. In Christ, both God and man, that price is paid, absolutely and finally.

Nowhere in the NT is it said that the wrath of God was satisfied by the death of Jesus. Rather, it is *God himself in Jesus Christ* who pays the cost for sin. I haven't the smallest spark of lyricism in me, but we need something like, but infinitely better than:

Till in the blood of his dear Son
The love of God redemption won.

## 4 The Spirit

It is well known that the Hebrew Scriptures use a word that may be transliterated as *ruach* and which means both 'wind' and (transcendental) 'spirit', and which is often used in the latter sense to denote the active presence and power of God among humankind. Especially in the book of Judges it means the transcendent power of God moving in human beings in deeds of special power: the Spirit of God falls upon, or even clothes itself with human individuals, empowering them. When Moses is bidden to delegate his administrative powers, a portion of this 'Spirit' falls upon the chosen 70 – even the two who did not come out to the door of God's presence. A great leader is spoken of as endowed with a spirit of various gifts. Prophets are spoken of as inspired by the divine Spirit. The disobedient are spoken of as 'grieving the Spirit'. In all these phrases the 'Spirit' is personal.

The case for the word's denoting a principle of life in creation is weaker: the *ruach* of God moving on the waters, in the first creation story in Genesis 1, is likely enough to be one of the features of chaos (a 'God-sized' hurricane) fuelled by the Creator.

In the New Testament the same enabling Spirit is imparted with renewed authority. According to John 20, the risen Lord visits a gathering of disciples in Jesus, breathes on them, and imparts the Spirit which gives authority to retain or lift away sin. According to Acts, the Spirit comes like a rushing wind, and fiery tongues, falling upon each head in a gathering of Christians in Jerusalem, enabling them to preach in many languages. In 1 Corinthians 12–14 the Spirit is recognized as the source of various gifts, including uttering sounds belonging to no known language. In the story of Apollos John the Baptist's baptism of repentance falls short of baptism in the name of Christ, which brings speaking with 'tongues'.

In short, the pre-Christian experience of the Spirit brought many powers: but the Christian experience was distinguished by the gift of tongues, in particular. Even that was probably not totally new. In the Hebrew Scriptures, the guilds of the prophets are referred to sometimes as possessed with special utterances: raving, one might almost say. Saul is said to have joined them (1 Samuel 10).

So what is new about Whitsun? Not tongues! Is the case of Apollos at the end of Acts 18 helpful? He knew the baptism of John (for repentance); what he didn't know was the spiritual power brought by trust in Jesus, raised from death – 'baptism' in the Spirit of God, through trust in Jesus. So what is new is the old phenomena *newly focused on the risen Christ*. That is veritably a new world, a new experience, incomparably more infectious, more compelling.


## 5  The Son of Man

*My thesis*. Jesus used the 'human figure' of Daniel 7 as a symbol of his own vocation, to which he also called his followers – that of total obedience to God's design, which is vindicated through and beyond death: a symbol rather that a title. (Note that in the Gospels 'the Son of Man' in any case does not stand for the humanity of Christ in contrast to his divinity, as in later 'two nature' Christologies.)

*Alternative proposals* have included (a) that 'the Son of Man' was already current by the time of Christ in Jewish apocalyptic thought, as a term for a transcendent Being; and (b) that it represents, in Hebrew and Aramaic, an idiomatic way of referring obliquely to oneself. (a) has gone out of fashion; (b) is popular.

*Facts* to which too little attention is generally paid. In the sayings-traditions in the Gospels (and Acts 7.56), 'the Son of Man' is used with nearly complete consistency (John 5.27 omits 'the' – the solitary exception). Conversely, in pre-Christian and Aramaic sources, whereas in the *plural* 'the sons of men' or 'of man' does occur, 'the Son of Man' in the *singular*, seems to be unexampled, with a solitary exception in the Dead Sea Scrolls (IQS xi.20), where the definite article has been added, over the line, as a correction apparently.

*Proposed interpretation*. The demonstrable fact of this consistency suggests an Aramaic sayings-tradition (Jesus almost certainly used Aramaic) in which an unambiguously *definite* locution was used. If some Aramaists deny that it is possible to distinguish definite from indefinite in the most obvious Aramaic equivalent, then why not postulate some *other* Aramaic locution that *was* (as is entirely possible) unambiguously definite? If so, to what did that definite phrase refer? The most plausible candidate is the human figure in Daniel's vision (Dan. 7.13) (Josephus provides evidence, in *Antiquities* 10.267, that Daniel was current at this period). The human figure in Daniel's vision ('one like a Son of Man') stands for the Jews who were loyal even to martyrdom – 'the saints of the Most High'. In the vision, their representative – that Man-like one – is vindicated and given an eternal kingdom. What more appropriate 'logo' for the aims of Jesus? (There is a parallel to the linguistic phenomenon in the *Similitudes of Enoch*, a Jewish apocalypse of uncertain date.)

*Note* (a) I am not competent to report on the Aramaic usage in the Targums, but, as they now stand, these are mostly much later than the time of Christ. (b) It is probable that not every instance of the term 'the Son of Man' in the Gospels goes back to the words of Jesus. Some instances look like a stylized use of it as a title (e.g. Matt. 16.13); some uses in St John look like adaption to the evangelist's interpretation of Christology. But this does not prevent one's finding an intelligible explanation for each of the main categories of its use in the Synoptic Gospels. The Johannine occurrences: 1.51; 3.13f.; 6.27, 53, 62; 8.28; 9.35; 12.23, 34; 13.31. John 5.27 is the solitary instance of 'Son of Man', without the article, in the whole sayings tradition. Outside the sayings tradition, it occurs in Hebrews 2.6 (from Psalm 8) and Revelation 1.13; 14.14 (from Daniel 7) – and without definite article. (c) For references, direct or oblique, to a 'collective' 'Son of Man', see Luke 22:30 (cf. Matt. 19.28; 1 Cor. 6.1f.; Rev. 20.4).

# 6 The beatitudes

The most familiar collection of what have come to be called 'beatitudes' is in Matthew 5, at the beginning of 'the Sermon on the Mount', so named from the statement in verse 1 that Jesus went up 'to the mountain' and sat down (as the rabbis are said to have done) to deliver it. What is meant may well be 'the hill country' – a generalized term, as it would seem (as in Matt. 15.29); but it is hard not to believe that a reference is also intended to the mountain on which the Law was given to Moses in the Old Testament. Here is the Christian parallel, to match the New Covenant.

The Sermon starts with a series of pronouncements about who are really to be congratulated. The word *beatus* is the Latin rendering of the original Greek *makarios*. This, in its turn, corresponds to the Hebrew exclamation *ashre* (Oh the blessedness of . . . !) and, no doubt, equivalents in the Aramaic probably used by Christ himself. The Hebrew exclamation is frequent in the Old Testament. The Queen of Sheba, in 1 Kings 10.8, uses it to congratulate Solomon's entourage on their privilege. Eliphaz offers Job the doubtful comfort of the thought that the man who is disciplined by God is fortunate (5.17). A Psalmist in Psalm 119.1 congratulates those whose behaviour is impeccable; and so on. In the New Testament too there are plenty of instances of the Greek word outside Matthew 5, the most obvious parallels being, of course, in St Luke's version of the beatitudes, in Luke 6, in what is sometimes called 'the Sermon on the Plain' because, in verse 17, Jesus comes down from 'the mountain' (v. 12) with his disciples, and stands on level ground. Both Matthew and Luke may be recalling the giving of the Old Law: Moses came down to the foot of the mountain to deliver it to the people.

The lists of beatitudes are not identical in Matthew and Luke. It makes sense to see the Lukan form as nearer to the original (though of course Jesus himself could have said different things on different occasions), because it seems to have in view the exceptional circumstances of the circle closest to the Lord – the Twelve. These were literally and materially poor, who were deliberately renouncing subsistence necessities, throwing themselves, as paupers, on anyone who would host them, as in the injunctions given to a special band of preachers in Matthew 10.9f. Such were the people to be congratulated – materially destitute, rich in what makes a true child of God. The Lukan version, unlike the Matthean, has some corresponding 'Woes': 'Woe to you rich and satisfied and happy and popular!' That's how it is with false devotees. They already have their reward, and there's nothing more to come.

However, not all those who accepted and revered Jesus and his mission were called to leave home and become indigent. St Matthew's version of the beatitudes is so phrased as to be compatible with a more ordinary material independence, which, however, is still just as much in need of that basic 'poverty' – the humility that recognizes its spiritual need and the blessedness of spiritual riches.

In both cases alike, the basic blessings attend upon freedom from self-seeking and self-vindicating and retaliatory, grasping attitudes, together with integrity, single-mindedness, compassion, and the courage to let God take over. The blessings that attend upon these attitudes of self-emptying are the abiding possessions – citizenship of heaven, 'possession of the earth', membership in the family of God and in the kingdom of God, the vision of God, comfort after suffering. It is like the dramatic exaltation that follows the divine self-emptying in Philippians 2.

If we are honest with our own unspoken longings, what shall we list among our 'beatitudes' – the blessings most to be desired? Health, wealth (or at least a competence), good looks, popularity, conjugal joys, nice children . . . ? Think of those 'sermons': poverty, tears, unpopularity because of faithfulness to Christ . . . ! It sounds perverse. Are we to believe that Jesus would not have contributed to the relief of poverty, had he had the means? Clearly, that would be a perverse interpretation. When an adoring woman lavished on him the entire contents of a phial of priceless perfume and was scolded for the waste of money that might have been given to the poor, he defended her but also showed approval of gifts to the poor (Matt. 26.8–11; Mark 14.3–9; John 12.3–8; see also Matt. 19.21 and parallels). How could he have congratulated the involuntarily indigent of the so-called third world, or the victims of world disasters? It is those who voluntarily embrace poverty for Christ's service, like St Francis, who are blessed. It was only the specially chosen Twelve who renounced a settled life. Another explanation offered for the Lukan extreme form is that it was only an 'interim ethic' for what was then expected to be a short interval before the 'return' of Christ after his death; but this has come to be discredited. It makes more sense to see it as a rigorous, exaggeratedly forceful enjoining of a consistent poverty and pacifism, presented as an individualistic ethic.

This seems, indeed, to correspond to as much as we know about Christ's own life-style. There seems to be no evidence that he ever espoused a social or political programme. The only references to his using force are nugatory. In John 2.15 he applies a home-made whip to the traders in the Temple. In comparable scenes in Matthew 21.12 and Mark 11.15 he overturns tables and chairs. In his teaching there is not a whiff of insurrection against the Roman occupation: his crucifixion seems to be the result of a totally mistaken idea that he might be a patriotic 'freedom fighter' who would attack the Romans. He makes no protest against the Roman army of occupation, on the contrary enjoining going the second mile when commandeered for labour by a soldier. He does not ostracize Jewish tax-collectors who worked for Rome. He enjoins submission to persecution. In John 18.36 he declares to Pilate outright that his kingdom is not of this world – otherwise, his assistants would indeed be fighting.

The people Jesus does attack, with fierce verbal lashings, are the scribes and Pharisees – though not for doing their job. The professional scribe was an interpreter of the Mosaic Law. The Pharisees were members of private fraternities of ultra-strict observant Jews. What Jesus attacked them for was for not following their convictions sincerely – for hypocrisy; and also sometimes for their actual teaching – see the tirade in Matthew 23, and also such passages as Matthew 15.3ff.; 16.12. These were not political attacks. As for the Temple hierarchy, they were hostile to Jesus (with the rare exceptions named in St John's Gospel). His response seems to have been to ignore or avoid them where possibie, and to defend himself verbally (and unanswerably) when attacked.

In parenthesis, and returning to the language of beatitude, elsewhere in the New Testament not only are beatitudes used but sometimes they actually echo the 'Sermons'. We have the beatitude to Peter, in Matthew

16.17, for recognizing the Messiahship of our Lord; in Acts 20.35, more 'blessed' to give than to receive; and in 1 Peter 3.14; 4.14 there is 'rejoice in persecution' for the Lord's sake. And there are other passages, including the 'Magnificat' in Luke 1.48, using the verb 'call me blessed', 'congratulate me'.

But the question is, what should our response be to the stringent demands of the beatitudes and the sermons that expound them. I would suggest that a responsible citizen today must combine a humble, self-searching submission to the *spirit* of the beatitudes with a responsible activity in the realm of public morals, in whatever manner will be most effective, given one's capacities; never self-seeking, never resorting to unjust force, but actively supporting what makes for peace and good order. It is fatal to lose sight of the spirit of the beatitudes; it is incumbent on us constantly to pray with their ideals before us – the Lord's Prayer itself is part of Matthew's Sermon. But then we must act, with pure motives and constant humility. After the beatitudes, the rest of the sermon is largely an exposition of how they work out. It is worthwhile to remember also John the Baptist's counsel in Luke 3.7–14.

*January 2005*

## 7 A difficult parable: Matthew 18.21–35

It is impossible to know how accurate are the traditions of our Lord's teaching. Is Matthew 18 self-contradictory, and was it so with the original? Peter asks our Lord how often he ought to forgive a brother – as many as seven times? The answer, 'Seventy times seven', seems to mean an unlimited number of times; forgiveness must be on offer always, and never withdrawn. However, the parable that follows, about the man whose master waived an enormous debt when he was unable to pay, but who was ruthless with a fellow-servant whose debt to him was nugatory, seems to suggest that such a one ought to have short shrift and to be at once consigned to a debtors' prison, complete with torture. This, it says, is how God treats the unforgiving – torture and all. So, is God himself, after all, unforgiving?

There are at least two considerations that are relevant here. One is the difference between public preaching and private teaching. The other is the difference between an offer of forgiveness and the ability to accept it.

Our Lord's public preaching, to vast crowds in the open air, much of it in parables, must have been couched in poster-style, huge black and white sentences without delicate discriminations. It was only afterwards, indoors, with the comparatively few seekers, that some finesse could enter the picture. May it not be that the wording of the parable belongs to the broad public preaching? In a smaller group it might have been explained (and this is the second consideration) that while the *offer* of divine for-giveness is indeed never withdrawn, the *reception* of it is possible only for the penitent, and that the precious gift of free will means that it is up to each person to accept or reject it. This thought is more awe-inspiring than any threat of revenge, and the unforgiving servant in the parable is self-declared as impenitent. And actually, our Lord's reply to Peter com-mands unlimited forgiveness specifically for the penitent.

However, offering forgiveness that is refused remains different from wreaking *vengeance* on the impenitent – something often attributed to God in the Hebrew Scriptures. It is the New Testament which, though not yet completely eliminating the concept of vengeance, has spun it to the circumference by the centrifugal force of the death of Christ as the complete and all-embracing implementation, in time and space, of the eternal love of God. So we must take note of 2 Corinthians 5.21, and ponder on Romans 12.19–21.

Is it possible that, in much of Matthew 18, we are listening to the outdoor rhetoric of the preacher, while other verses might contain a combination of the more intimate style of teaching?

*A respondent reacts: On your opening sentence: among the evangelists Matthew is the moralist and the one who emphasizes divine judgement and even hell, and he likes to drive home the point. Would it not have been more like Jesus to stop with verse 33, the point powerfully made?*

## 8 Self-interest in sayings attributed to Jesus

Countless pages of research must have been written on the source or sources peculiar to St Luke's Gospel (so-called 'L'), but there is prob-ably always more to add. One noteworthy fact is that this material includes literary gems such as chapter 15 (lost sheep, lost coin, lost son) side by side with passages so badly written as to be, at least in some manuscripts, ungrammatical.

The teaching of Jesus in the 'L' source includes sayings that may be described as worldly-wise, not to say selfish, reminiscent of some of the 'wisdom literature' in Hebrew tradition; and far from what we have come to reckon as distinctive of the Christian message of self-abandon for the kingdom of God. Luke 14 contains two examples. Invited by a Pharisee to a meal, Jesus notes how guests choose for themselves the most honourable places at table. Don't do that, he says; it may only lead to humiliation, when the host has to displace you, in favour of someone more honourable. Choose, rather, a humble position, and then you may glory when invited to move to a more honourable position. In other words, plan for your own glorification! Compare Luke 18.14. Again, he says, when you give a party, don't invite your rich friends, but the indigent who can't repay you: then you will be rewarded by God. Are these appeals to self-interest compatible with the way of the cross? Have they come into the sayings-tradition from elsewhere, or did our Lord really speak in this way?

Again, whereas the unconditional love of God for us, which we believe was implemented in time and space in our Lord, excludes the idea of *punitive revenge*, however severe are the *consequences* of rejecting it, it is in Luke (12.7f.) that the saying occurs that the guilty will be beaten severely, whereas the guiltless receive only a few strokes (why any at all?!).

Was our Lord deliberately coming down to the level of quantitative justice and self-interest, and saying, 'If that's your purpose, use your intelligence'?

## 9 Criticisms of St Paul

It is fashionable today to decry St Paul. Some who do so scrupulously avoid reading the Epistles but quote opinions they have heard. Others do read the Epistles but tend to read even more between the lines. St Paul, they say, was dictatorial; he tyrannized over his converts and tried to manipulate them. He was conceited, irascible, a misogynist and, of course, hopelessly obscure. Also, some would add, he knew little and cared less about Jesus, the historical person. It was Paul really, they say, who invented the Christian religion, and it has little to do with the man of Nazareth.

How do these opinions stand up to scrutiny, in the light of careful reading of such genuine epistles as have survived? There is wide agreement on the genuineness of 1 Thessalonians, Galatians, most of 1 and 2 Corinthians, Romans, Philippians and Philemon; and I submit that an attentive reading of these is enough to dispel many of the features in the unacceptable face of the Apostle as it appears to the imagination of many.

Not that there is nothing here that is unacceptable to a thoughtful reader; there is a good deal. It is easy to draw up a considerable list of difficulties – the following, for a start:

(1) In Romans 13 St Paul declares that obedience to the civic authorities of the Roman state is a duty for Christians, because, he says in a sweeping statement, all who are in authority have been appointed by God. It is pretty evident that Paul is addressing a situation where some recently converted Christians are tempted to exploit their new status – free from law and under grace – to justify sitting loose to their responsibilities as citizens. It is this that St Paul is curbing. But *as a generalization* about all secular government, it is self-evidently untenable.

(2) So, too, the acceptance of the institution of slavery, and the admonitions to slaves to be submissive, are completely out of tune with today's Christian conscience. (See 1 Corinthians 7. 21–3 and Philemon – not to include the Pastoral Epistles, see 1 Timothy 6.1f.)

(3) Notoriously, again, there are passages that seem to declare that women, as such, are subordinate to men, and which limit the scope of a woman's ministry in church. In the acknowledged Epistles, there is 1 Corinthians 11.3–10; 14.33b–35, though considerable obscurity attaches to both these passages, and in the second the text is not stable. But there's enough there to disturb us. And, as before, there would be still more to be reckoned with in the doubtfully Pauline Pastoral Epistles: see 1 Timothy 2.11–15.

(4) Another difficulty, in addition to these *ethical* problems, is presented by *doctrinal* problems. For instance:

(a) the eschatology is difficult for any reader today to fit into any intelligible pattern. I am thinking especially of 1 Thessalonians 1.10; 4.13–18; 1 Corinthians 15.23, 51–3; Philippians 3.20f. Even if we allow that much of this is consciously pictorial and symbolic language, not meant to be taken with prosaic literalism, it is still difficult to get away from what seems to be the expectation of an individual return of Christ very soon, to take charge and put the world to rights (Rom. 16.20); and this goes, it seems, with the expectation that, at that climax, the Christian dead, who have been somehow waiting, as it were in sleep, will be resurrected. (1 Thessalonians 4.13; Philippians 3.20f. – though Philippians 1.21–3 might mean something different; and 2 Corinthians 5 may reflect a change of mind.) Can we conceive of the realization of the kingdom of God on earth in any such terms? As I see it, it is only in 2 Corinthians 5 that there seem to emerge more realistic conceptions.

Then (b) some of St Paul's christological formulations do not conform to the ecumenical credal consensus – the most obvious instance being the explicit subordination of Christ to God in 1 Corinthians 11.3 and 15.28. Is this Trinitarian? Also, of course, there is 1 Corinthians 8.6, with its subtle distinction between God and Christ in respect of their relation to the act of creation: and, outside the most widely acknowledged genuine Epistles, there is Colossians 1.16, where 'the firstborn *of* all creation' is ambiguous, and might mean, not God's eternal Son existing *before* creation, but the eldest Son existing *within* creation. If the Apostle had lived to the period of the ecumenical Councils, yet without changing his language, he might have been anathematized as a heretic.

Some, if not all, of these reservations must be reckoned with, if we are to presume at all to estimate the great Apostle. Yet, all this being said, I submit that what is really impressive in his doctrinal consciousness is not this element of looseness and imprecision in formulation, but the amazing *height* (if I may use the metaphor) of the overall christological convictions reflected in the acknowledged Epistles, which were written, remember, only some 20 years after the death of Christ.

Before we consider this, however, there is that other serious allegation (c), in which many well informed scholars concur, that the historical Jesus is given little prominence in the Epistles. What is at stake here is whether there is, for St Paul, a firm *continuity* between the historical man and the transcendent presence of the believer's experience, without which his Christology would, indeed, be incompatible with any orthodox stance. My own belief is that this objection can be satisfactorily met. In the first place, one needs to remember that all his letters are addressed to confessing Christians; and it is not usual for one Christian writing to another to recite the historical story of Jesus all over again: naturally, it is taken for granted. What is remarkable, though, is that in the two cases where Paul feels driven to recall to his hearers their initial instruction – what they were taught by him when they were first being brought to faith – the material suddenly becomes a narrative, and begins to look like a fragment of a Gospel. I refer, of course, to 1 Corinthians 11.23–5, the earliest surviving narrative of the institution of the Eucharist, and 1 Corinthians 15.1–7, the earliest surviving record of the traditions about the resurrection appearances. Both of these are explicitly described as part of the tradition that had been handed on to him, as he, in turn, had passed it on to them. Note, too, the reference to his vivid portrayal of the crucifixion to the Galatians (Gal. 3.1); and, in Galatians 2.2, his reference to his checking his way of proclaiming the gospel with the Jerusalem apostles – an impressive testimony, considering that it comes in a context in which his main theme is precisely his independence of Jerusalem. Another striking pointer is Galatians 2.19f., where he speaks of 'the Son of God who loved me and gave himself up for me' – a reference to the crucifixion of a known individual in history, which is the more impressive for its being coupled with a reference to St Paul's present, personal involvement (some would say mystical union) with the unseen, transcendent, divine presence. This suggests to me very strongly that, for all his visionary devotion and spirituality, St Paul had a firm grasp on the continuity between the man of Nazareth and that transcendent presence. Certainly some good scholars (including Bultmann, though not his great predecessor F. C. Baur) were *mistaken* when they supposed that, in 2 Corinthians 5.16, Paul is disclaiming any continuing concern for the physical man of history. That is not his meaning at all. When Paul says, ' from now onwards, we do not know anybody "according to flesh". Even if we *have* known Christ "according to flesh", yet now we no longer do so', how could Paul cease to know *anybody* as a historical person? The fact is that 'according to flesh', 'fleshwise', clearly qualifies the *verb* 'to know', not the *noun* 'Christ' or 'any other person'. 'According to flesh' does the job there not of an adjective qualifying a noun, but of an adverb qualifying a verb: it describes a *manner of knowing*. The converted Christian looks at Christ, and, for that matter, at everybody, with new eyes and in a new attitude; but he or she doesn't cease to look at the person's human history.

To this might be added, if there were time, a few 'straws in the wind' blowing in the same direction; but I mention further only one significant fact: in 1 Corinthians 7.10, when advising about marriage and celibacy, he makes an express distinction between a traditional saying of Jesus Christ, and his own opinion, showing that he knew at least some of the traditional sayings material.

So much, by way of responding to some of the allegations against St Paul's thought, while acknowledging defects in it, as judged by later conclusions. What of (5) the popular ideas about his character – irascible and dictatorial? Of course it is possible to quote chapter and verse for stern and sometimes sharp words, not to say harsh judgements, not to say coarse (almost Luther-like!) exclamations. He does sometimes reprimand severely, even fiercely; but it looks as though many of his critics, when speaking of his arrogance, are thinking chiefly of 2 Corinthians 10.1 – 12.7, that long survey of his 'track record', forgetting that this is explicitly described by him himself as an ironical exhibition of the sort of boasting that he *could* indulge in, if it came to a competition in the same game between himself and his rival boastful evangelists, but which in fact he scorns and derides. It is in his weakness that he finds a divine strength not his own; it is in physical distress and abasement that he learns to trust God; and the only true boasting is to boast in the Lord (2 Cor. 10.17). Again, I am simply not convinced by those who find evidence that he tries to manipulate his converts – that seems to me to lie, if anywhere, *between* the lines. And what does stand out is his passionate affection and gentle concern for his friends: 1 Thessalonians 1, 2; Romans 16; Galatians 4.19.

So, now, to an attempt at a positive estimate. The fact is that Paul's courageous originality towers over the other NT writers. One must concede, I am sure, that the Apostle is no *systematic* thinker. What we have from his pen (or rather his mouth) is, after all, only a few pastoral letters, directed at particular situations and not purporting to be a systematic exposé of his belief, even if the Epistle to the Romans goes some way towards being a personal confession of faith.

(1) Think, first, of Christology. The marvellous thing is that what shows through this rather loosely assembled, incidental writing, is a massive conviction about Jesus Christ, containing (I would say) all the implications of the developed fourth-century creeds, though not expressed with perfect consistency, nor with *their* philosophical precision. Indeed, so remarkable is this that (as my friends so often hear me say) it seems to me inexplicable that anyone in his situation could possibly have reached such convictions, unless they do *match the reality* of Christ. By this I mean that I cannot conceive of any alternative explanation of how St Paul reached these convictions than that this is how he found Christ to be. The idea that they were generated by the well-known process of 'deification' or 'apotheosis' – that is, the enthusiastic

imagination of the devotee lifting the hero step by step to the stars – is ludicrous, when you consider how far St Paul's conception of Christ and of his 'work' surpasses any known example of the standard types of imaginary deification, and when you consider how specially unlikely it was, humanly speaking, that Paul of all people should come to such convictions. The complete revolution that changed him from an ultra-observant Pharisee into a pioneer of an opposite and totally new way is described by him as due to a revelation of Christ (Gal. 1.12, 16), to a commissioning by Christ (Gal. 1.1), to a realization of the superiority of the knowledge of Christ (Phil. 3.8), and to a grasping of Paul by Christ (Phil. 3.12); and I can conceive of no other adequate way of describing it. It results in an amazingly profound and subtle Christology, more comprehensive (I dare to say) than that of any other NT writer, although the others reflect the implications of what they do not explicitly spell out. The Johannine corpus, like Luke and Acts, always (I think it is true to say) speaks of Christ as an individual. Even as the true Vine, his relationship with disciples is 'branch by branch'. Even when he is transcendent in post-resurrection glory, he is still conceived of as an individual, and localized – not on earth when he is in heaven. Paul, by contrast, combines the most vivid knowledge of Christ as an individual person (I have already quoted that phrase in Galatians 2.20) with a corporate understanding of him and an acceptance of his ubiquity: he *is* in heaven, but *also* in all the world. *He* is the One *in* whom Christians are incorporated and in whom they are integrated into a mutually coherent body. Does 'became flesh' take us further? This is an extraordinary achievement of thought, and can hardly spring from anything other than deep, personal experience. Implied in it is the universal validity of the reconciliation achieved by God in Christ. Thus, to be '*in Christ*' (somehow incorporated in him) is to be fully and completely 'in Israel', in the chosen vehicle of God's kingdom. St Paul saw that a baptized Gentile was as fully a member of the people of God as a circumcised Jew, and that Jewish ritual could not render anybody more completely so. You could not get further into the people of God than by baptism in the name of Christ and trust in him. St Paul's consistent stand on this principle caused much scandal among less percipient, less consistent Jewish Christians, including St Peter (Gal. 2.13f.); but Paul risked ostracism, and eventually death, in consistently abiding by this new and radical conviction. Paul did not invent Christianity; but he was a very potent factor in what set the Christian Church on its catholic, universal way. (It is interesting to consider the relation of the first martyr Stephen, and his group, with this radical break away. There are close affinities, and, according to Acts 8.1, Paul was in on that martyrdom.) Other NT writings recognize universal salvation in Christ (1 Peter is a striking example): they reflect the implications of the Pauline position; but none shows so comprehensive and percipient a grasp of the all-inclusiveness, the cosmic scope, of the One who, at the same time, remains the vividly known individual of history, and a personal guide and counsellor. So it is that Christ retains his individual, Jewish, personal name, yet is spoken of in the same breath with the Almighty: 'grace and peace from God-and-Jesus': *astounding!*

(2) So it is with St Paul's conception of how person is related to person. Quite apart from any religious tradition, it is an observed fact of human nature that a reconciliation after an alienation can occur only if, on the one hand, the wronged person is ready to offer undeserved forgiveness, and, on the other hand, the aggressor is ready to admit the wrong and repent and accept forgiveness. So it is (as St Paul saw) that on the universal, eternal and all-comprehensive scale, a putting right (justification) with God can be alone by repentance and trust: *sola fide* is the only recipe; and it is in Christ as both man and God that such a relationship is already completely recognized. (That is about as 'high' a Christology as can be imagined. The titles used by Paul for Christ *are* highly significant: 'Lord', 'Son of God', 'Messiah' – these, in their respective contexts, take us far. But the great corporate and collective conceptions of Christ as the Body in whom believers are incorporated, and through whom come reconciliation and healing, go even further.) It is thrilling to watch St Paul's grasp of reconciliation as achieved by God in Jesus Christ beginning to oust systems of quantitative justice in which he must originally have been trained, with their demand for retribution and punishment. Paul does sometimes, it is true, retain allusions to retribution, he does still speak of the punitive anger of God (though 2 Thessalonians 1 is not generally regarded as Pauline); but it is striking that they are driven to the periphery, so that he revolutionizes the notion of propitiation. In the acknowledged Paulines, although he still uses the word *propitiation*, there is no instance of the language of propitiation used with God as its *object*. Instead, God is

the subject of the action. It is not that Christ or humans propitiate God – try, by sacrifice or other means, to make him propitious and forgiving. On the contrary, it is God who initiates reconciliation: God in Christ was reconciling the world to himself (2 Cor. 5.19) – a pronouncement of the most far-reaching importance. Even in Romans 3, where the actual language of propitiation is used, it is still God who originates the action, as its subject, not its object. Only in Ephesians 5.2, which may not be Pauline, is there a mention of Christ's offering himself as an acceptable sacrifice to God, as though God needed to be propitiated.

(3)  A further remarkable aspect of the Apostle's relationship with the risen Christ is the way in which his belief in the Holy Spirit is enlarged and redefined by it. In the Hebrew Scriptures, 'the Spirit of God' usually denotes the presence of the transcendent God among his people and within individuals. For St Paul, in his Christian experience, it becomes the Spirit of Jesus Christ within a believer, uttering the words of personal relationship and trust: 'Abba, dear father, your will be done!' (Rom. 8.15; Gal. 4.6). It is the 'mind' of Christ – the outlook of the Son of God – created within the believer. As believers are incorporated in Christ, so the Spirit is within believers, guiding and admonishing, and imparting moral strength. Thus Christians may claim to have the 'mind' of Christ (1 Cor. 2.16; cf. 1 Cor. 7.40): the 'outlook' of the Spirit (Rom. 8.6) is what brings life to the Christian. In this kind of language, St Paul is, I believe, reflecting realities that lie behind the later formulation, in more philosophical terms, of the doctrine of the threefold unity of the deity. The texture of the Apostle's language thus reflects, however unsystematically, a profound and wide-ranging experience of the manner of God's contact with humankind, which was eventually going to be crystallized in the more philosophical and less experiential language of the ecumenical creeds; and although it is Johannine language that is more commonly quoted in the great doctrinal debates of the patristic period, my belief is that it is the Pauline experience that is the more comprehensive.

If we now look back at the portrait of Paul in the Acts, perhaps the beloved friend and adored leader is, after all, more realistic than hagiographical.

It would not be difficult to add to this. For example, we might discuss Paul's conception of Christian mission, which seems to be unusual and original; and as a coda I should like to touch on this topic within his theological thought. I mention this, not because it is in an area where the Apostle is disparaged in popular thought about him, because I doubt whether those who attack him are even aware of the area; but I mention it because what he has to tell us in relation to it belongs to the great and often unrecognized riches of what he has contributed to Christian life and thought. Owing much to Paul Bowers, I touch on four aspects of the theme of mission in Paul.

(1) The first is his conception of the task of mission and of his vocation to it. A scholar, F. Watson (1986), suggested that 'Paul turned to the Gentiles only after he had failed as a Christian missionary to his fellow Jews' (W. P. Bowers' summary in his article 'Mission', in *Dictionary of Paul and His Letters*, ed. G. F. Hawthorne, R. P. Martin and D. G. Reid (Downers Grove, Illinois/Leicester: IVP, 1993)). But this takes little account of the evidence, which seems to show that St Paul's failure to make more than a very little impression on his fellow Jews was due precisely to his already firm conviction that Jesus, who had been known for violating the ritual code of Jewish law, was himself the climax of the vocation of Israel. In other words, what offended his fellow Jews was Paul's conviction that the Gentile mission was not an alternative, adopted after failure with a Jewish mission, but part of the newly revealed conception of what Judaism meant; and that this conception was indeed a revelation, and sprang from the Apostle's divine commission, received in personal encounter with Christ.

(2) The second aspect is his understanding of the relation of the Gentile mission to the purposes of God for human history. It is only, he believes, when the destined number of Gentiles has been brought into the People of God that the purposes of God for the entire People of God can be fulfilled (see especially, Romans 9—11).

(3) The third aspect is St Paul's method of mission. He sees himself as only one among other evangelists, recognizing the Jewish mission of Peter and John as another valid activity, and recognizing Apollos and others as fellow-evangelists in his own area; and he seems to see this area of mission in which he works as, roughly, a crescent from Antioch to Macedonia, and then, if possible, on to Rome and Spain. And within this area, it is remarkable that he seems to see his vocation as that simply of planting churches in strategic centres and moving on. His is not the task of preaching

to every individual he can reach, but of founding communities in strategic centres. On this assumption, he can declare (Rom. 15.19) that he has 'completed the good news of the Christ' from Jerusalem to Illyricum, although we know that this meant nothing more comprehensive (gigantic achievement though this was) than establishing ten or a dozen Christian communities over the area. Vincent Donovan, *Christianity Rediscovered* (1978, 1982), writes: '[Paul] evangelised just a few centres in each province . . . and considered his work done' (p. 36). Donovan concludes that missionary work today 'must be planned and carried out in such a way that it is finishable in the shortest possible time, not in some vague future, but *now*' (p. 39).

(4) The fourth aspect of the Pauline mission that I wish to name is the originality of its method. We know something about Jewish proselytism, and something about the itinerant preachers of philosophy and mystery religions, and these have often been invoked as antecedents to the Christian mission. But W. P. Bowers (in 'Mission', pp. 610f.) questions whether these present close parallels. 'The public evangelist seeking to plant churches territory by territory is hardly discernible in early Christian history after Paul' (says Bowers, in 'Mission', p. 611 and in 'Paul: Religious Propaganda in the First Century', *NT* 22.4 (1980), pp. 518f.), and he seems to show that it was probably unknown also before him. Interestingly, Bowers has shown also that Paul seems not to have expected of his own converts a comparable energetic, aggressive, mobile missionary outreach like his. Certainly, their behaviour is to *attract* others to their community; and their Christian life may become widely known abroad through hearsay, and may thus be a far-flung witness to the gospel; but that is not the same as the task to which St Paul is divinely appointed, this being as an *Apostle* (see especially W. P. Bowers, 'Church and Mission in Paul', *JSNT* 44 (1991), pp. 89f.). Donovan himself refers to Roland Allen, *Missionary Methods: St Paul's or Ours?* (1913), an influential Anglican contribution.

## 10 Mary the Mother of Jesus Christ: A response to the Report of the Anglican–Roman Catholic International Commission

A high proportion of the world's finest paintings are devoted to Mary, and deep and genuine devotion frequently attends the cult. But the fact remains that to ignore critical investigation and to indulge in credulous fancies is to undermine the authority of Christian doctrine.

Let it be said, first, that a Christian estimate of the person of Christ, an estimate that justifies our worshipping him as 'one' with God, issues from critical examination of the earliest and most reliable evidence, and that there is enough evidence of this sort, even if we were to discount the infancy narratives of Matthew and Luke. Besides, without calling in question the authority of these narratives, it may be remembered that some of the great figures of history have been of obscure – even disreputable – origin, like Jephtha in the Old Testament (Judges 11). Even if the sad fact had been (as scandalously suggested by opponents from early days) that the mother of Jesus was raped by a Roman soldier, goodness – perhaps even transcendent goodness – seems not to depend on forebears. Whatever may be the facts about genes, and whatever we may believe about supernatural agency and virginal conception, lineage seems not to have the last word. 'Born of the Virgin Mary' is part of the ecumenical creeds; but even without it, the rest of the evidence still points to the worship of Jesus Christ as 'one' with God. Whatever the transcendent glory of the annunciation, whatever the facts may be about the wondrous birth, the independent evidence about his life and nature carries its own weight.

But that said, to what in fact does the Gospel material about the mother of Christ point? St Luke tells the matchless story of the annunciation by the angel Gabriel to Mary, a girl espoused to one Joseph, that she was to be the mother of 'the Son of the Most High', of the king of an eternal kingdom. It is a promise and a divine command that, after initial alarm and puzzlement, since she is not even married, she meekly and devoutly accepts, being told by the angel that the Holy Spirit will come upon her and the power of the Most High will overshadow her. It is a story for all time of a more than heroic rising to a unique vocation. That at the very least is what is reflected. The 'Magnificat' (as it has come to be called, from the first word in a Latin translation) may have been intended by the evangelist as the utterance of Elizabeth, Mary's cousin (there are textual variants); but, on any showing, it is a fine statement of the consequences of divinely inspired courage and obedience – the turning upside down of human ideas about honour and power: it is God who is in charge.

The eventual birth, in Bethlehem, is heralded, in St Luke's story, to some shepherds, by an angelic spokesman and a choir of angels, who announce a Saviour who is to be the Messiah. In St Matthew, the same message is given in a dream to Joseph, the man to whom Mary is espoused, and confirmed by the Magi, led by the Star.

What follows? At whatever stage one places the Matthean flight to Egypt, according to St Luke there is the Jewish rite of ransoming the firstborn child in the Temple, when old Simeon greets him with prophecy about his world-wide shining, and with a warning to his mother of coming anguish; and another worshipper, the aged Anna, speaks to others of the Wonder Child.

Yet, in spite of all this, and in spite of Mary's devout cherishing in her heart of all this witness and prediction (Luke 2.19, 51), the next event reported by St Luke finds Mary rebuking her 12-year-old son for staying behind in Jerusalem, after the Galilean party, having celebrated the Passover, had started back. But it is he who has the last word, with his own gentle rebuke of her. Worse is to follow. Mary is found, with the rest of the family, trying, unsuccessfully, to rescue Jesus from the preaching and healing vocation he has just embarked upon (Luke 8.19–21; Mark 3.31–5; Matt. 12.46–50). According to Mark 3.21, some at least of the family even said he was out of his mind, though in this verse his mother is not mentioned.

And that, in the Synoptic Gospels, is all. Mary is not even among the women who view the crucifixion from a distance, nor those who visit the empty tomb, though in Acts 1.15 she is with the believers in the upper room in Jerusalem after the resurrection.

In the Fourth Gospel, there are no nativity stories, but the mother of Jesus is at the Cana wedding. In spite of what sounds, to English ears, like a rebuke from her son for interfering, she loyally bids the servants to obey him implicitly, command what he may; and it is in this Gospel alone that she is at the foot of the cross and is committed by the Lord to the care of the beloved disciple.

In Revelation 12 there is a majestic vision of the woman robed with the sun and crowned with 12 stars, and with the moon beneath her feet, giving birth to the Messiah. But this is a symbolic figure of majesty, who may be the Judaeo–Christian Church, as much as any historical individual.

In short, the Mary of the New Testament, divinely chosen for the unimaginably high destiny, and initially heroic and devoted in the extreme, appears seldom after that, and then not conspicuously to her credit. Where, then, in all this, is there so much as a breath of adoration of the Virgin or of assumption into heaven? By all means, let us imagine her tenderly cherishing the precious child. Let us glory in her initial obedience to the stupendous divine mandate and promise. Also, let us honour and celebrate the divine gift of motherhood. But the Universal Mother, a goddess, a consort for a supposedly male God, one whom one worships, one to whom one offers prayer – for this there is no warrant.

Steps in that direction, however discreetly described, must surely be resisted. We are told little in the New Testament about the mother of the Lord. Let us rejoice in the glory of her initial stupendous commitment, but not invent what is not evidenced.

It might seem that such austerity would quench the warmth and affection of devotion. But there is plenty of evidence to the contrary. Here, for instance, is a familiar hymn which, while perfectly compatible with an orthodox trinitarian faith, has the reverent tenderness and affection of an *Ave Maria*:

*Whom having not seen, ye love (1 Peter 1.8)*

Jesus, these eyes have never seen
   That radiant form of Thine;
The veil of sense hangs dark between
   Thy blessed face and mine.

I see thee not, I hear thee not,
   Yet art thou oft with me;
And earth hath ne'er so dear a spot
   As where I meet with Thee.

Yet, though I have not seen, and still
   Must rest in faith alone,
I love Thee, dearest Lord, and will,
   Unseen, but not unknown.

When death these mortal eyes shall seal
   And still this throbbing heart,
The rending veil shall Thee reveal
   All glorious as Thou art.

Ray Palmer, 1808–87

## 11 Judas Iscariot

There can be few figures of history round whom have collected more speculation and controversy. This, from *The Times* of 17 January 2006, is a random sample:

> While on Catholic matters, what about the Vatican's plan to 'rehabilitate' Judas Iscariot because he was 'fulfilling God's plan' when he betrayed Jesus? To me the logic seems decidedly dodgy. Does man not have free will? Aren't we accountable for our actions? Are murderers, muggers and molesters also 'fulfilling God's plan'? According to Rome-watchers, the subtext to this move is the new Pope's desire to 'improve Christian/Jewish relations'. As Judas was Jewish, it's now considered politically incorrect to make him the scapegoat for

the Crucifixion. Which is a bit odd. With a few exceptions, such as Pontius Pilate and the Good Samaritan, *everyone* in the Gospels was Jewish – Jesus included. The Vatican ought to stick with its original story. After 2,000 years, it's a bit late to start fiddling with it now.

Ignoring superstitious legend, what may be said convincingly about this tragic person? That he was one of the twelve disciples of Jesus and that he turned traitor is an indispensable part of the tradition. (For New Testament references, see at the end.) But why did this happen?

A plausible suggestion runs as follows. The Jewish Temple aristocracy – the High Priest and his colleagues – had the delicate task of combining the prosperity of the Jewish community with maintaining good relations with the Roman army of occupation and the Governor. Such a tightrope act would, of course, be threatened by any popular nationalist Jewish hot-head likely to raise a rebellion and lead an attempt to throw off the yoke of Rome. Jesus of Nazareth was in fact exactly the opposite of such a one, being a pacifist and a consistent teacher of the love of God for Jew and Gentile, good and bad alike. But his healings and his popular teaching won him such a passionate following that, contrary to his intentions, he could have been the spark to explode a national rising. The time came when exactly this seemed to the Temple aristocracy an imminent threat, rising to a flash-point at the Passover season, when Jerusalem was full of ardent nationalists. Jesus must be stopped, or Judaism would be extinguished by the Romans. But stopping him was easier said than done. Any attempt to arrest Jesus in daylight among the Passover throngs would only be the fatal spark leading to an explosion. He would have to be secretly taken by night. But where and how to apprehend him? Only a disciple would know where to look, and would be able reliably to identify him in the dark.

Judas Iscariot, one of the Twelve, seems to have become disillusioned with Jesus. Why, we are not told; but might it not be that Judas was an ardent nationalist, and found that Jesus was not his man? Judas Iscariot wanted a new Judas Maccabaeus, a fiery leader of a violent rebellion. Jesus steadily refused to lift a finger. So Judas decided to remove him. The Temple leadership offered him money, if he would guide them, together with a detachment of the Roman army, to the hiding place out-side the city of Jerusalem where Jesus and his group spent the night in the Passover season, and could readily identify Jesus in the dark. He did so; and, although there were a futile couple of swords among the dis-ciples, when Jesus himself quietly gave himself up, what could his fol-lowers do but (after one badly aimed slash with a sword) run away? It was a total success for the plan to arrest Jesus without a loyalist mob.

It may be that the offer of reward sealed Judas' diabolic decision to turn traitor, but he must already have reached disillusionment.

Inevitably, stories about the tragedy were quick to spring up. It was said that, in remorse, Judas flung his coins back at the Temple Jews (obscure passages in the Jewish Scriptures were invoked as a prediction of this) and hanged himself; or, alternatively, that he came to some ghastly end when his bowels burst in rivers of blood. Inevitably, too, people would speculate on the divine judgement drawn down upon treachery. Dante, among others, consigned him to nethermost hell. For many, he is the embodiment of unforgivable sin. What ought Christian opinion to be? In view of the determination of Jesus Christ, as the embodiment of God on earth and for love of humankind, to give himself away in an almost inconceivably appalling death, divine forgiveness would seem to stop at nothing: the offer of it, so defined, could never be withdrawn. The only conceivable bar to forgiveness would be inability to accept it. Can a person become so callous by long refusal to repent that God can do no more without violating human freedom? Is it to such a one only (or is this too facile?) that may be applied the terrifying saying attributed to Jesus: 'The Son of Man goes his way as it is written of him [where?], but woe to that man through whom the Son of Man is betrayed! Better for that man if he had never been born!' (Matt. 26.24; Mark 14.21)?

What must we say?

### The chief New Testament references

*Judas traitor*: Matt. 10.4; Mark 3.19; Luke 6.16; John 12.4; Acts 1.16.
*Decision to arrest*: John 11.47ff. – but secretly, Matt. 26.5; Mark 14.2.
*Judas bribed*: Matt. 26.14–16; Luke 22.3–6.
*Betrayal, arrest, sword*: Matt. 26.47–51; Mark 14.44–7; Luke 22.38, 47–51; John 18.3–12.
*Judas a thief*: John 12.4–6.
*Judas' diabolical decision*: Luke 22.3; John 13.27.
*Death of Judas*: Matt. 27.3–5 (cf. Zech. 11.12f.; Jer. 32.6–9); Acts 1.

## 12 Alleged anti-Semitism in the New Testament

Especially since the horrors of the Holocaust, it has become fashionable among students of the New Testament, Christian as well as Jewish, to speak of anti-Semitism in it. This calls for close examination, since it is all too easy to be content with imprecise statements, not least among

Christians who are deeply ashamed not only of the appalling wickedness that led to the death-camps, but also of the centuries of persecution of Jews by Christians. Naturally, they are eager to make whatever
amends may be possible, by confessing Christian misdemeanours.

But what are the facts about the New Testament? First, it is important
to distinguish between hostility to Semitic races as such, and criticism of
Jewish convictions. The odious pride and deliberate evil of those who
have pretended that Semites are racially decadent and contemptible over
against a supposedly superior Aryan race – an attitude for which the
term anti-Semitic should, strictly, be reserved – is, of course, nowhere
to be found in the New Testament, which, indeed, is almost entirely the
work of writers who were themselves Semites. What critics of the New
Testament sometimes call anti-Semitism is, strictly speaking, hostility
to certain Jewish individuals or to certain convictions of Judaism. But,
obviously, that does not in itself constitute anti-Semitism.

The only words in the New Testament that seem to constitute a
sweeping condemnation of the Jews as such are in 1 Thessalonians
2.15f., where Paul unleashes a ferocious attack on Jewish persecutors
of Christians (among whom he had himself once been, 1 Cor. 15.9;
Gal. 1.13; Phil. 3.6; 1 Tim. 1.13; cf. Acts 8.1; 9.1f., 13f., 26; 22.4f.;
26.9–11), declaring that the ultimate wrath of God has begun to over-
take them. This can only be seen as an outburst of anger, inexcusable
no doubt but understandable perhaps, in view of the way Paul had been
hounded all but to death by his opponents. But his considered attitude
towards his non-Christian fellow-Jews is expressed at length in Romans
9–11, in which he rebukes Gentile Christians for triumphing at the
expense of Jews, and affirms the divine promises made to Israel, and
his confident expectation that Israel will realize its glorious destiny. It
is true that this optimism seems to depend on his conviction that Judaism would ultimately be brought to confess Jesus as its true Messiah –
something that, to this day, has not been realized; but it is far from a
disparagement of Judaism as such. Admittedly, the Jewish olive tree in
the metaphor of Romans 11.16ff. has only Christian branches left in
it (just as, in Romans 9 also, St Paul reckons as part of real Israel only
those Jews who accept Jesus as Messiah); but the stock itself is still Israel, loved by God and never to be abandoned (11.28).

What is, for Christians, as against Judaism, a non-negotiable conviction, expressed by both Paul and the writer to the Hebrews, is that the
Covenant made by God with Moses has been superseded by the new
Covenant sealed by the death and resurrection of Jesus as Messiah
(2 Cor. 3; Heb. 8.13). It has become customary with many Christians,

out of courtesy, to avoid the use of 'the Old Covenant', over against 'the New'; but the fact remains that Christians cannot, as Christian believers, deny the newness. But that newness is the newness not of negation but of fulfilment, and, although that is still not acceptable to the non-Christian Jewish believer, at least it is very different from the newness of negation. Christianity is claimed to be the climax and realization of the essence of Judaism, not its extinction. What Paul blames the Jews for, in Romans 10.1–4, is not recognizing Jesus as the end (and goal?) of the Law.

In St Matthew's Gospel (27.25) there is the terrible cry from the Jewish crowd, in reply to Pilate: 'His blood be on us and on our children', misused by Christians down the ages in their rejection of the Jews, as though it meant that the charge of deicide attached, on the authority of Scripture, to all Jews. But all the evangelist actually says is that this is what the Passover crowd shouted on that occasion. It does not constitute evidence that the evangelist himself believed it, nor does it lend the authority of Scripture to an all-time, universal sentence against Judaism. It is in Matthew again that the fiercest attack by Jesus on the scribes and Pharisees occurs (23), but what they are attacked for is not being devout Jews! – in which connection one has to remember the extraordinary words in Matthew 5.17–20:

> Do not suppose that I have come to abolish the Law and the prophets; I did not come to abolish, but to complete. I tell you this: so long as heaven and earth endure, not a letter, not a stroke, will disappear from the Law until all that must happen has happened. If any man therefore sets aside even the least of the Law's demands, and teaches others to do the same, he will have the lowest place in the Kingdom of Heaven, whereas anyone who keeps the Law and teaches others to do so will stand high in the Kingdom of Heaven. I tell you, unless you show yourselves far better men than the Pharisees and the doctors of the law, you can never enter the Kingdom of Heaven. (NEB)

The Gospel according to St John is a special case. Notoriously, it frequently uses 'the Jews' as a general term for the opponents of Jesus. It even goes to the length of representing Jesus as in heated controversy with 'the Jews' in which he speaks of 'your law' (8.17; 10.34), as though he himself no longer shared it, and even calls them children of the devil (8.44). Yet, it is this Gospel that shows us Jesus telling the Samaritan woman that salvation belongs to the Jews (4.22). It is John, too, who reports that many Jews had come to believe in him (2.23; 8.31; 11.45), including, evidently, Nicodemus and Joseph of Arimathea (19.38–42).

St John's Gospel, indeed, is in many respects the most Jewish of the Gospels, in spite of the extraordinary dissertation in chapter 6, where Jesus insists that the only way for a disciple to receive spiritual strength is to eat his flesh and – a concept that could hardly be more un-Jewish – drink his blood.

It is worthwhile to note that in the Acts 'the Jews' is a term used in much the same way as in John. In the appropriate context, it denotes the Jews who were hostile to Christians (Jewish and Gentile alike); but equally, in another context, it can denote Christian Jews, like Paul himself (cf. Acts 21.20), or friendly non-Christian Jews.

At any rate, what this adds up to is that St John's Gospel uses the term 'the Jews' in various ways, which must all be taken account of in any fair estimate of its attitude to the Semitic. It may be that St John's Gospel has chosen to put into a narrative framework, comparable to that of the Synoptic Gospels, language that belongs to a later period in which a 'high' Christology, holding Jesus to be the divine and glorified Son of God, is in conflict with non-Christian Judaism. If so, the recognition of Jewish fundamentals already mentioned – 'salvation belongs to the Jews', for instance – becomes the more remarkable. The Gospel is not anti-Jewish in an unmodified way, though severely critical, like St Paul and others, of Jews who failed to see Jesus as the crown and climax of Jewish destiny. What we have here is a basic, non-negotiable conviction of the Christian faith; but this conviction is that Judaism is not negated but fulfilled and crowned by Christianity.

Looking at the four canonical Gospels together, it is sometimes urged that they misrepresent the facts so as to implicate the Jews unjustly in the death of Jesus. It is indeed true that it is impossible to piece together from the Gospels a fully coherent story of the Last Supper, the betrayal and arrest of Jesus, and the trials before the Sanhedrin and Pilate. Yet there seems to be nothing improbable in the broad conclusion that the Temple aristocracy did hand Jesus over to Pilate as a potential revolutionary. Even though Jesus himself constantly lived and preached a pacifist attitude, identifying himself not with a militant Judas Maccabaeus but rather with the Maccabaean martyrs, symbolized by 'that Son of Man' who, in Daniel 7, symbolized non-resistant obedience to God, which would be given the eternal kingdom, yet the majority missed the point. The story of the so-called 'triumphal entry' shows how an enthusiastic crowd could hijack a peaceful demonstration on a donkey and make it into an aggressively nationalist occasion. The High Priest and his colleagues could well have decided that Jesus was a liability to the delicate balance between themselves and Pilate: John 11.47ff. says as much. It is natural that they should have seized the opportunity to shunt responsibility for removing him onto the shoulders of the Romans. If so, the Gospels are condemning that particular Temple aristocracy: it would not make them anti-Jewish in a general sense.

The Revelation is emphatic in announcing that God is making everything new, including 'Jerusalem'. If any New Testament writing could be claimed as predicting the replacement of an outworn Judaism by something different, it might be this. Yet, it is the more striking that the 'new' city is still called Jerusalem, and that the elect are, it would appear, somehow identified as the tribes of Israel (Rev. 7). It is true that in Revelation 2.9 (the letter to Smyrna) and 3.9 (the letter to Philadelphia) the Jews are bitterly called 'the synagogue of Satan'; but (as in John 8.44, already noted) this seems not to be a general term for Jews, but a reference to the hostile Jews in a particular situation.

These reflections are deliberately restricted to the canonical New Testament. A review of Christian attitudes towards Judaism in early extra-canonical writings, including, for instance, the Epistle of Barnabas and Justin's Dialogue with Trypho, would take us far afield; but it would confirm, in varying degrees, a hostility, not to Jews as such, but to a non-Christian Jew's refusal to accept Jesus as Christ and Lord. However regrettably harsh and heated, this is not itself anti-Judaism. Hatred is always wrong; but the fact remains that religious hatred is not the same as racial hatred. This is spelt out (but in terms not of hatred but of loving regret) in Romans 10.

# 3

# Christian Practice and Belief

## 1 What constitutes a distinctively Christian faith and practice?

A large number of people imagine that Christianity means an attempt to follow Jesus of Nazareth. But although of course the Jesus reflected by the earliest traditions is indeed an unsurpassable 'icon', and although he did astonish his hearers by preaching a radical moral code which went far beyond the current norms, Christianity is still infinitely more than an effort to follow it.

Christians believe that through Jesus they can be united with God. '*Through* Jesus' (not just *because of* him) is a term central to Christian faith. How can this be? It is because Jesus, the man of Nazareth two thousand years ago, though truly human, was also God, so far as a human being can be God. That is the astonishing conclusion to which the earliest evidence points. Though no genuinely human being can possibly be the whole of God, the whole of Jesus was God: he was God so far as God could be incarnate – that is, within human flesh and blood of that period. His death by crucifixion was, as again the earliest evidence shows, due to his following the path of love for all alike, regardless of the consequences, meaning that the offer of the forgiveness of God for sins of all alike, before and since, is an achieved reality. Therefore, the aliveness of Jesus and his presence with his followers beyond his death – this also seems well evidenced – offers to all generations a supreme and unique way to God for humankind, and a way to humankind for God – a uniquely comprehensive and ever-present way of spiritual contact with God; a channel for the undeserved, stupendous love of God for us, and for our all too feeble response: 'through Jesus Christ our Lord'.

Of course it is right that Christians should respect other religions; but it does not follow that they are all to be seen as equally comprehensive revelations of God. The Christian claim is that Jesus (called 'Christ', meaning, in Jewish idiom, the one 'anointed' as universal king) is the most comprehensive way in which ultimate reality has ever been revealed, and remains the most effective ladder between heaven and earth. It follows that a Christian is always eager to 'evangelize', that is, share this good news which transcends all others. Missionary work sometimes gains a bad name because of insensitive and condescending attitudes; but real evangelism is essentially loving, respectful and sensitive, though nonetheless ardent.

So, to embrace Christianity and to be embraced by it is not just a determination to live like Jesus; rather, it means being brought, through Jesus, into touch with God. This contact takes an endless number of shapes. Formally, it is by the sacrament of baptism (whether in infancy or in adult years), conveying forgiveness of sins and membership in the Christian community. Sooner or later, this means a personal and (where possible) conscious commitment to Jesus as Lord of one's life and as the mediator between oneself and God in the community of other believers. It means believing that the divine–human person, though invisible, is still accessible, here and now, precisely because he has passed through death, to be restored to life: he is for ever 'the human face of God'. We can feel after him, find him and be found by him: praying to God through him, listening to God through him, trusting him, loving him and in him united with fellow worshippers. He is for ever the accessible presence of God.

Thus, although this access is for every individual, it is necessarily a communal reality, each believer being constituted a limb or organ, as it were, of the whole body, giving and receiving spiritual growth and vitality through public worship and mutual prayer, focused in particular on the Eucharist and bonding all to Christ. There have always been Christian hermits, believing themselves called to solitary, intensive concentration on God through Jesus Christ; but they would claim that they are still members of the Body, spiritually linked to the whole Church and sharing its heartbeat.

It must by now be evident that what it means to be a Christian is a question that has to come to terms, sooner or later, with what constitutes an authentic Church. The Church of Rome claims to be the only genuinely 'catholic' Church (that is, the authentic Church 'throughout' the world), on the strength of an unbroken chain of valid ordination of 'priests' (authorized to consecrate the eucharistic elements) by imposition of hands from the apostolic beginnings. At least in the Anglican Church, there are many who do not believe that there is convincing evidence for uninterrupted tactual continuity; but they still believe that the Anglican Church is catholic, in the sense that its structure and creed are in authentic continuity with the beginnings. In some more independent Protestant bodies there is less regard for such continuities.

In any case, what is at issue in this note is the nature of distinctively Christian experience. This means confessing Jesus Christ as Lord and worshipping God through him, both alone and in company with others, and receiving from God, through Jesus Christ, the love and spiritual strength that he provides when his Holy Spirit lives in us. It is a trinitarian reality.


## 2 The Bible and the guidance of God

The Bible is sometimes treated in a superstitious way as an oracle: open it and you will read the will of God! Indeed, it is often itself called 'the word of God'. But that is a misnomer. In the passage in Ephesians 6 about the Christian warrior's armour, 'the sword of the Spirit which is the word of God' (verse 17) is almost certainly *not* the Bible. If it were, it could refer only to what Christians call 'the Old Testament', for the New Testament did not then exist. Rather, the weapon that delivers the winning stroke is simply obedience to the will of God, however found. The function of the Bible is not to speak God's will directly to us, but to bring us into touch with Jesus Christ, and to make us open to his guidance: he it is who, in his living presence, speaks the 'word' or utterance of God to us, if we are sensitive and thoughtful. It is Jesus Christ whom the New Testament calls the 'Word' of God (e.g. in John 1 and 1 John 1); actually Ephesians 6.17 does not even use the standard word, *logos*, but *rhema*, 'utterance'. Patient study of the Jewish Bible, 'the Law, the Prophets and the Writings', which Christians often call 'the Old Testament', tells us of the People of God – their aspirations and ideals, their disobediences and failures. In the New Testament we meet Jesus of Nazareth and the New Covenant inaugurated by his fearless teaching, his persistent love for all in need, the terrible death to which it led him, and his rising again and palpable presence as king of that people of God. The way to God's will is through Jesus Christ, and it is he – the living will of God – to whom the Bible leads us. We need to study the Bible patiently and persistently and with disciplined care, both individually and collectively, both at the study table and in communal prayer and worship. So we may find and be found by Jesus Christ, the living 'Word' of God, and be given the moral courage to obey. Of course we know the freak stories of guidance direct from the written page – the wayward seeker in North Africa, overhearing the mantra of a child at play, which led him to pick up the book and read, or the defeated evangelist at Cambridge, held to his duty by the words that leapt off the page; but normally it is not that way. It is the unromantic, obedient slog, both alone and with fellow seekers, in disciplined prayer and study, that makes the command audible and the moral strength accessible. That is how the will of God is strenuously discerned. If one could read it off from the page, whatever one makes of the homosexual questions, one would have to start by stoning to death one's disobedient son! (Deut. 21.18–21). Is *that* 'the word of God'? It is a dangerous mistake to imagine that the words of Scripture can speak with direct authority, outside the complex context of a community believing in Christ and inspired by the Holy Spirit. We need to take into account reason and tradition as well as the Bible as a whole, and to be discriminatingly alert to all the channels by which the Holy Spirit may reach us. Elsewhere I have suggested that the Bible is not so much a compass or a chart as instructions for finding the Pilot.

## 3 Prayer: a non-interventionist 'miracle'

It seems more reasonable to believe in a Creator who, though infinitely beyond his creation, acts from within it, than in one who intervenes from beyond it. Intervention implies interrupting the consistency of what is created, as well as seeming arbitrary, when one prayer is answered and another ignored. Immanence, by contrast, means that, having given humankind a measure of freedom, God himself shares the disasters caused by its abuse, not intervening to reverse them, but transforming them from within – a principle that reaches its climax when Christ is not rescued from the cross, but, by enduring it, creates new life. The evidence points to the conclusion that this one achievement has, fully and for all time, implemented in time and space the eternal forgiving nature of the Creator.

Reflecting on this supreme achievement, one begins to grasp that at the heart of such transformation of evil into good – a transformation worked out not by intervention but from within – there lies the willing acceptance of the will of God by humankind. It is noteworthy, therefore, that Mary's prayer near the beginning of St Luke's Gospel (1.38), 'Be it unto me according to your word!' corresponds to the prayer of Jesus near the end (22.42), 'Not my will but yours be done!'

And why should not prayer be understood as literally a factor in the structure of things, so that every prayer of obedience is the clearing of a

blocked artery or the opening of a sluice-gate in a dam? It is marvellous –
a 'miracle' – and no less so for being achieved within the consistent
working of creation.

*November 2006*

## 4 Petitionary prayer

The glory of the Christian faith is the incarnation. Astoundingly, we are
privileged to know the human face of God! But this carries with it the
danger of 'anthropomorphism': we are tempted to conceive of God as
a human Father – the 'Old Man in the sky' of the cartoonists. And this,
in turn, may spoil our prayer.

'Prayer', in this context, is used in its strict sense of 'petition', 'request'. It is not the whole of worship, for there are other ingredients
too, such as penitence, adoration, meditation. How, then, are we to
conceive of our petitioning? Our conception of prayer may be all too
like a vast family, besieging a harassed parent with conflicting demands –
a farmer praying for rain, while a vicar wants fair weather for the church
fête. No wonder if we begin to think that answers to prayer are erratic,
or that prayer just isn't answered, even when it is so obviously in line
with the divine will as prayer for the enlightenment of an unbeliever!

The New Testament does indeed picture God as a parent, and insists
that, as his children, we must persist in our requests and never give up.
Does a father give his son a scorpion when he asks for an egg (Luke
11.12)? Indeed, will even a surly, godless judge refuse a widow her
rights, if she pesters him for long enough (Luke 18.1–8)? Persevere in
prayer, urges St Paul (1 Thess. 5.17; etc.).

Yet why, then, do prayers so often seem to be disregarded – only
some spectacularly answered, but others simply ignored? Perhaps two
considerations may help.

First, we have to recognize that the family analogy – good as far
as it goes – is too narrow. Perhaps we have to ask how the universe
works – stupendous in its dimensions, incomprehensible in its com-
plexity. Does it help, at least a little, if the human will turns out itself
to be an ingredient in its working? What if our prayer is, in effect, an
offering to God of our obedience, as an active force in the universe,
that opens sluice-gates through which the power of God may stream?
(Compare James 5.16–18.) What if prayer takes its place among other
forces in the dynamics of the universe? A case has been made for this

belief. It would make prayer of vital importance in God's mode of action, and yet with workings too complex and too far-reaching to be containable within simple analogies drawn from human experience, such as a mere 'yes' or 'no' in family life. It would lift our prayers to the honourable level of a link in the structure of God's designs. It would be the humble offering of a human will for his unimaginable purposes, with results far beyond our range of vision. Instead of expecting to get just what *we* want, we are offering our will-power for God to use in his mysterious and infinitely far-reaching design. It will not rob our prayers of confident expectation, but it will rebuke our narrow conceptions of their scope. Of course it is a shattering experience when a godly person prays earnestly, but the request is not granted. It feels like something no better than indeed receiving the scorpion instead of the egg. But it need by no means be a denial of the value of the prayer: genuine love of God, in the offering of obedience, can never be wasted.

But, second, there is an even deeper reality to be reckoned with. I have just used terms of power – 'active force', 'dynamics' – in describing God's purposes; but the deepest Christian truth of all is that Christ's way is the way of self-emptying (Phil. 2.5–11) – the way of what the world sees as weakness and failure. Christ took no account of achieving and winning, only of serving and giving and loving. It may be that sometimes our prayers are misconceived because, even at our best, we are still not fully accepting the way of the cross. As St Paul says (1 Cor. 1.18–25), the way of the cross looks foolish to the worldly-wise. It is difficult for even the best of us fully to take on board the extraordinary truth that, in a deep sense, weakness is the way of God's strength.

Yet, however far we may still be behind the way of God, it is still important that our requests should, at least sometimes, be specific. In order to make our prayer strong and realistic, it often needs to be precise. But if it is to be an offering of loving obedience, it must then be conditional. It must be marked by a 'DV' – 'if it be the will of God'. Our Lord's prayer in Gethsemane is the model: 'Father, let this bitter cup pass me by: yet, not my will but yours be done!' It must be specific, but wide open to God's better judgement. He will use it to fulfil his wise purposes, whether or not by granting our particular request.

Does all this rob prayer of its thrilling immediacy? It need not. Of course we long for our wish to be fulfilled; but too often it will fall short of the demands of self-giving love; and we can rest content, most of all, to know that God accepts the best we can offer, and will use it for the working out of his designs. Our prayer, granted or not in the shape in which we offer it, has helped to make the world go round. If we can believe that, perhaps we shall find strength to persevere.

## 5  The sacraments

The ethos of the Church of England is not, by and large, legalistic; but with regard to the sacraments there are at least guidelines in the Thirty-Nine Articles, the Book of Common Prayer, and the Catechism, pointing to a position distinct, on the one hand, from Rome (or what is usually defined as Roman), and, on the other, from Presbyterianism and other Reformation Churches.

In the first place, Anglicanism gives the name of sacrament only to baptism and the Holy Communion or Eucharist, the two 'sacraments of the gospel' (i.e. those deemed to have been inaugurated in some sense by Christ himself), whereas the Church of Rome recognizes seven, including, for example, matrimony. But that is not much more than a matter of nomenclature.

More importantly, it is usual in the Anglican Church to repudiate the doctrine, usually attributed to Rome, of transubstantiation in the eucharistic elements (seeing the bread and wine in some sense as actually changed by consecration). Equally it repudiates mere 'memorialism' (seeing the ritual of the Eucharist as nothing more than a reminder of the original event), attributed to some of the Reformation Churches and often called Zwinglianism (after the reformer). According to Anglican belief, the rite not only recalls the Last Supper and all that it meant, but actually effects a spiritual change in the worshipper. A sacrament, accordingly, is sometimes called 'an *effective* sign'.

It is important to recognize that the sacrament is not the bread and wine. The sacrament is the *use* of them in an act of worship. Strictly speaking, therefore, there can be no such thing as a 'reserved sacrament'. What is reserved – if this practice does obtain – is simply bread and wine once used in a sacrament. The consecration does not, as it were, 'stick': the elements have not themselves been altered. The direction in the Book of Common Prayer to consume what is left over of the consecrated elements after worship is simply to secure reverence, and precisely to prevent their being used as objects of worship. (The water of baptism, often 'blessed' or consecrated in current rites, is not 'reserved'.) Perhaps a valid principle along the same lines can be recognized in the difference between when a young man gives a rose to his lady love with a kiss and a declaration of love, and when, later, she simply keeps the rose and looks at it: in the first instance, a sacrament; in the second, a reminder.

It is common now in the Church of England to sanction the administration of the once consecrated elements by a lay person, as an alternative, especially at a sick-bed, for the sacrament. No doubt this may be pastorally valuable as awaking precious memories and bringing home the presence of God; but though it may thus be a helpful rite, it cannot but encourage the superstitious idea that the elements themselves are somehow charged with holiness. This is precisely what Cranmer's rubrics in the 1662 Holy Communion are designed to eliminate. Deep down, what is involved is the avoidance of subtle and refined sorts of idolatry.

## 6  The New Testament and Eucharistic thought

These reflections attempt to identify the contributions of the New Testament to Anglican eucharistic liturgy. They take no account either of critical investigation of the various streams of tradition behind the New Testament or of the vast area of research in the post-biblical developments of doctrine. In some types of these latter, 'the Mass' is understood as in some sense a re-enactment by the presiding priest, by virtue of ordination, of the sacrifice of Christ on the cross.

For the reformed Churches, including the Anglican Church (which nevertheless stoutly claims to be catholic as well as reformed), the Eucharist or Holy Communion or the Lord's Supper constitutes a memorial, not a re-enactment, of Christ's self-offering, since this latter, as Hebrews 9 declares, was once for all and unrepeatable.

Nevertheless, in Anglican doctrine, the Eucharist is more than *merely* a memorial, a reminder. It is a sacrament, and, as such, an effective reminder and *active application*, though not a re-enactment, of what the Lord did once for all. Every time it is celebrated it is, as St Paul says (1 Cor. 11.26), a 'declaration' of the death of Christ. It is thus, every time, a re-application of what he did, and, in response, a renewed acceptance of what he gave, and an obedient re-dedication of the worshippers. This is the rationale behind the 1662 Prayer Book rite and all the other – now many – Anglican forms of Eucharist. It is the various themes contributing to this that the following investigation seeks to define. It is not surprising that a wide range of meanings should have accumulated round the poignant and dramatic story of the Last Supper. Here is an attempt to identify and locate at least some of them as they are to be found in the New Testament.

In the New Testament there are five accounts of events and words at the Last Supper of our Lord with the Twelve (and perhaps other participants besides?), namely, in the four Gospels and in 1 Corinthians 11.23ff. In the Johannine account (John 13) the Last Supper is described as 'before the feast of the Passover', and is not itself the Passover meal, unless an anticipated one, and there is no reference to bread (except the 'sop' offered to Judas) or to cup. Instead, the story is told of the washing of the disciples' feet by our Lord. In John 6.32ff., however, there is a discourse that says much about the Lord's own flesh and blood as life-saving food and drink, essential to eternal life; and this has contributed emphatically to eucharistic interpretation.

In the Synoptic Gospels, Matthew (26.20ff.), Mark (14.17ff.) and Luke (22.14ff.) and in 1 Corinthians 11.23ff., there are sayings of Jesus at the sharing of bread at the supper and of the cup after supper, though Jesus himself abstains from sharing the cup, or declares that he will abstain thereafter – which looks like a Nazirite vow, and perhaps explains his refusal of the drugged wine at the cross (Matt. 27.34; Mark 19.23). In Luke only (Luke 22.17ff.), there is mention of a cup before as well as after the bread (at least in some manuscripts), from which Jesus himself expressly refrained from drinking.

Disregarding further details and variant readings, these sayings fall into two types: (a) Luke and 1 Corinthians amount, essentially, to 'This (bread) is my body, given for your sake', and 'This cup is (? i.e. affirms) the New Covenant in (? i.e. inaugurated by) my blood.' (To this the words 'which is poured out for you' are ungrammatically added in Luke, at least in some manuscripts)

(b) Matthew and Mark amount, essentially, to 'This is my body' and 'This is my blood of the Covenant, shed for many' (Matthew adding 'for the forgiveness of sins').

That is to say, (a) relates the drinking of what is presumably wine, to the inaugurating (or affirming?) of the New Covenant, while (b) speaks of what is in the cup as the life-blood of Jesus 'of' (i.e. constituting?) the [New] Covenant. Form (a) also enjoins the repetition of the eating, or of both eating and drinking, in the future, as a memorial of Christ. In none of the accounts is there any mention of the Passover lamb.

The discourse in John 6 aligns itself with (b) in respect of drinking the blood, but emphasizes not a covenant but the idea of nourishment: Christ's body and blood are life-giving food and drink.

The form of words in (a) is compatible with Old Testament ideas of the sealing of the covenant by a shared sacrificial meal (Exod. 24.3–8; Gen. 31.46): the flesh of the victim, drained of blood, constitutes the food, and the blood may be thrown or sprinkled on the participants as in Exodus 24 (? compare 1 Peter 1.2). If there is drink, it will presumably be simply part of the meal confirming the covenant inaugurated by the victims' death. If so, the bread of the Last Supper can understandably represent the Lord's sacrificed self (compare 1 Corinthians 5.7), and the eating of it might be like the eating of a sacrificial victim at a covenant-feast; but the cup is not his blood for nourishment; it is wine, as part, simply, of the meal affirming the covenant sealed by the blood of his self-sacrifice, which is not drunk. The form (b), by contrast, is concerned not only with the Covenant sealed by the blood of the Lord, but with the drinking of the blood; and John 6 connects the drinking of the blood and eating of the flesh with nourishment and sustenance, rather than with a covenant: the body and blood of the Lord are declared the food and drink of eternal life.

Eucharistic tradition has chosen form (b) for its 'words of institution', adding the theme of memorial and specifying the Covenant as New from (a), thus retaining the idea, spelt out in John, of sustenance and nutrition, alongside the inauguration of the New Covenant and its constant remembrance at every repetition of the words and actions. All three Synoptic Gospels speak of Christ's saying he would drink the wine 'new' eventually.

The idea of drinking blood is, of course, alien to Jewish thinking, as well as to the sensibilities of many worshippers also who are not Jewish at all; but somehow it came into John 6 (could it have been under Gentile influences?), and from there it has come to stay in eucharistic interpretation. Present in the worshipper's consciousness may also be the passage in Revelation 7.14, where the martyrs' robes are, paradoxically but powerfully, washed white in the blood of the Lamb. This is alluded to in the 1662 Prayer Book's beautiful Prayer of Humble Access: '. . . that our sinful bodies may be made clean by his body, and our souls washed through his most precious blood . . .'.

Here, then, is a rich assemblage of suggestive metaphors, which sacramental theory reads as far more even than just that. Except in traditions that do not go beyond the merely symbolist and memorialist, the Eucharist is a potent sacrament, an 'effective' act of worship, in Anglican thought, though not an actual repetition of the death of Christ as a trans-substantialist interpretation seems to imply. But the purpose of these reflections is mainly to assemble meanings, not to debate sacramental theory.

Perhaps even on this limited level we should try to organize prosaically this complex texture of metaphors. On the other hand, clarification
can promote devotion; and in particular it may help to bring home
the challenge to respond to the demand of the divine Covenant, which
is easily forgotten behind the perhaps more prominent and dominant
themes of forgiveness, comfort and sustenance. It is good that the second post-communion prayer of the 1662 Book speaks of membership
in the mystical Body, which is not far from the covenantal obligations
of community; and the first post-communion prayer, echoing Romans
12, speaks of our offering ourselves, however unworthy, as a sacrifice –
a costly and demanding response to the goodness of God. Such aspects
of communion ought not to be sidelined. If we receive into our selves
the amazing gift of Christ's self, we cannot but give ourselves in response to be members in the Body of Christ.

In Common Worship (2000), in six of the eight options for the consecration prayer, A, B, C, D, F and H, we offer the sacrifice of thanks and
praise (echoing Hebrews 13.15f.). In all eight, the cup is identified as
the blood, and in all except D it is called the blood of the new covenant,
while in G we are to be built into a living temple (as in 1 Peter 2.4ff.) – a
metaphor, again, not far from the mystical Body and Covenant.

In none of the prayers of consecration, in 1662 or Common Worship,
is the Blood spoken of, in so many words, as refreshing or reviving;
but as has already been said, nourishment, both by the Body and by
the Blood, is alluded to in the Words of Administration and in After
Prayers. In T. S. Eliot's 'East Coker' come the terrible words 'The drip-
ping blood our only drink', which bring us closer to John 6. In the now
famous prayer 'Father of all . . .', in the Common Worship Prayer after
Communion, we, more euphemistically, 'drink his cup'.

What seems to have fallen from view in reference to the Supper, both
in 1662 and in the other orders of service now on offer, is the deeply
moving theme of John 13, where the Master and Lord kneels to wash the
feet of his disciples. (It is hinted at in Luke 22.27, 'here am I among you
like a servant'.) Is it beyond the linguist's skill to work this into the many-
coloured embroidery, or is it better to keep it as a separate celebration?
After all, in St John's Gospel, as has already been said, the Supper is not a
Passover celebration. Indeed, there is no mention of food or drink, except
that 'sop' given by the Lord's own hand to the traitor (John 13.26).

In terms of subtraction, not addition, it would be a relief to some
worshippers if at least the drinking of blood, if not the eating of the
flesh, might be withdrawn without loss of power; but the discourse in
John 6 is very insistent, and a crassly cannibalistic motif is drowned

out by the deeply devotional thought of daring to take the whole Christ into oneself – 'that we may evermore dwell in him, and he in us', in the words of the 1662 Prayer of Humble Access (echoing, in its turn, the words of John 6.56 and 15.4).

How, then, may the several themes of the Eucharist be summed up? How should we respond?

### (1) Christ's redeeming sacrifice, cleansing from sin

With humble and thankful penitence, we renew our acceptance of forgiveness and cleansing through the self-giving of God in the total dedication of Christ, who shed his blood 'under Pontius Pilate', actualizing in history the eternal forgiveness offered by God.

### (2) Nourishment, sustenance

We accept Christ into our lives as spiritual nourishment and strength. In the Words of Administration, we are to feed on him by faith with thanksgiving, and in the second post-communion prayer we thank God for feeding us with the spiritual food of the most precious Body and Blood. This is comparable to the bestowal of living water promised to the Samaritan woman in John 4.10ff.

### (3) Challenge

In response we dedicate our selves in active obedience, to belong to the Body of Christ. Christian life is never merely private. We belong with each other; 'we are very members incorporate of the mystical Body' of the Son of God, and are to exercise our calling for the benefit of all.

### (4) Memorial

We must never lose sight of the good news of our redemption and calling. Every Eucharist is an active reminder.

## 7 Solitary and collective in the Christian Church

Christianity, like the Israel of the Hebrew Bible, has an essentially social structure. It is not a private or solitary religion. It is true that there are Christian solitaries – hermits deliberately cultivating withdrawal from society; but they would insist that their withdrawal (in obedience to a 'call') is only to concentrate on prayer and meditation, and that they still depend on their spiritual link with the community, and belong in what St Paul called the Body of Christ (1 Cor. 10.17; 12.12ff.). Every Christian is, as it were, a limb or organ of the collective body, which is Christ. All Christians, as such, are bonded together as parts of this great Body. It follows that – apart from those dedicated to physical withdrawal, but all the more linked on the spiritual level – all Christians have a duty to worship regularly with fellow-Christians, in addition to their private prayers. The Epistle to the Hebrews (10.25) urges its recipients not to neglect regular meeting for worship. Thus it is that, throughout the world, Christians know themselves as belonging to one another, with a duty to worship together, however different or even alien their traditions and style of worship may be. Perhaps the only style of worship that should be protested against (as well, of course, as anything not truly Christian) is what is culpably inferior in language or music. Children may sometimes know no better; but it is all the more sinful to offer them anything but the best – not to mention the blasphemy against God!

In short, private and public worship are both essential ingredients in a normal Christian life, and Christians should be conscious of their obligations as belonging in the world-wide Body of Christ.

As a footnote – it has recently become fashionable in certain Christian circles to speak of 'being Church'; but is not this a meaningless affectation? I may say 'I am a Christian' or 'I am Christian' or 'I belong to the Church'; but what can 'we are Church' possibly mean?

## 8 Sunday

To a devout Jew the observance of sabbath is important. The word essentially means cessation, stopping. After six days of creating the Creator stopped on the seventh day (Gen. 2.2f.); and in the version of the Ten Commandments in Exodus 20, the sabbath-commandment is associated with that: as God stopped, so must we. After six days' work, it is a religious duty both to cease from activity ourselves and to allow others, both human and animal, to do the same (vv. 10f.).

Jesus rose from the dead on the day after the sabbath, the first day of the week, which we call Sunday; and when Christianity found itself to be not just a peculiar Jewish sect, but a distinctive religion, no longer bound by Jewish rites but with new commitments of its own, it transferred the special day of the week from Saturday to Sunday. Immediately it could be a new day of special recollection, though it was not at first a 'sabbath', since it remained a working day – not least for slaves. If there was any collective worship, it would have to be before the working day began or after it was over. In Acts 20 we are given a glimpse of what may have been late-night Sunday worship. They were gathered 'to break bread', which, in Jewish idiom at least, could mean simply 'for a meal'; but St Paul spoke at it, and it was quite likely a Eucharist with a sermon. The preacher 'went on a bit', and a weary lad sitting on the window-ledge dozed off and fell to what might have been his death.

When a country had become broadly Christian, Sunday could be a public holiday, and, for Christians, a day of 'cessation' and of collective worship. Of course George Herbert was right to say, 'Seven whole days, not one in seven, I will praise thee'; but that does not obviate the importance, still, of a special day. I was brought up in a rather strict, though gentle, evangelical family, in which we were expected to give up our everyday occupations: no games, no 'secular' activities. Even reading had to be 'special', and drawing and painting had to be related to religion: you might decorate a biblical text but not just do a 'secular' picture! No doubt that is manifestly absurd; but I remain grateful for the idea, if only because it encourages me to make room regularly for meditation and for specialized religious reading, which might otherwise get postponed in favour of something more immediately appealing. I was also taught to go regularly to public worship, and I remain convinced of the value of making the whole of Sunday, if possible, worship-oriented. It is not the same to be a most faithful and regular worshipper on late Saturday night or early Sunday morning, but to forget about worship for the rest of the day, and to cram every remaining corner of Sunday with activity.

Besides, I am convinced that the cessation every seventh day from being busy, remains, in itself, a salutary habit. In the end, it tells on our reserves of energy and reduces our effectiveness if we have no regular times of quiet and contemplation.

For a practising Jew, observance of the sabbath is an identity-marker and a stringent obligation, rooted in the Hebrew Scriptures. In addition to the injunction in the Ten Commandments, there is the terrible story of the man who was stoned to death for gathering sticks on the sabbath day (Num. 15.32–6); there is the story that the manna miraculously ceased every seventh day – some went to collect it, and found none (Exod. 16.27); and there are the tirades against sabbath-breakers in Jeremiah 17.19–21, and in Nehemiah 13.15–22. In addition to the

Scriptures, Judaism has a huge rabbinical literature, interpreting and applying the Mosaic Law.

The Christian has no comparably authoritative Sunday-command; and Jesus himself, while in the main observing the Law, let works of mercy override the sabbath-law (e.g. Luke 13.15f.), and appealed to the way in which the needs of domestic animals were habitually met on the sabbath – though we now know that the strict sectarians of Qumran disallowed even this. Incidentally, a remarkable saying, allegedly of Jesus, occurs in Luke 6 in just one (eccentric) manuscript: Jesus saw someone working on the sabbath, it says, and said to him: 'If you know what you are doing, you are blessed; but if you do not know, you are accursed and are breaking the law.' Thought-provoking!

At any rate, with all their freedom, Christians do well to ponder over the sabbath-law and to ask how best to transpose it, rather than merely ignoring the matter; and even without the religious concern for worship, regular 'cessation' remains important. The movement called 'Keep Sunday Special' deserves support when it champions unbelievers and believers alike who claim Sunday from their employers as an island of peace in the reverberations of workaday life.


## 9 After death, what?

In some forms of the eucharistic liturgy in the Christian Church, worshippers are called upon to join in the triumphant cry: 'Christ has died, Christ is risen, Christ will come again.' The first clause, as a literal, prose statement, is as well evidenced as any item in history. The second, startling though it may be, is, as we shall see, surprisingly difficult to deny. Of the third, the very meaning is enigmatic.

In *Hope against Hope* (1999), Richard Bauckham and Trevor Hart observe that readers of the Bible, as much as of any other literature, need to be alert and to recognize when it is plain, factual prose and when it is something else – poetry, symbolic speech, metaphor, parable, myth and so forth. Of course that in itself does not justify us in arbitrarily choosing, for our own convenience, to interpret what was *meant* as literal truth as something, instead, which we need not accept literally. But it might mean that, if what was originally meant literally is no longer credible, it might be allowed to suggest, for us, a way forward in our thinking.

What, then, may 'Christ will come again' mean for us? The 'Synoptic' Gospels (Matthew, Mark and Luke) represent Jesus himself as saying that, though the day and hour were known only to God, it would happen within his own generation (Mark 13.30–3 etc.; St John's Gospel has its own equivalent: 14.2f., 28; 16.16). Since that time, two millennia have passed, and cosmology has seen the cosy world of earth, sun, moon and stars expand to the mind-boggling dimensions of what the spacecraft Hubble can see – with more still to come. Was Christ mistaken? If he was, that is no reason to give up the central conviction of the Christian creed – that in Jesus of Nazareth God was incarnate (that is, enfleshed), meaning that, uniquely, Jesus was both perfectly human and perfectly divine. To be perfectly human is, most emphatically, *not* to be omniscient or infallible, though to be a perfectly divine man must mean a uniquely perfect perception of what divine love means.

However, even if we were to allow that, through a human error, the earliest expectations merely got the timescale wrong, that, by itself, would not solve the problems. There are indeed signs that St Paul, while starting with the expectation that he would still be alive at the 'return' of Christ, began later to change his mind: contrast 1 Corinthians 15.51, 'we shall not all die' (literally 'sleep'), and 1 Thessalonians 4.15, 'we who are left alive', with 2 Corinthians 5.1ff. A little later, 2 Peter 3.4ff. is clearly fighting a rearguard action against what, by that time, had become loud cries of ridicule against the whole idea of Christ's return. But by our day, any theory of mere postponement has become farcical. Besides this, the very concept of lapse of time *beyond death* is itself problematical. (What might be meant when, in 1 Peter 3.19f., we are told that, between his death and resurrection, Christ 'went and preached to the spirits in prison'? See also 4.6.)

What are the implications of the belief – which we shall consider further directly – that Christ alone has already been raised from death, while the rest of us must 'await' his return? This is the standard New Testament faith, as Dr C. Cocksworth noted in *Prayer and the Departed* and Dr N. T. Wright in *The Resurrection of the Son of God*.

Whatever we make of the difficult concept of 'waiting' after death, as though in some sort of limbo, the idea of a 'general resurrection at the end', as a single, simultaneous event yet to be realized, points to the vital belief that there is no such thing as a solitary Christian. Even the strictest of hermits is spiritually part of the 'Body' of Christ.

Christian reality has to accommodate itself *both* to a deeply individual and personal relation to God *and* to a constant concern for collective and universal unity. More still, as Romans 8.22f. implies (and compare Ephesians 1.20ff.), our completion is bound up, in the purposes of God, with the renewal of all creation. All alike 'waiting' to the end is a powerful symbol of this conviction. There is a hint of this also when we are told in Hebrews 11.39f. that the heroes of the Old Covenant cannot be completed until the faithful Christians of the New Covenant have fulfilled their destiny; and it is possible that something of the same principle appears when St Paul speaks (perhaps?) of his contribution to the completing of the necessary tale of sufferings (Col. 1.24), and the waiting martyrs in Revelation 6.10f. are told that their vindication must await the completion of the destined number of martyrs. In short, when the New Testament speaks of 'the End' as a single event, that is an intelligible message about a great collective and all-inclusive event.

Christians often – perhaps more often than not – think of death as the gateway directly into their ultimate destiny, 'eternal' life. *Mors Janua Vitae* ('Death the Gateway to Life') is inscribed on crematorium gateways. But the New Testament demands that we take seriously a two-stage process – first to 'sleeping' or 'being with Christ', and only after that to resurrection, to the remaking of ourselves, at 'the End'. It is Christ Jesus alone who has already been 'raised' from death into bodily life, but bodily life of some mysterious new kind. To think of death as the gateway immediately to our ultimate fulfilment is nearer to the essentially 'pagan' dualism, which sees an individual person as a self entrapped in a body, so that at death it is released from the body, like a bird from a cage, and simply goes on living. By contrast, the Jewish–Christian doctrine of the remaking after death of the whole person goes with belief in a Creator, for whom re-making, re-creating, is the climax of the pattern of salvation.

## 10 Life after death

There is a widespread belief, going back to the ancient world, that there is an immortal component in humankind (if not in other life also – for that question note Ecclesiastes 4.21), which, at the death of the body, simply escapes like a bird from a cage, and continues to live and perhaps be reincarnated. More typical of Judaeo–Christian thought, however (though the dualistic idea does sometimes surface), is the belief that a human individual is an indivisible whole, for which any life beyond death can only be by resurrection: the person has died as a whole, and as a whole must be raised to life, if at all – even from the ashes of incineration, an idea no less reasonable than creation from nothing.

We know, from Scripture and other sources, that such resurrection was believed in by some Jewish thinkers at the time of Christ, including

Pharisees as contrasted with Sadducees. What such thinkers did not – so it seems – believe was that any resurrection had *yet* occurred. The dead would return to active life only at some supposed climax of history. Meanwhile, they were kept in some kind of suspended animation, awaiting the Last Day. It was a startlingly new conviction, therefore, when the followers of Jesus claimed to have encountered him already active, after crucifixion. They found him subtly different from what he had been – able to come and go suddenly, not always immediately recognizable, mysterious. Yet, that it was he and that it was the whole of him they were convinced: 'He has risen indeed!' As Dr Tom Wright, among others, has insisted, except for this highly eccentric conviction, there is absolutely nothing that can account for the genesis and continuation of the Christian community. That it did arise and that it stood by this belief, gaining momentum instead of fading out as an eccentric flash in the pan, is strong evidence for its truth. It seems well established that, at least in the early days of Christianity, Jesus and he alone was thought to be already 'raised'. He was 'the first fruits' (1 Cor. 15.23). For others there was, to say it again, some kind of suspended animation.

In considering what lies beyond death and ultimately the resurrection, we have to face the controversial subject of hell. The Hebrew Scriptures say much about retribution for sinners, both in this life and in some nether world; and there are passages in the NT where eternal punitive torture is envisaged. The rich man in Luke's story is 'tormented' in a 'flame' and is in a 'place of torment' (Luke 16.24, 28). In Mark 9.49 (with an echo of Isaiah 66.24) there is an image from the place outside Jerusalem, Gehenna, where there was perpetual incineration and the horror of maggots for ever consuming rotting flesh. Revelation 20.10 refers to endless torture in a lake of fire; and so on. If, however, one judges simply by the nature of love – love divine – it is obvious that love, though never condoning wrong but firmly condemning it, will inflict only *corrective* suffering (Hebrews 12.5–11, with reference to Proverbs 3.11ff.), but *retributive* suffering never. Retribution and punition as such are not part of love's concern, which is for correction and education. The danger is not that love can ever be retributive or punitive in intention, but that the sinner become too callous to repent – and love can, by definition, never impose itself. 'Conditional immortality' thus seems conceivable. The elimination of the retributive ought to be a concern of criminal law. Of course fines and imprisonment for offences and compensation for victims are right; but they function only on the surface: deep down, in personal relations, constructive reconciliation ought urgently to be considered.

What, then, may these reflections mean for a Christian hope? The resurrection of Jesus establishes life beyond death as a reality: it constitutes an anchor for our hope that will not slip or drag (Heb. 6.19). Perhaps we may say also that life will be life 'at home'. In John 14.12, the disciples, deeply unsettled by the threat of their Lord's departure, are assured that, in the beyond, there are plenty of places where one may 'stay', not rove about like exiles. On the other hand, one cannot imagine that there will be no satisfaction for the born adventurer: that that life should be dull is unthinkable. Above all, there will surely be unplumbed depths and measureless breadths of loving relationship. In this earthly life, marriage ideally is exclusive; but St Paul (Rom. 7.1–3) refers to the Roman law by which the exclusive union of a couple in this life is transcended by the death of a partner, dissolving the exclusiveness. And according to a saying attributed to Jesus in Luke 20.35f. (and parallels in Mark and Matthew), 'those who have been judged worthy of a place in the other world and of the resurrection of the dead, do not marry, for they are not subject to death any longer. They are like angels; they are sons of God because they share in the resurrection' – a saying which of course was intended to be understood as though it were in 'inclusive' language.

Strictly inconceivable in many ways as is the 'life beyond', we may venture confident statements within limits such as these, though never presuming on divine forgiveness as though it were 'God's *métier*'. To use a phrase lifted out of a commentary on the Psalms by John Eaton, may we 'at last take wing to your holy dwelling, where we shall see you face to face'.

*July 2007, two months before he died.*


## 11 Advent

We have considered (above, no. 9) the congregational response in most of the forms of the consecration prayer in Common Worship: 'Christ has died; Christ is risen; Christ will come again' (Form F has: 'we long for his coming in glory. Amen. Come, Lord Jesus') but are still asking what could that third sentence mean? If we believe that Jesus was truly human, we are bound to believe that his knowledge was limited; and a devout Jew of his period, ignorant of the cosmos as we now know it, and of the nature of human history, even to the limited extent of our knowledge of it today, could believe that the triumph of the will of

God, for which he himself had lived and was about to give up his life, would quickly and decisively be manifested.

The tradition preserved in the Synoptic Gospels shows him assenting with great emphasis that the divine triumph, his victorious return, would be achieved within his own generation. As time passed, and it seemed to delay, one can see rearguard actions being fought to vindicate this hope, despite all: within the canon of Scripture John 21 and 2 Peter provide examples. But today, with 2,000 years between the life of Jesus and our own, and with a cosmology of awe-inspiring infinity and a timescale new to our generation, a divine 'return' to Planet Earth has become inconceivable.

In my early days, there was a slogan: 'the evangelization of the world in this generation'. If it is almost impossible now to believe that such a hope ever existed, I can bear witness that it did.

So, how might: 'Christ will come again' be reinterpreted in today's terms? It should be mentioned that there are a few passages in the NT that seem to hint at the Stoic idea of a climax at which the old world is burnt up, and, Phoenix-like, a new world emerges (2 Pet. 3.12f.; Rev. 21.1). But these are exceptional. We know of the cyclic idea of a return of the Golden Age (Virgil's fourth Eclogue, echoed exquisitely in Sears' hymn 'It came upon the midnight clear' with its doubtfully Christian last verse – is Acts 3.21 possibly an echo of this idea?).

The most obvious way might seem to be in terms of social progress. That would mean an expectation that (quite apart from anything on a cosmic scale), on Planet Earth at least, human society would improve, becoming nearer and nearer to the ideal community with every generation that passed. And there were, about 60 years ago, those who maintained that progress of this sort was a reality: every wave of history came further up the shore, and the tide was coming in. Not so any longer! No sane claim could possibly now be made for such a credulous faith, even if the total of persons on the globe calling themselves Christians has increased. All one seems to hear now is the sound of Matthew Arnold's dismal outgoing tide on Dover Beach, or no sound at all from the stagnant sea of (non-)faith.

So what? 'Christ will come again' can now be conceived neither in terms of an individual presence (parousia) nor in terms of social progress. It is perhaps possible to believe that individuals will slip away at death to a better life 'with Christ'; but that Christ should somehow return to earth and reign is inconceivable. The great season of Advent is stultified. 'Lo, he comes' seems beyond interpretation. There is a crack in the Christian Creed, 'We must all stand before the judgement seat of

Christ' remains deeply credible in individual terms (perhaps at death?),
but in what other sense? Where lies hope for the world?

The conclusion of these reflections, rightly or wrongly, is that we
have not the wherewithal to conceive of a second Advent. The first Advent – the Christmas story – is the only Advent story that makes sense.
But that does not mean that we are cast adrift: the incarnation is itself
an anchor sure enough to hold our faith (Heb. 6.19). As has been said,
the question of a second Advent is prominently raised by the congregational response in the consecration prayer.

So, how might 'Christ will come again' be interpreted in terms of
today? Can we frame an Advent faith at all in terms that carry credence
today. Individually, that we must all stand before the judgement seat
remains still awesomely real: divine judgement is most surely 'coming'
to us all. It is possible to believe that, individually, we shall each be
confronted by the climax of that all-seeing scrutiny. But it seems impossible to frame a meaningful doctrine of a new divine visitation. Perhaps
it is not for nothing that, in the Church's year, Advent *precedes* and
slides into Christmas. That supreme 'coming' we do hail with believing
wonder and thanksgiving. And it is that first coming that enables us to
rest in hope. The first Advent, the Epiphany, is a sufficient anchor to
our hope, even if we cannot give a worldly shape to it.

Advent meditations, literary and musical, such as are exquisitely rendered by splendid choirs, undoubtedly have a compelling power and lay
a spell on the heart. But it cannot be contrary to the will of God that we
should dare to ask how far they can be ultimately spelled out in praise.
God forbid that we should give up reverent questioning!

## 12 The Great Tribunal

There are clear statements in the New Testament that it is God's desire
that everyone should have life. The best known is in John 3.16: 'God
loved the world so much [or 'in such a way'] that he gave his only Son,
that everyone who has faith in him should not die but have eternal life';
also verse 17: 'it was not to judge the world that God sent his Son into
the world, but that through him the world might be saved'. There is
also 1 Timothy 2.3f.: 'God our Saviour, whose will it is that all men
should find salvation and come to know the truth'.

Over against such statements, one can collect statements not only
about the severity of God's judgements, but about their punitive and
retributive character. To take a random example, St Paul speaks in

Romans 1.18 of 'divine retribution . . . falling upon all the godless wickedness of men'. In the Gospels there are parables attributed to Jesus that give the same impression. In the Lukan story of the rich man who disregarded the beggar at his door, in the afterlife the beggar is seen in the distance, enjoying a feast with Abraham, while the rich man is in torment (Luke 16.22f.). In the Matthean story of the sheep and the goats, the 'goats' are sentenced to torment, while the 'sheep' enter into joy because they are the people who were sensitive to the needs of the poor and distressed: in helping them, they had been doing it to Christ himself (Matt. 25.41). In Revelation, the retributive theme reaches a white-hot fury, especially in chapters 19 and 20, with the Great White Throne and the lake of fire and the eternal torment of the devil and his angels. In Revelation 16.6 the vindictive cry is heard: 'they deserve it'. (See further such passages as Matthew 12.31; 2 Timothy 4.14; 1 John 5.16.)

On the other hand, St Paul is famous for his teaching of 'acquittal' for the guilty who renounce all claim to being worthy, and simply trust in the forgiveness that is offered to them, although of course the guilty must be genuinely penitent – that is part of 'trust' or 'faith'. Perplexingly, there are also references to being already 'in the book of life', meaning, it would seem, that such a one is declared acquitted and rendering the final judgement superfluous. (See Philippians 4.3; Revelation 3.5; 13.8; 17.8; 20.12, 15; 21.27 – though the references in chapter 20 might mean that the name is entered in the book *on acquittal* before the throne.)

Whatever the uncertainties, however, in this pattern of hope and apprehension, the central conviction is that God is love, which, though it cannot for a moment imply that God condones evil (quite the reverse!), does mean that the love of God is not revengeful but is a redemptive force that never fails to offer reconciliation – the very meaning of the cross.

Perhaps one needs to lean heavily on what is axiomatic. It is axiomatic that love, by definition, can never force itself on anyone: it can be accepted freely or not at all. Otherwise, it would not be love. If, then, there is anybody who stubbornly persists in rejecting the approaches of pure love, it is theoretically conceivable that such a person might ultimately become too calloused to be *able* to receive love, even though love cannot cease to offer itself. Therefore, never to doubt the love of God, but always to be on the watch as to one's response, would seem to be the right approach to the question of heaven and hell.

Perhaps this is as far as we can go for the time being, in contemplating the meaning of 'Christ will come again'. What, now, for 'Christ is risen'?

## 13 The resurrection of Jesus

That Jesus was put to death by the appalling cruelty of crucifixion, was wrapped in grave-cloths and laid in a tomb, there is no doubt: all four canonical Gospels and 1 Corinthians 11 are unanimous; and given the circumstances, there is nothing improbable in the story, unless it be that Jesus is said to have died more quickly than the average tortured victim. (See Mark 15.44f., and John 19.33.) What is startling is the tradition that, after two nights had passed, the tomb was found empty, and he was seen alive and, according to some accounts, even touched by some of his followers, and seen eating food; yet, also that he seemed in some ways to be different – not always immediately recognized, and able, it would seem, to appear and disappear at will. According to Luke and the Acts, after appearing intermittently for a period, he was raised to heaven, and destined to come again. (See Matthew 28.8–10; Luke 24.13–50; John 20.14–29; 21.4–22; with numerous references in Acts: 1.3–11; 2.31–6; 3.15, 26; 4.10; 5.30; 10.40f.; 13.30, 33, 37; 17.31; 23.6; 25.19; 26.23.)

Admittedly, these traditions are by no means without their difficulties. They do not agree in details, and the oft-repeated suggestion that this only shows that they are not fabricated, because, had the story been made up, care would have been taken to see that it was self-consistent, only works if they were all the work of a single narrator or of writers working in mutual collaboration, which is clearly not the case. Also, there is the curious question, where did our Lord get the clothes to wear? That may seem frivolous, but it is a genuinely teasing problem. However, there is the weighty witness of St Paul in 1 Corinthians 15, where he recites traditions already current before his own startling U-turn from persecutor of Christians to devoted follower of Christ. St Paul's are thus the very earliest traditions we have, and are clearly independent of the Gospels. It is significant, too, that St Paul himself claims to be one of the eyewitnesses (though peculiar, as a kind of after-thought or irregular birth, much later than the original witnesses). He insists on distinguishing *visual* encounter, to which he here refers, from *visionary* experience: contrast 1 Corinthians 15.8–11 and 9.1 with 2 Corinthians 12.2–5. (But what do we make of Galatians 1.1, 16?)

But, above all (a matter emphasized by Dr N. T. Wright in *The Resurrection of the Son of God*, 2003) there seems to be no plausible explanation for the very origin of the Christian Church and for its development and survival as an independent body, except its foundational distinctiveness. We know well enough that certain Jewish groups, in particular the Pharisees, as attested by the Gospels and the Acts, believed that there was to be a general resurrection at 'the End'; but only Christians believed that one man alone, Jesus the Messiah, had already been raised from death – the sole forerunner and 'first-fruits' of the general resurrection. This belief seems to be without parallel, and inexplicable unless based on fact. Accordingly, it is irresponsible just to dismiss it as 'legend'. This is still not to deny that language swings between plain prose and many other levels of meaning. To say that the risen Christ was raised 'to the right hand of God' or that he 'ascended into heaven', is the language of devotion, compatible with a foundation of plain prose, and, indeed, part of the Christian's interpretation of its meaning.

## 14 Easter

There are good reasons for believing that the canonical Christian Scriptures contain the earliest and most authentic traditions about Jesus of Nazareth. That he was put to death by crucifixion is as firmly established as anything in history. Theories depending on his resuscitation are worthless. What, then, can be said for belief in his resurrection?

First, the meaning of resurrection must be clarified. It is to be distinguished from survival. The idea that an indestructible 'soul' is released from a mortal 'body' – that the 'soul' cannot die, and that, on the death of the body, it escapes and continues to live – has been widespread and persistent in many systems and many periods. The Christian (and, in some cases, a pre-Christian Jewish) claim is different: it is that the whole person, undivided, dies but is brought again to life; and there is well-known evidence that certain groups of Jews contemporary with Jesus already believed that this could happen.

What Dr N. T. Wright (for one) seems to have established is that this was not expected by anyone to happen until the climax of time and history – all the dead would be kept in some state of 'waiting' until the climax of the ages. Among those who believed in an embodied 'afterlife' at all, there is no evidence of any other form of the belief in resurrection until followers of Jesus insisted that *Jesus* – and so far Jesus alone – had already returned to *full, embodied life, ahead of the climax* (whatever that might be). That is the distinctiveness of the belief among the followers of Jesus; and it constitutes the only known explanation of the survival of the Christian community. Without it, it must have petered out after a time, simply as one more Jewish sect. Instead, claiming to be the fulfilment and crown of Judaism itself, it gathered momentum and grew. The distinctively Christian conviction was that Jesus, alone already restored to active life, was the sole forerunner of the climax.

The canonical Scriptures agree that the conviction that Jesus was already alive after death was based on visual and aural and factual contact between him and various of his followers; but it is impossible to build a single, coherent, self-consistent account of these occasions on the early traditions contained in Scripture. In this area no sharp line can be drawn between legend and history; and not until Paul of Tarsus is any *opponent* of Jesus confronted by him.

As for the when and how of the cessation of what we may reverently call 'sightings', there is no agreement. Luke and Acts are the only writings that offer a story of the termination of the contacts on the level of sight, sound and touch – a separating of the master from his disciples like the ascension of Elijah in the Hebrew Scriptures (2 Kings 2). Luke seems to place it on the same night as the Emmaus supper; Acts, 40 days later. St Mark's Gospel is almost certainly defective (in the best manuscripts), and we cannot say how he ended his story, although that Jesus will show himself to his disciples is absolutely declared (Mark 16.7) before the abrupt end at verse 8; all continuations are from later manuscripts. Matthew ends with an appearance (doubted, it says, by some) on a hill in Galilee (whether visionary or not, who can say?), and the promise of the Lord's constant presence to the end. John's 'appendix' leaves us with Jesus walking off-stage, followed by some disciples.

In sum, then, details of 'sightings' of the Lord after his death are impossible to reconstruct into any single, coherent story; but *that he showed himself alive, as a whole, living person, ahead of the climax of time*, is essential throughout the traditions. To none but believers is he shown until the case of Paul of Tarsus, which Paul himself regards as exceptional, and in which there is dazzling light and a voice and a fall to the ground, but no reference to tactual experience (1 Cor. 9.1; 15.3–8; Gal. 1.16; Acts 9; 22; 26.12ff.).

Thus, the earliest traditions establish that he 'showed himself alive' (Acts 1.3; 10.41) ahead of the climax of history; and without this there is no explanation for the genesis and continuation of the Christian Church. Mortal humanity is manifested united with eternal deity, and God thus makes himself accessible to us. But why, just then, and not before or after? That is a question impossible to answer. If it was to be in history at all, then it had to be at a particular time – with reference, among all else, to the history and evolution of Judaism. These are incalculables beyond our reach: St Paul calls it simply the time for ending our 'minority' (Gal. 4.4) and entering on our responsible adult status.

Considered with critical rigour, have we not here material of compelling force? It is the story of a manifestly human individual found to be transcendent.

*May 2007*

## 15  The language of Christian experience

According to the New Testament pattern of Christian belief Jesus Christ alone of all human beings was raised from death to life almost immediately after death. For the rest of us, whatever we might believe about what was immediately to follow death, there would be no resurrection until 'the Last Day', when Jesus was to 'come again'. If at first this 'return' of Christ was expected very soon, it is now clear, after two millennia (if not after a century), that the language of devotion must change; but it was noted that, nevertheless, the concept of 'waiting' after death for a simultaneous *general* resurrection at 'the Last day' carried a vital message. We had already noted that there was a rich diversity in the language of religion, and that some never can be treated as factual prose. We need to be on the alert to words that are poetical, symbolical, parabolic, and so on; and we noted that one vital message from the idea of a resurrection 'postponed' to the end – no matter what we may say about the difficulties of any concept of the lapse of time in 'the beyond' – was that God's plan of salvation was collective and communal, not solitary; the life of 'the world to come' is a great climax of festive celebration: we are members together of a single great community – limbs of the very Body of Christ himself. We cannot go forward alone – indeed, we are bound even to the remaking of the rest of creation and of what we have come to call 'the environment'.

Meanwhile, however, to use (if we must) the language of time, there is a special kind of life to be lived after death, and a special range of language is employed by the New Testament. A common description of death, carried over from the language of the Hebrew Scriptures ('slept with his fathers', etc.) is *sleep*. Stephen the Christian martyr 'fell asleep' (Acts 7.60 in the Greek). When St Paul is musing on the possibility of living on until the 'return' of Christ, he says 'we shall not all sleep' (1 Cor. 15.51); in another context (Rom. 14.8f.) he says, either way, 'whether we wake or sleep' we all belong together to the Lord; and yet again, when wondering whether his own death is imminent, he declares he does not know which to choose – to be *'with Christ'* which is by far the better, or to live on (Phil. 1.23f.). According to St Luke, the Lord on the cross says to the man on the next cross, 'today you shall be with me in Paradise', that is, in a place of peace and beauty (Luke 23.43).

Thus, much Christian metaphorical language speaks of a kind of oblivion or of an intensified presence with Christ. Either way, we have to come to terms with the language of the lapse of time in the hereafter, which itself is not easy. 1 Peter 3.19 speaks strangely, as we have seen, of Christ, between death and resurrection, going and preaching to 'the spirits in prison' (and compare 4.6).

More than this, the fervent language of devotional life ranges through the concept of 'death' with Christ *before* 'life', to being with him in the hereafter: Colossians 3.3f.: 'you died; and now your life lies hidden with Christ in God. When Christ, who is our life, is manifested, then you too will be manifested with him in glory' (so, too, 1 Thessalonians 4.14, explicitly). Again, Galatians 2.19f.: 'Through the law I died to law – to live for God. I have been crucified with Christ: the life I now live is not my life, but the life which Christ lives in me: and my present bodily life is lived by faith in the Son of God, who loved me and gave himself up for me (NEB).'

Then, in 2 Corinthians 5.1ff. we find St Paul wrestling with an extraordinary weave of ideas related to metaphors of changing abodes or changing garments (compare 2 Peter 1.13f.): we already have a heavenly dwelling; we wish it could be put over us (like a tent, perhaps, or an outer garment?), rather than our having to suffer the discomfort of taking something off, in exchange for something else, and risking the horror of nakedness. Yet, we know that to be in the present abode or covering is to be away from the Lord, and to be away from it and present with the Lord is better – a momentary flash of 'pagan' dualism? In the yearning to *add* rather than *exchange*, there is possibly a recollection of 1 Corinthians 15.54, where indeed there is no divesting: 'Death is *swallowed up* . . .'.

In a different idiom, there is the jubilant expectation expressed in 1 Peter 1.3–12 looking forward rapturously to seeing the unseen but beloved Lord – words caught up in Ray Palmer's hymn of adoration, 'Jesus, these eyes have never seen / That radiant form of Thine . . .'.

We could go on, but this is enough to give us a glimpse into a vibrant language of faith and hope, which it would be impossible to build prosaically into a totally coherent and wholly self-consistent statement. It would seem that, in these great tides of devotion, it is right for us to swing at anchor on the great, basic verities – a situation referred to so memorably in Hebrews 6.19f. Is it not firm anchorage enough to know that if God continues to own us, we are alive? 'God . . . said, "I am the God of Abraham, the God of Isaac, and the God of Jacob" . . . God is not God of the dead but of the living' (Mark 12.26–27).

## 16 The incarnation of God in Jesus Christ

Of the millions who know something about Jesus of Nazareth and admire him as one of the spiritual giants, it is a fair guess that the majority think of him as 'inspired' – exceptionally 'full' of the Spirit of God. Why do Christians go further? The Christian conviction does not stop short of 'incarnation', a word strictly meaning that in Jesus God became flesh. It was not just that the Spirit of God as it were 'entered the human being', but that the whole person *was* God. Not that the whole of God (to speak in crude quantitative terms) was 'in' Jesus, but that the whole of Jesus was God.

The term 'incarnation' is not always so limited. It is used in English language descriptions of Hinduism in senses nearer to inspiration. But in Christian technical usage it is carefully limited and distinguished.

So, where has so extraordinary a conviction arisen? What could be more implausible than that a single individual of a particular sex and citizenship and period and place – a Jewish male of first-century Galilee – should be 'one' with God? Everything was hostile to its genesis. The Jewish monotheistic tradition was intolerant of identifying man with God. The Pharisaic thinkers believed in an embodied life beyond death, but not until the End, the Climax of the divine plan. Yet here was a group of Jews whose most authentic traditions, in the New Testament, show that in Jesus they had found one who, during his lifetime, brought with him a powerful sense of divine presence, and who, after his terrible death and entombment, was seen alive – perhaps even touched – *already*, only two nights later. All this is flat contrary to their traditions, and the last thing one would expect to be fabricated.

Moreover, without these bizarre and unlikely convictions, there would have been no distinctive Christian group. Even though the narratives in the Gospels and the Acts do not add up to a self-consistent, smoothly reading story, it is very difficult to believe that such a series of alien ideas was arbitrarily invented. In addition, St Paul, who in

1 Corinthians 15 gives us the earliest traditions of all, as he received them, is able to add a statement of his own encounter with the risen Lord, leading to a dramatic about-turn from furious opponent to devoted servant. To dismiss so much smoke without searching for fire is, to say the least, irresponsible.

And here is another point, often overlooked. The liturgical phrase, '*through* Jesus Christ', scattered through the New Testament, cries out for comment. *Because of* (say) Socrates, I may be a wiser person. But it is *through* Jesus that I am given access to the living God, as through a living presence, not through a past body of teaching.

This experience of access to God through the living Presence is sometimes also expressed in terms of the Spirit of God. In pre-Christian Judaism, God is present among his people as Spirit when he speaks through a prophet or does some striking work of power. In the New Testament, the presence of the risen Christ is sometimes spoken of in terms of the Holy Spirit, especially in Luke and Acts and in the special idiom of St John. This bears independent witness to the same reality.

These few words are but a cockleshell in which to sail fathomless waters. I dare believe they are as seaworthy in construction as a larger craft.

## 17 Incarnation – climax of creative love

*Prayer*

O Jesus Christ, our Lord, you emptied yourself, you were born in the likeness of humankind, you became obedient, even to death, and so you became the Son of Man, crowned with glory and honour. Lift us up, we pray, to our full stature as children of God, and enable us, by the power of the Holy Spirit, to pray our prayer: Abba! Father! Your will be done! – to the glory of God the Father.

*Address*

If it is not arrogance but a realistic reading of evidence to see human personality (or personhood) as of paramount value, as the norm by which we should organize our priorities; and if love, the characteristic of personal relations, is the 'highest' activity of a Creator who is personal, then incarnation can be seen to be totally appropriate to a universe so ordered – perhaps, to be inevitable in such a system, however little any human mind might have dreamed, in advance of its possibility.

When I speak of incarnation, I am aware of Rowan Williams' essay in the Anglican essays collected by Robert Morgan in commemoration of *Lux Mundi* (Bristol Classical Press, 1989). In this searching chapter, 'The Incarnation as the Basis of Dogma', Rowan Williams, commemorating and recalling Moberly's *Lux Mundi* essay under that title, proposes, as a refinement of Moberly's title, something like 'Conversion and Judgement as the Basis of Dogma', since he cannot see the full weight of the doctrine that God united a human individual decisively and wholly to the divine life as intelligible outside this context (p. 87). Putting it in a slightly different way, he says: 'The question, "Do you believe in 'the incarnation'?" is a quite futile one in itself unless it has something to do with the serious question, "How do you proclaim, and how do you hear proclaimed, the judgement of Christ?"' (p. 90).

I think one must agree wholeheartedly. But I still believe that, if we do encounter in Christ a judgement that searches us as only a divine judgement can, we are thereby still driven, sooner or later, to ask ourselves the doctrinal question, 'Who, then, and what is this Christ?' And to that I still find it impossible to give an answer that does anything like justice to the evidence of the New Testament and of subsequent Christian experience, except in terms that do not themselves occur within the New Testament but are borrowed from a philosophy that uses abstract terms of essence and being. And Rowan Williams himself, alluding to the doctrinal approach of Bonhoeffer, says, 'It is the nature of this encounter in the preaching of the Gospel that prompts Christology to foreswear the solutions both of a "gnostic" supernaturalism and of the teacher–pupil, hero–emulator scheme. And when we have said that . . . we have come to the point at which the Chalcedonian problematic still faces us.'

I take it that Rowan Williams' point is similar to Eberhard Jüngel's, when he is reported (in *The Tablet*, 6 June 1992, p. 708) as saying that another doctrine, namely that of 'justification by faith', should be seen. 'not as a doctrine but as a message'. Clearly, a merely doctrinal formulation is useless, unless it brings with it the living confrontation. But, with all due concern to avoid using abstract ontology as a way of escaping concrete confrontation, I think that a doctrine of incarnation still has to be stated, if we attempt to formulate what is central to Christian faith.

Now, concerning the antecedents of this doctrine, it is well known, of course, that Judaism had many spokesmen who firmly declared that God acted in history and was involved in what went on in the world – in the world both of the animate and of the inanimate, both of humans and of other animals. It is equally well known, however, that Jewish thought, on the whole, stopped short of *incarnation*. Philo, who spoke often and elaborately about the *Logos*, or utterance of the one God, and who personified that Logos as God's eldest son and as an intermediary between God and the world, yet repudiated the possibility of the identification of any human being with God. (Notoriously he calls Moses 'God', but that is only, I think, with reference to Exodus 4.6, where Moses is to Aaron as God is to his prophets. It is only an analogy and a metaphor.)

The passage in Philo most often quoted to illustrate this personification of the *Logos* is *Quis rerum divinarum heres* 205f. (translation in C. K. Barrett, *The New Testament Background: Selected Documents*, SPCK, 1956 (since then revised), pp.184f.):

> To his Word, his chief messenger [Greek, 'archangel'], highest in age and honour, the Father of all has given the special prerogative, to stand on the border and separate the creature from the Creator . . . neither uncreated as God, nor created as you, but midway between the two extremes . . .

On this theme in Philo, A. Edersheim wrote an epigrammatic comment, in his long study on Philo in (surprisingly!) Smith's and Wace's *Dictionary of Christian Biography*: 'Thus, so to speak, *the Logos of Philo is a medium of disjunction, the Logos of the New Testament one of conjunction. In Philo it is because God is so far, in the New Testament because he is so near*: in Philo the Logos is an unreal, in the New Testament a real and essential Personality' (iv.380a). That may be too slick and tidy by half; it may be a determined Christian's over-emphasis: but I believe that it does underline what is a fact.

It is not surprising, then, that when the followers of Jesus eventually reached a description of their convictions in terms of *incarnation*, pushed to this conclusion as they were by experience and events, this was seen by many Jews as a betrayal of monotheism and a decline into the beginnings of a pagan polytheism – as it was also subsequently to be seen by Muslims. Some of the early stages of the conflict that arose seem to be reflected in the fierce and contorted dialogues of the Fourth Gospel.

But in the face of attack, mainstream Christianity held tightly to monotheism, while yet convinced that Jesus was one with God, and that, if the whole of God could not be in any human individual, yet this human individual was wholly God – the whole of him, that is, was one with God.

And when once this was shown, perhaps it was natural to ask how, indeed, creative love *could* stop short of this complete union. Was it not in character with a personal Creator constantly to express himself personally, in persons, and sooner or later, in the whole of a person and in every corner of his being? Rowan Williams rightly calls for a relocation of the meaning of incarnation, in terms of the divine call to penitence. But incarnation, relocated by all means, remains, I believe, central to a Christian faith.

The Word became flesh and dwelt among us; he was not comprehended; he was rejected; but, persisting in being himself, he triumphed in death and defeat, and is for ever glorified and for ever life-giving. This not only fits the pattern drawn by all the evidence of God's way and will; it makes sense of the relation between the Creator and his creation, as a mere blurring of the two does not. In 1 Corinthians 8.6, St Paul said, 'for us there is one God, the Father, from whom are all things, and we exist for him: there is one Lord, Jesus Christ, through whom are all things, and we exist through him'. These are the beginnings of a credal statement, groping after ways of expressing the paradox of experience. In 1 Corinthians 15.45, there is a neat double contrast between humankind, 'the first Adam', and Christ, 'the ultimate Adam': 'the first Adam became a living individual (a *psuche*); the ultimate Adam [became, was?] a life-giving spirit (or spiritual being)'.

I find myself, therefore, questioning the position of a writer like A. M. Allchin, who writes (in his book about Celtic Christianity, *Praise Above All* (1991):

> western Christianity, both Catholic and Protestant, has tended to harden [the] distinctions between divine and human and make them into separations. The religion of redemption seems to have become divorced from the religion of creation, and sometimes completely to have overshadowed it. Christianity which is a religion of incarnation seems to have become curiously disembodied, and more and more restricted to a narrowly religious sphere. In a situation such as this there is an instinctive turning towards the tradition of the Celtic Christian world which offers us a different picture of things, a picture in which the whole creation is seen as touched by God and full of God . . . (pp. 10f.)

In a similar vein, a writer in *The Tablet* (9 May 1992), Walter Schwarz, says that the Judaeo–Christian tradition 'is found wanting by many, who explore a return to paganism or New Age practices because they believe that Judaeo–Christianity is too wedded to belief in the separate existence of God from creation'.

I believe, on the contrary, as I have been trying to say, that a true understanding of the immanence of God within the created universe is reached precisely by *observing* the distinction between divine and human and by seeing, as paradoxical but actual, the union of both in the incarnation. I believe that a right relation between humankind and its environment is going to be reached, not by humankind's abdicating from a special position in creation, as made in the image of God, but precisely by accepting the responsibilities that this brings and recognizing its culmination in the incarnation; not by blurring the distinction between Creator and created, but by embracing the tension between the two and recognizing its culmination in incarnation as the paradoxical and astonishing, yet necessary, result of the divine love between them.

In the light of the new Christian experience, certain strands in Old Testament thinking about humanity and morality are reinterpreted by New Testament writers in a way that is both revolutionary and constructive. The famous vision in Daniel 7 of 'one like a son of man' – or, in plain prose, 'what seemed to be a human figure' – is, within that very chapter, interpreted with reference to the Maccabaean martyrs. The interpretation seems to say that, whatever command the tyrant may have of the apparatus of force, the figure that comes out on top in the end is the human being who obeys God, no matter whether it costs his life – or *her* life, in the case of the mother of the seven sons. That is the one to whom God gives kingship over all the world for ever and ever, just as he gave it to Adam at the first. Humankind *is* designed to be in a special position; but the essential human wins that position in the end by being essentially human, that is, by being a child of God.

This Son of Man of Daniel 7, the unarmed human who triumphs by obedience even to death, is, I believe, the symbol adopted by our Lord to denote his vocation; it was, if you like, his 'logo'. There is a strong tradition in the Gospels that represents Jesus as referring to '*the* Son of Man'. The consistency of the use of the definite article in the Greek phrase makes it difficult to believe that the original Aramaic behind it, which Jesus must have used, was not also an unmistakably 'deictic' locution – a phrase referring, that is, to a particular figure that would be well known to the hearers and recognizable; and for this Daniel 7 is the most likely 'referent'. Daniel 7, in its turn, may well have been exploiting passages such as Psalm 8, which expatiated on the glorious destiny promised by God to humankind, and the exalted status, at the head of creation, bestowed on him.

This sequence of ideas – man, crowned by God with glory; man, learning that this glory meant obedience even to death; Jesus, perfectly implementing this reality in his own obedience and death, and taking humankind with him – is taken up by the writer to the Hebrews. In chapter 2, he quotes Psalm 8 with its exultant estimate of mankind's supremacy, and then adds, ruefully, 'We do not yet see all things subject to humankind' – far from it! An understatement! 'But', he goes on, 'in Jesus we do see one who, precisely because of his acceptance of death, is crowned with glory and honour.' Only the man who is totally one with God and obedient to death realized – and pioneers – the way to true human existence. Incarnation, with its vulnerability, is the way by which love rescues us from lovelessness. And, says the writer to the Hebrews in another passage (2.16), it is not angels, it is the posterity of Abraham, that God 'takes hold of' – that is, perhaps, with his redemptive power: humankind, exercising Abraham's trustful obedience, is the medium through which God works out his design for creation.

In the famous Philippians 2.5–11, Christ accepts vulnerability *in spite of* (so most commentators, at least) his divine status; but the call to accept vulnerability *because* it is the divine way seems to surface, if not here, at least in 2 Corinthians 4.10f. There St Paul seems to be saying that, if his daily apostolic hazards – the death that he lives with – are embraced as 'the dying (*nekrosis*) of Jesus', then they become also a sharing of his life – the life which Jesus lives: 'we are always carrying with us in our body the dying of Jesus, in order that the life of Jesus also may be seen in our body . . .'.

This is, I believe, an advance on Paul's position in 1 Corinthians 15.54; and it is no morbid falling in love with death – no false asceticism. It is a facing of the fact that death is constantly near ('in the midst of life we are in death'), and an affirmation that the acceptance of this fact *for the sake of Jesus* turns it into a means of life. I was reading (*The Tablet* 25 April 1992) of a Dutch Jewess, Etty Hillesum, who died in Auschwitz in 1943, but whose diaries during the last two years of her life have been recovered. She knew perfectly well what was ahead of her; but even without a Christian faith, she discovered that to look death in the eye and accept it actually enhanced life. So far from this diminishing life, it taught her that, on the contrary, it would have been by a *failure* to be thus realistic that life would have been diminished.

There is a line of Judaeo–Christian tradition that sees physical death and decay as due to sin, and as something *from* which we may be rescued by Christ. But I believe it is more authentically in line with all the implications of incarnation to see death and decay as that *through* which, not *from* which, we are redeemed. And this, I believe, is what St Paul is discovering in 2 Corinthians 4 and 5.

So, if humankind, made in the image of God, is at the apex of creation, so far from arrogantly assuming privilege, it means the most awe-inspiring demand and call to service; and to find in Jesus the 'proper man', the real human being, is to find the clue to its realization. Being in the likeness of God, he went to death as mortal man, and therefore he reaches the true end of humankind and we in him.

*Launde Abbey, July 1992*

## 18 The Christian doctrine of the Trinity

From Anglican pulpits on Trinity Sunday most sermons will declare that Godhead is an impenetrable mystery, but few will attempt to probe it. A popular Trinity hymn is Reginald Heber's 'Holy, holy, holy . . .', an address to God as he is portrayed in Revelation 4, which, in its turn, draws upon the triple acclamation in Isaiah 6, and other language of adoration; but again there is no attempt to go further in understanding. However, worship withers and becomes superstitious unless the convictions behind it are rationally investigated; and while there is much to be said for doing theology on one's knees, so conversely worship gains depth by association with investigation. That a mystery is impenetrable does not exempt the worshipper from trying to understand, and there is nothing irreverent about humble enquiry. Christian belief needs to be constantly under scrutiny. What, then, of the mysterious doctrine of the Trinity?

The Christian creeds start with the affirmation that the God we worship is the Almighty Creator, alone, without rival. So in the Hebrew Scriptures, Deuteronomy 6.4 declares the Hebrews' God to be one, in deliberate contradiction of competing polytheisms such as are reflected, sometimes without disapproval, in other parts of those same Scriptures. For instance, in Psalm 82, the High God appears to be presiding over an assembly of the gods. It is a great step forward when there emerges a clear belief in a one and only God, and this great faith is particularly associated with the later stages of the Hebrew religion, though we are told of an earlier sign of it in the fourteenth century BC, when the Egyptian King Akhnaton worshipped the Sun alone. Much later, in the seventh century AD, Mohammed introduced his special type of monotheism.

After the emergence of Hebrew monotheism, however, comes the distinctive creed of Christianity, often severely criticized by the other monotheistic faiths. The Christian creeds, starting from common ground, immediately introduce highly distinctive beliefs. A child was born (in about 6 AD, as we now reckon years), a Jewish child, Jesus of Nazareth. He died young, by the terrible death of a Roman crucifixion. By his followers he came to be called 'the Son of God', but – more than that – worshipped as God. In Jewish idiom human individuals could, in certain circumstances, be hailed as 'children of God' without any implication that they were divine. When Hosea 11.1 represents God as calling his son out of Egypt, he is referring simply to the exodus of the Jewish people. But it was amazingly soon that Jesus came not only to be called 'Son of God' or 'the Son of God', but to be worshipped by his followers. There seem to be incipient signs of this attitude even during his lifetime: certainly it was happening shortly after his death. That was an almost unbelievable happening, yet happen it did. The development of belief in Jesus as the 'Christ' or anointed 'Messiah', and then as a divine figure, was spectacularly rapid. The Epistles of the new Testament (mostly earlier than the Gospels) are full of evidence for it. How could this have happened in a monotheism so austere as the Mosaic creed, and in what sense was that creed modified?

Without going into the whole long story, perhaps one of the most revealing facts, as has already been noted, is that, already in the first Christian century, according to the New Testament Epistles, worshippers were finding access to God *through* Jesus Christ (Rom. 5.2) – the formula is frequent. This meant much more than that, by his example and teaching, he had 'explained' or 'shown' God to them, as inspired prophets and preachers had done. It was not just because of what he had taught them: it was *through* him, as through an invisibly present, living person, that they found themselves in the presence of God. Their prayer and praise and their very selves went to God *through* him – which means that, though distinguished from God, he was not separable from God. St John's Gospel phrases it, 'I and the Father are one' (10.30). It is a duality that does not destroy the unity. Conversely, according to St Paul in 1 Corinthians 2, it is through the Holy Spirit that God converses with humans. The Spirit is distinguishable from God but not separable from him: the Spirit is, as it were, the self-consciousness of God, entering our consciousness (1 Cor. 2.11). Thus God Almighty, the Son of God and the Spirit of God are all one, but distinguishable aspects of the Unity; and this threefold analysis, so far from pluralizing the one God and contradicting monotheism, offers an insight into the one God's mode of being single and acting as single. It has to be recognized that, in the New Testament, this analysis is not rigid or mechanical. There are passages, for example Romans 8.9–11, where 'Christ' and 'the Spirit' are used almost interchangeably; but that the New Testament uses 'the Spirit' simply as a name for the risen Christ is not true. The two are usually given distinguishable roles – a fact that throws important light on the nature of the Trinity.

Thus the unity of God is revealed as a rich unity. The deity is not a being with, as it were, a uniform 'texture', but a vibrating, living unity, in dialogue with itself (as is a human person, on a miniature scale) and with others. This analogy of the human individual's inward dialogue was used from early days. One might also perhaps take, as a parable (no more) of the plural unity of God, the plural unity of the physicist's matter – single, yet when hugely magnified, found to be a shimmering assembly of dancing particles, like small-scale stellar systems; or one might think, perhaps, of white light with its spectrum of colours; or perhaps of music harmonized.

The Christian threefold analysis of the living unity of God is thus very far from suggesting merely that God is a 'composition' (!) of three parts: nothing could be a less apt parable than the shamrock attributed to the preaching of St Patrick.

Similarly, we must be cautious of laying too much weight on the three men of Genesis 18, or the triple formula of adoration in Isaiah 6, the 'thrice holy', or even, striking as they are, the triplets of the New Testament (1 Cor. 12.4ff.; 2 Cor. 13.13; Eph. 4.4–6; 2 Thess. 2.13f.; 1 Tim. 5.21; 1 Pet. 1.2; Rev. 1.4f.). These deserve careful consideration and may indeed be signs of an emerging sense of a threefold structure in the divine unity, but they do not, in themselves, constitute a doctrinally conceived statement of the tri-unity in the being of God. Even the baptismal formula of Matthew 28.19, anticipating the universal Christian usage, is not necessarily thus truly doctrinal. The language of a properly doctrinal understanding was forged after the New Testament in the complex debates of the following centuries, in the acrimonious church councils and the vast so-called 'patristic' literature – the mainly Greek and Latin writings of the Church 'fathers'. It is this long-continued debate that issued in the successive creeds of the various councils, with their anathemas against recusants – the leaders of heresies whom modern research sometimes shows not actually themselves to have held the doctrines attributed to their followers.

But one still asks: Why the number three? One can understand, at least to some extent, the subtle conception of a plural singularity; but if plural, why *three*? Why not limit the plurality to two, or, alternatively, not limit it at all?

Furthermore, it is difficult to recognize 'spirit' – a term that seems in this context less obviously personal than Father and Son – as an equal 'member' of the divine Trinity; but such is the majority belief in centuries of profound reflection. And it may be worthwhile to note that Dorothy Sayers was not only a superlative writer of detective novels in a class of her own, nor only an innovative, self-taught translator of Dante, but also the author of a penetrating study of the nature of creative art, visual or literary (*The Mind of the Maker,* originally 1942; reprinted subsequently with introduction by Susan Howatch, 1994), which found it to be essentially threefold in structure, in a way relevant to the study of the divine Trinity.

Relevant to these thoughts but beyond the range of the present investigation is the vexed question of gender. Why Father and Son? Why not Father and Mother, and why not Son and Daughter? And is it significant that, in Hebrew, spirit is feminine? (The latter fact is of doubtful value, both because in Latin it is masculine and in Greek neuter, and because in Hebrew feminine and neuter are bracketed together.)

Whatever we make of abstruse questions, and even if we go no further than we have so far gone, we may well find ourselves asking: But does it make a difference whether we are trinitarians or not? It does make a difference, if only in the way in which one approaches God and learns to listen to him and find his will and worship him. The trinitarian 'Gloria', in Christian worship, is infinitely more than a decorative formula. It is a serious reminder of how to grasp, with all God's people, what is the breadth and length and height and depth of the love of Christ which surpasses knowledge, for only so shall we be filled up to the full measure of God (Eph. 3.18f.).

The following meditation by Brian Wren, from *Piecing Together Praise* (London: Stainer & Bell, 1996, p. 167) may help us.

I met three children in the street.
They did not give me trick or treat
but whispered, laughed and
    called my name.
I nearly walked away,
but something made me stay
and join them in their game

The second child moved so
    fast
I hardly saw her spinning past
as all around she sang:
'I'll dance the dance of destiny
till you are all as real as me:
I made you. I know you.
I love you.'

'Now let's pretend that we are God,'
they said, and ran to where I stood.
They danced around me in a ring

The third child took my hand
and whispered 'yes, we
    understand.

and sang, 'You must agree
to give us questions three,
so ask us anything.'

They waited, sitting on the ground,
and did not move or make a sound.
I thought and puzzled long that day,
and then, to my surprise,
I looked into their eyes,
and knew what I would say:

'Now listen to my questions three,'
I said, 'and you must answer me:
*What is your name?* and *Are you
    real?*
and *Can you see and know
how humans think and grow,
and fathom how we feel?*'

The first child stood up tall,
and suddenly I felt quite small
as solemnly she said:
'We never give our name away,
but listen hard to what I say:
God is not a she, God is not a he,
God is not an it or a maybe.
God is a moving, loving,
knowing, growing mystery.'

I know what children think
    and do,
for I have been a child like you.
I know how it feels to walk
    and run,
to sing and shout, and play in
    the sun,
or cry in the night,
or fall to the ground,
or tremble with fright,
or be lost and found.
I know how it feels to look at
    the sky
and keep on asking why and
    why.'
I met three children on my
    way,
and never knew, in all our play,
their age or name or why
    they came,
yet all the world is new,
and everything I do
will never be the same.

God is not a she,
    God is not a he,
        God is not an it or a maybe.
God is a moving,
    loving,
        knowing,
            growing
                mystery.

## 19 The problem of evil: some tentative thoughts of a perplexed Bible-reader

The unfairness of life is notorious, and notoriously there is no satisfactory explanation. Frequently, the best people suffer horribly, while the least deserving get away with it. The poet of Psalm 73 knows all about that (verses 2–12). Were the sufferers, then, wicked in some previous life, and are they paying for it now? That will not satisfy a Christian investigator, since there is no room for reincarnation in a Christian creed. Again, even if you promise the sufferer compensation in a future life (like Lazarus in Luke 16), there is still no answer to why a person should suffer undeservedly in any life.

There are promises in the Bible that those who pray resolutely enough will be rescued from their distress (Matt. 7.7–11; Luke 18.1–8) and a great deal besides; and there is ample supply of stories to illustrate this faith, in Exodus, Joshua and Judges, Daniel, the Gospels and elsewhere. But, as Hebrews 11.36–8 confesses realistically, there seems to be no consistency about this: some are relieved, some simply are not. In the wonderful saga of Joseph, Genesis 37 and 39–45, the upright man suffers but eventually comes out on top; but that is by no means always the story.

In any case, quite apart from the matter of unfairness and inconsistency, where does evil and unfair suffering come from? The story in Genesis 3, taken up by St Paul in Romans 5.12–14, traces it to a primal disobedience in the first couple of human beings. But not many today could take on board the idea of a genetically transmitted evil will; and in any case Genesis 3 offers no answer to the question where the serpent came from, whose evil persuasiveness did the damage. The book of Job has an introduction and a termination in prose, telling us that God inflicted misery on a blameless man, just to prove to 'the Satan', the Public Accuser in the divine assembly, that Job really was a disinterested worshipper; but what sort of answer is that, and what sort of God does it reflect? In the body of the book, the great poem with Job's impassioned complaint, the answer finally vouchsafed by God is to call attention to the strangeness of some of the marvellous things in creation – ostrich, hippopotamus, crocodile, the storm, the dawn, and so forth. Does that really help someone *in extremis*?

Yet, if there is no coherent answer to the problem, there are some considerations that may mitigate our sense of outrage.

(1) One may ask, Can one imagine any sort of personal existence that would be preferable to what at present obtains? Is there anything more precious than moral freedom – ability to choose for oneself in making decisions? Or again, is not mutual interdependence and a social sense very important? Would it be preferable to run on rails and be mechanically programmed never to do wrong? Surely life without moral freedom or mutual responsibility would be infinitely the poorer,

not deserving to be called personal. To be a person, and human, seems necessarily to be vulnerable and able to hurt others.

(2) Life genuinely personal, yet always protected from the resulting hazards, would imply an 'invasive' Creator, constantly intervening to rescue someone from trouble or suspending the regular and consistent working of the Creator's structure. It would mean a string of miracles rather than the consistent working of a Creator from within his creation. Mark well, above all, that Christ himself – 'one' with the Creator, as we believe – prayed fervently to be delivered from agony, but the prayer was not granted. He was taunted by his enemies with his inability to come down from the cross, and himself felt deserted.

(3) This seems to suggest a conclusion so astonishing, so demanding, that nobody has a right lightly to declare it, but which the event seems indeed to establish: what St Paul dares to express when he counsels 'Be not overcome by evil, but overcome evil by good' (Rom. 12.21).

Does it not seem possible to believe that the human will is built into creation as a force in the structure of being, so that believing prayer and prayerful obedience actually does (to use the cliché) 'change things'?


## 20 Exorcism

The Pope has lent his support to exorcism. Is this something to be welcomed? There is no doubt that Jesus of Nazareth believed in the existence of evil spirits: there is ample evidence that he practised exorcism with spectacular success. He also believed in a king of demons, a personal opponent of God, called 'the Satan' (a Semitic word for 'the Opponent') or 'the Devil' (a Greek word for 'the Slanderer') or 'Beelzebub' (the name, variously spelt, of a pagan deity, used derisively). But Jesus, Christians believe, was not only truly God but also truly human; and no genuinely human person is omniscient. As well as exorcism, Jesus is said to have used spittle for his healings, and even dust from the ground, without regard for hygiene in the modem sense. We today have more factual knowledge than anyone did in the days of Jesus, and our additional or corrective knowledge, however defective it still is, makes it difficult to believe in the existence of non-human *personal* beings, charged with evil or identified with it. Indeed, is not evil precisely what destroys personal being? Is not the ultimate evil just that lack of love that extinguishes personality? It is all the more terrible for being essentially negative – the fatal 'Evil, be thou my good'.

Thus, to most of us, it seems more reasonable to identify what is called demon-possession with psychological or moral derangement. Some, in fact, of the seeming results of exorcism can be achieved by treatment, chemical or manipulative, based on psychological systems, even if none of them is invariably successful or as spectacular as exorcism described in the Bible.

Is it wiser, then, and safer and more rational (not to say more devout, given our knowledge) to remove credence from religious or quasi-religious exorcism (though in no way giving up prayer to God) and transfer it to one or another of the 'scientific' approaches? This is a valid question, even if, in discussing exorcism, we exclude from its genuine practice abuses such as physical or psychological cruelty. Would it not be better, if we had faith enough in the power of God, to pray to him for healing, rather than addressing orders in his name to a supposed demon? Obviously, for a Christian, even if he or she cannot believe in personal demons or a personal king of demons, the duty of devout prayer remains unquestioned. The difference is that one no longer delivers a hostile command to a supposed evil being, but all the more believes in positive prayer for the victim, combined with the best scientific therapy available. In fact, is it ever right to pray *against* anybody or anything? Must not prayer always be *for* all persons concerned? Positive prayer is no less devout than the exorcist's attack in the name of God. It involves just as much faith and sincere dependence on God: it involves just as much resistance to whatever hinders health; but it is not a personal address to what we believe is impersonal. It is prayer to God for the patient, to enable that patient to expel the evil.

It could, perhaps, be argued that, if the patient is conscious and can hear the exorcism, it may stiffen his or her resistance against the evil. But is the use of such fiction desirable? Are there not more realistic ways of fortifying the will?

With respect, then, the Pope's judgement must be resisted.

*October 2005*

## 21 Sacrifice and propitiation – do the words belong in the proclaiming of the Christian gospel?

These reflections concern only one section of Christian doctrine. They presuppose, without discussion, the conviction that Jesus is, in a special sense, 'one' with God, and, mysteriously, 'one' also with the whole of humankind. Granted these tremendous presuppositions, this is an attempt to interpret the use of the word 'sacrifice' in a Christian context.

In St Luke 15 comes a story (generally known in English-speaking contexts as 'the parable of the prodigal son') of a generous father who eagerly welcomed home his younger son though, insultingly, he had demanded his legacy before his father's death and squandered it. He then returns home penniless, asking for a menial job on the farm; but his father, without a word of blame, restores him to his place in the family. The story was probably told by Jesus originally to defend himself against criticism for consorting with irreligious, non-observant Jews rather than the respectable conformist ones represented by the obedient elder brother. But it has been widely adopted as a picture, simply, of what generous, free forgiveness of an offender looks like. Using it in this way, a friend once asked me what I thought the ashamed, penitent son saw, when at last he dared to lift up his eyes and look at his father. A plausible answer was: He would have seen a change. An unfeeling father would probably react merely with anger and a desire to 'take it out of' the son: he would not have suffered great emotional stress. But a father who could greet the son with love and forgiveness would be bound to have suffered emotionally, and this would have registered visibly – in greying hairs, perhaps, and lines of suffering on the face. The boy would be bound to notice a drawn look that would not have been there when he left home. He could read off something of the 'cost' of this forgiveness.

You don't need to be 'religious', only observant of human nature, to realize that forgiving is a 'costly' process – it 'takes it out' of you. For consider what has to happen. Most estrangements are not between one wholly good and one wholly bad person. Usually, a plurality of persons is involved, with some shades of grey on both sides. But, for simplicity's sake, let us think of two individuals, one entirely innocent, the other guilty. For reconciliation to be possible, the injured, good party must *give up* (you might say 'sacrifice') his or her rights, offering to let the guilty one off free – which is what forgiving means. Equally, to *accept* such an offer, the offender must swallow his or her pride, admit to being at fault, and recognize that forgiveness is a pure gift, wholly undeserved. That, too, could be called 'sacrifice'. There is 'cost' or 'sacrifice' on both sides.

This is quite different from a *transaction*. The guilty party doesn't *buy* forgiveness by making an offering. It is simply that free (and costly) forgiveness can't be accepted without the acceptance itself also being a sacrifice.

On the superficial level, there may indeed be a transaction. The injured party can accept compensation. The offender must be penalized. But this can be entirely devoid of feeling. The offender need not be penitent, the injured person need not feel forgiving. It will be no more than a legal settling of the case. But if it is a reconciliation, on the deep level of personal relations, it can be spoken of in terms of 'sacrifice' or 'cost' on both sides alike. 'Sacrifice' and 'cost' are metaphors appropriate to mutual reconciliation; and they will not be metaphors for a gift to propitiate an angered person and buy his or her favour: they will represent the emotional expenditure in a genuine reconciliation.

This brings us to what is manifestly a misunderstanding of the Christian gospel. From the top of a London bus, I once caught sight of a 'wayside pulpit', as they used to be called: a bill-board outside a place of worship with a 'sound bite'. The awful words proclaimed: 'God doesn't hate you any more.' They reflected the crude idea that the death of Christ 'bought off' an angered God. The death of Christ imagined as a sacrifice of himself by a loving Saviour to pacify a God of vengeance is not unknown in crude versions of the gospel. There is even a tiny hint of the idea in the New Testament itself, when, in a passing phrase in Ephesians 5.2, Christ is spoken of as handing himself over as a sacrifice to God – as a sweet fragrance (a term borrowed from Old Testament language of sacrifice). But this is almost unique in the New Testament. The conviction at the heart of the Christian good news is summed up in the tremendous words of 2 Corinthians 5.19, that God was offering *himself* in (or by) Christ, in order to eliminate the estrangement caused by our sin. Christ on the cross was the expenditure of love by God, in forgiving us and welcoming us home. To call it a sacrifice is to use the word not in a ritual sense such as it would bear in the context of a sacrificial system. It means simply 'expenditure'; and that in its turn here means the release of psychological energy. The importance of this is that it gets rid of the fatal idea of propitiating or pacifying an angry Being. Many early doctrinal debates had trouble with the question, 'To whom was the sacrifice made? Was it to the devil? Was it to an alienated God?' Instead, we are now describing the psychological compensations involved in the emotional processes of reconciliation.

Thus, although it is true, as is often pointed out, that the language of propitiation is occasionally used in the New Testament, it is never used with God as the recipient; rather, the action referred to is itself the work of God: he is not the recipient of propitiation, but its instigator. Even in the Old Testament there are not a few statements such as 'thou desirest no sacrifice' (Ps. 51). In our analysis of the 'sacrifice' that both sides of a reconciliation need to make, the sinner sacrifices his pride and his reluctance to admit the wrong. And if Christ indeed is 'one' with humankind as well as with God, then his self-surrender is the human side of the sacrifice as well as the divine: the death of Christ is the whole cost of reconciliation.

Perhaps we may still find ourselves asking: But if all this is true, how comes it that God is already a God of forgiveness before the climactic and definitive 'sacrifice' under Pontius Pilate? The Old Testament declares that God is a God of forgiveness, long before the Christian era. The answer clearly lies somewhere in the great mysteries that I have already said are presupposed by the present discussion. If Christ is mysteriously 'one' both with God and with humankind, then what he achieves in time is one with the eternal realities of the Holy Trinity. God is 'beyond time' a forgiving God because, within time, in Christ, he 'pays' the full 'cost' of reconciliation; and vice versa.

What the historical causes of the death of Christ were, is much debated. One proposal is that he died because, on the one hand, he refused to become a 'freedom fighter' against the Roman occupation, like Judas Maccabaeus against Antiochus Epiphanes. Equally, he refused to share with the Temple aristocracy in the diplomatic game of holding the balance between submission to Rome and maintaining Jewish identity. Instead, without swerving to right or left, he lived to offer the love of God impartially to all who would accept it, and so was trapped between the two. In any case, his death embodies the 'sacrifice' or 'cost' of ultimate forgiveness, received by ultimate repentance.

In certain types of preaching, the cross of Christ is presented as a special device, applied, as it were, from 'outside', by God. Here it is shown as divinely basic to the very structure of human relationship.

## 22 On the cost of reconciliation (2 Corinthians 5.19)

From the top of a London bus I once caught sight of a 'wayside pulpit', a board outside a place of worship with a 'sound-bite' on it. It said: 'God doesn't hate you any longer'. This appalling message meant that the death of Jesus Christ was a sacrifice that had pacified an angry God. But that is not a Christian message. It is a straight contradiction of the marvel at the heart of the gospel, which is that – astoundingly – Jesus Christ is 'one' with both God and humankind – perfectly divine and perfectly human. He didn't give his life to placate an angry God.

It is God himself, in Christ, who was making the sacrifice: 'God was in Christ reconciling the world to himself'.

But if so, why bring the word 'sacrifice' into the picture? And why the word 'reconcile' which is already in our text? Well, it is true that technically 'sacrifice' does belong in a religious system that dedicates (makes sacred, sacri-fices) a gift, to propitiate an alienated deity. But the word is often used in a non-technical, secular way, so as to mean simply costly expenditure; and every 'reconciliation' between estranged people is indeed an eminently costly business, not because God demands a price, but because the process itself of overcoming estrangement is demanding. Think of it. The wronged party must offer forgiveness, free. That is an eminently costly business, emotionally speaking. Equally the offender has to swallow his pride, admit to being in the wrong, confess – a very expensive job. Reconciliation isn't a bargaining process, in which the offender compensates the injured party. That does have to happen: there will be some sort of fine and compensation. But that is on the surface, not emotion-deep. The offender will be fined, but that doesn't necessarily mean he repents. The injured party's compensation doesn't guarantee forgiveness. Reconciliation is a deep-down, emotionally costly process, and ever since human intercourse began, this kind of demanding emotional adjustment has been necessary, if antagonism is to be healed. That is the 'sacrifice' we are talking of.

The whole life of Christ, powered by absolute love going all the way to death, is the output of what it takes to heal an alienation. It is the absolute offer of forgiveness by Christ as 'one' with God, and the absolute response of repentance by Christ as 'one' with humankind. It is the climax, in a person, in history, of the work of the eternal, timeless, love of God. God always has been a God of forgiveness; that is why one day in one Person he brings the costly process of reconciliation completely to fulfilment.

Thanks be to God, through Jesus Christ our Lord!

*Local Church Magazine, April 2004*


## 23 Greed as wanting more

In the New Testament there is a word *pleonexia*, meaning 'greed', 'acquisitiveness' (literally, 'having more'), which occurs several times, and, in Colossians 3.5 (cf. Eph. 5.5), is strikingly equated with idolatry: to be acquisitive is nothing short of worshipping possessions. This exactly matches what has already been quoted – our Lord's telling the rich man that if he wants eternal life he must give his wealth away (Mark 10.21). Similar is the saying 'You cannot serve God and Mammon' [? the god of wealth] (Matt. 6.24). It is this passion for more that is rejected in the words of St Paul, quoted in a previous comment, that, by the power of God, he is enabled to be independent: he can live both with poverty and affluence (Phil. 4.11–13). In Proverbs 30.15 there is a saying of which the text is uncertain; but as it stands it provides a caricature: 'the leech has two daughters, [who say nothing but] "Give, give".' (The NEB renders it well: '"Give" says one, and "Give", says the other.') There's *pleonexia* for you! Blood-sucking, wealthy concerns must give heed.

Perhaps it is the right *attitude* to possessions that underlies both forms alike (Matthean and Lukan) of the beatitude.

*26 February 2005*

## 24 Repentance as against expressions of regret

It has become fashionable for the descendants or representatives of those who have committed some great wrong to make a public apology to the representatives of the wronged – apology for the 'Holocaust', for the slave-trade, for the persecution of aborigines, for the Crusades. This has been contemptuously called 'contrition chic'. Do these gestures deserve such scorn?

Perhaps they would if the public gesture were claimed to be repentance. It is one thing to express regret; it is another to repent; and is it possible to repent of something that one has not oneself done? Equally, is it possible for anyone but the victim to forgive the perpetrator? Perhaps the scorn should be reserved for a mistaken claim for regret to serve as penitence.

The Christian belief is that the divine Creator is himself the ultimate target of all wrongdoing, and that Jesus of Nazareth, as uniquely 'one' with the Creator, has implemented in time and space the absolute suffering love which is divine forgiveness. This forgiveness can be received only by the penitent perpetrator of the wrong: representatives can receive no more than acknowledgement of disapproval and regret. Jewish thinkers maintain correspondingly that none but the victim can offer the divine forgiveness. If there is a sense in which Christians differ here, it is only because they believe themselves to be united with Jesus, who is the ultimate victim and in whom is embodied the divine and absolute offer of forgiveness.

Two biblical stories may be placed side by side. The story of the first Adam in Genesis 3 shows disobedience to the will of God as the root of all wrong. The story of Jesus of Nazareth, the last Adam, presents the divine answer to that wrong, namely, the ultimate unconditional forgiveness of love absolute, implemented in history in the total obedience of Jesus. It is unconditional but not compulsory: by definition, love cannot impose itself. It still leaves the sinner the option of rejecting it. But, given true repentance, divine forgiveness is assured. Others can regret; only the sinner can repent. Others may hope and pray for repair; only the victim can forgive, together, perhaps, with those who are willingly united with the ultimate divine victim of the sin of the world; for may not all such constitute a channel for the material of repair?

*24 November 2006*

## 25 The treatment of offenders

I am no expert in criminal law or prison management, though I have read some of the literature; but I believe that mere retribution ('tit for tat', quantitative justice) has no place in the motivation behind a Christian system of law or of the treatment of offenders. The deliberate application of suffering or loss to an offender may be justified if its purpose is to reform; but simply as an exercise in quantitative justice, as a 'squaring of accounts', it cannot, I believe, be justified or be of any constructive value to victim or offender. In other words, punishment as such, retribution, has no valid place in the handling of crime, even if severe treatment may be justified as reformatory.

Where an outrage has been committed, there is always a big proportion of the public that bays for the blood of the offender and cries for revenge; but this is disastrously wrong-headed. Self-protection, and protection of the vulnerable, are, of course, justified motives; but retaliation is a different matter.

In the Old Testament there is a great deal about punishment and retribution. In the New Testament, without the smallest concession to the condoning of sin, the appeal for retribution is substantially reduced. It is as though the centrifugal force of the gospel of redemption from sin has spun it to the circumference.

But why should revenge be thus disparaged? Why should a lust for retribution be disallowed? In one of the few New Testament passages about revenge, it is explicitly attributed to God (Romans 12.19, in a quotation from Deuteronomy 32.35). It is the more remarkable that St Paul here explicitly forbids Christians to follow suit, bidding them, instead, to shame an enemy by generously helping him, and adding: 'Do not be overcome by evil, but overcome evil by good.' A famous saying attributed to Jesus himself (Matt. 18.6) declares that it is better for a person to be drowned in the depths of the sea rather than that he should do harm to 'one of these little ones who believe in me'; but even that extreme severity does not advocate revenge, it highlights the wickedness of harming a 'little one'. So in Luke 10.12–14, the towns that rejected Christ's message will at the last judgement fare worse than the famously wicked cities of antiquity; but when the disciples want to invoke a curse on a hostile town, they are rebuked (Luke 9.54f.).

Even if a convicted offender may complain that the infliction of the sentence feels no different, however little retribution there may be in its intention, the principle remains, and, in the long run, the motive behind law and practice is bound to tell. Reform is a valid intention, as retribution and revenge are not.

As things are at present in English law and procedures, imprisonment notoriously tends to make offenders worse. Ideally, offenders should be helped to realize the harm they have done, and to begin to be concerned about their victims; and it seems that the systems of some other countries are more successful than the English system in bringing offender and victim face to face, and sometimes even effecting reconciliation. The option of community service may be a step in the right direction. Of course there are no facile answers; and of course it is a duty to the public to protect them as far as possible by restraining dangerous offenders; but it still matters a great deal whether the principles and motives behind legislation and practice are merely negative, or are positive and reformatory in intention.

Christians have a duty to do all in their power to promote these ends, and to support all the creative ministries of prison chaplaincies.

Notoriously, the application of penalties can be only external, and does not necessarily lead to any inward reform of character: an offender may pay a fine without a trace of remorse, and a victim be compensated without forgiving. But the motive behind legislation and practice should be to bring the external and the internal together, so as not merely to repress evil but to encourage good, and to work towards reconciliation. This will be achieved not by facile talk, but by a radical change of mind.

## 26 Christianity among world religions

There is much confusion about the status of Christianity. Exclusive 'fundamentalism' quotes texts: 'no one comes to the Father except by me' (John 14.6); 'There is no salvation in anyone else at all, for there is no other name under heaven granted to men, by which we may receive salvation' (Acts 4.12). At the opposite end, extreme liberalism sees the Christian faith simply as one of the planets circling the central sun: all ways lead to God.

Attention to facts, however, points to neither extreme. A strong case can be made for the belief that Jesus of Nazareth was, in a special sense, the fullest possible embodiment of God in a human individual. (For a more detailed statement, see 'The Incarnation of God in Jesus Christ'.) If this is true, then Christianity has the only revelation that offers what has been called 'the human face of God'. Without any diminution of the awe and supreme majesty of God – indeed, with their greatest possible enhancement – Jesus brings to believers a unique revelation. It is the revelation of a God whose 'almighty' power is constituted, not by overruling force but by self-giving love and by a compassion which, enhancing rather than diminishing supreme moral demand and judgement, goes all the way in paying the absolute cost of reconciliation between humankind and God. Is not this a unique and compelling understanding of power, all too little regarded and reflected by the Christian Church itself?

Judaism, for its part, presents God as a God of forgiveness and redemption, yet does not run to the length of incarnation. Islam offers an austere world-ruler. All three faiths insist on the unity of God: despite contrary claims against Christianity, it is in reality as staunchly monotheistic as the others.

Some of the eastern religions avoid personal and monistic representations of God, refusing a sharp distinction between Creator and creation, and thinking rather of influences permeating everything and distributed through an indefinite number of forms. One thinks of Wordsworth's 'deeply interfused' pantheism.

Of 'paganisms', it might be true to say that the chief aim of a cult is to gain control over circumstances, using techniques for getting rather than giving. If this is a fair estimate, 'paganism' can reasonably be excluded from the present investigation.

Of the others, it must surely be said that all are in some measure valid understandings of the divine. It would be false to suggest of any of them that it is not, in some degree, an authentic revelation of God, and does not lift humankind above itself and call for worship.

But – and this is a point sometimes overlooked – that is no reason for grouping them all as equally successful revelations of the divine reality. While recognizing them all as 'ways to God' and, in their degree, valid revelations, it is still not unreasonable to claim for one of them that it is the fullest, most comprehensive, most illuminating revelation. And that, in a word, is where the Christian faith stands. Rejecting the validity, in its degree, of none, it claims that the fullest and most comprehensive revelation is in Jesus Christ. Of all the planets circling the central sun, Christianity is the brightest. More sophisticated statements have been proposed by Christian philosophers. If the one here presented is crude, let it be at least a stepping-stone to something better.

To claim that the Christian revelation is fuller than Judaism is in no way anti-Semitic. It was indeed precisely Semitic writers who themselves first put the Christian claim in writing. It is sadly true that St Paul spoke bitterly about Jews in 1 Thessalonians 2.15f., but, in the context, it is clear that these were only the particular Jews who attacked Christians and tried to stamp out their movement. About Israel as a whole, one only has to read Romans 9 – 11 to see St Paul's passionate love and eager hopes for his own nation. Christians saw the Church as the natural crown and fulfilment of all that Israel stood for. The Old Covenant is indeed superseded, but only because it is transcendently fulfilled by the New (1 Cor. 3). If the Christian Church were faithful to its calling, the truth would be better understood.

## 27 Gospel truth

If we think rather hazily and not too precisely about authority, we may find ourselves the victims of all sorts of doubts and feelings of guilt. For instance, if we vaguely think that Scripture is somehow evenly permeated with divine authority (Isn't it called the 'word of God'? Isn't it supposed to be 'different'?), then we shall be upset if we can't respond to every bit of it. For instance, the systems of Bible reading (the Bible Reading Fellowship, the Scripture Union, etc.) serve up a daily crumb of the large cake. If this small crumb seems to be lacking in nutritive quality or even tasteless, we ask ourselves 'What's gone wrong?' Even worse, if we find in the verse or the passage for today something that we frankly cannot believe, or perhaps cannot even approve of, again we're perplexed: isn't the New Testament meant to be authoritative? Doesn't it speak with the word of God? Or again, is our perception hopelessly distorted? If we are preachers and having to handle the word of God in public, are we to expect the readings for that particular day always to carry a message for us to share with the congregation? And then all the enormous problems of how the New Testament *is* meant to speak: is it cheating if I go back to a very old practice, and use the passage not literally but as a kind of vehicle in which to convey some truth from elsewhere, or as a peg on which to hang some message? If we do that, the kind of authority becomes a really urgent question, because what we are putting into, or hanging onto, the passage clearly does not derive its authority from there (unless we can believe that God designed that verse from the beginning to be used non-literally in the way we are using it now – which *is* a bit of a strain on the credulity!). Or, finally, if we look in a commentary and find some distinguished scholar telling us that what we are reading is unlikely to be the words of Jesus himself, and is more likely to be an alteration and adaptation by the later Church, then what sort of authority are we now left with? If it is not our Lord's, then is it the early Church's? Or is it even the commentator's? The verse seems now to be coming at us on all sorts of different levels simultaneously: on what storey of this high-rise building are we going to come to rest?

I don't pretend for a moment that there are slick or easy answers available to any of these questions. But I propose one very simple exercise, which does seem to me to blow away a good deal of fog: ask very simply – 'What is distinctive about Scripture (or, in this particular case, about the New Testament)?'

In attempting to reply to that question I submit that we have first got to face the fact that inspiration is not at all distinctive. If to say 'Scripture is inspired' means that we believe the writers of Scripture were inspired, if we're using inspiration in a normal and fairly intelligible sense, then that is not by any means peculiar to the New Testament. I suppose no religious person would ever deny that all great art – literature or music or visual arts – is dependent on something special, given from beyond to the artist. Genius comes from beyond: it is something breathed into the artist. So, if writers of Scripture were inspired, that puts them in the class of genius, but along with many others in many different religions and even in completely non-religious traditions – though, actually, I find it very difficult to believe that all writers of Scripture were inspired all the time; some of the things that they write are very pedestrian. 'Oh but', you'll say, 'that is outrageous because we are using inspiration in a special way when speaking about the Bible. It is not just that the writers were inspired in that general sense, lifting them above themselves. It is much more than that. God's Spirit possessed them completely; they

were kept from error; it is as though the Almighty were dictating.' (Yes –
and, no doubt, dictating which books subsequently should be chosen
for the 'canon'?) Well, of that I can only ask, 'Who said so? And on
what authority?' I can see no trace of evidence to support that position.
It doesn't appear from other areas of experience to be God's way to
rob people of free will and of the freedom to make mistakes. Neither is
there evidence, so far as I know, that the New Testament is in fact free
from error; neither is there any evidence to show that church councils
are always free from error. The list of those authoritative Scriptures
that were chosen was not an infallible list; neither, I think I am right
in saying, did those who chose them announce that they were chosen
because they were infallible.

What they did do was to declare them normative, the standard. But
that's not the same thing as saying they were kept from error; nor that
everything in them is found independently of the rest to utter Gospel
truth. What the early centuries of Christianity meant by choosing them,
and, as it were, drawing a circle round a certain lot of books and excluding others, was just what Article VI of our Thirty-Nine Articles says –
that nothing outside this selection of writings may be declared necessary for salvation; and, conversely, that everything that is necessary to
salvation may be found somewhere within these writings (which was to
cut the ground from under the feet of those who, in doctrinal or moral
controversy, were appealing to a great range of apocryphal and unau-
thorized writings). Article XX moreover declares that the Church may
not 'so expound one place of Scripture that it be repugnant to another',
which seems to imply quite clearly a view of the authority of Scripture
as belonging not to each part inherently, but to its total witness.

So, the term 'inspiration' appears to be less than useful for our present
purpose. Talk about the Scriptures being inspired (or being 'the word
of God', i.e. God's self-expression), however true, says in itself nothing
wholly distinctive or true exclusively of the New Testament. What, then,
is distinctive about the New Testament? Back to our original question!
If it's not the only inspired utterance and if it's not uniformly inspired,
that approach isn't going to help. There are other writings, there are
other works of art that also speak of God and from God.

But then neither does it help to change our words slightly and say
that Scripture is *inspiring*. It is inspired, but we found that isn't highly
distinctive. Can we say then that it is distinctive in its inspiration? It is
uplifting, it is searching, it is suggestive in a high degree that is undoubtedly true. But other literatures of other traditions and of later Christian
traditions are also inspiring, searching, suggestive and uplifting, at least

in some measure. The New Testament has no monopoly of these functions, even if it performs them in a supreme degree. That only makes it the best of the bunch – not distinctive.

So what is wholly distinctive about the New Testament, what is it or what does it do that no other body of literature is or does? The answer is that it is the earliest and most authentic evidence for what led Christians to their distinctive conviction – the conviction that Jesus is uniquely one with God and one with mankind; and the New Testament is the earliest and most authentic evidence for what caused the launching of the Christian Church. Not only did the Church of the first four centuries declare this collection of writings to be normative, to be the standard of belief and practice, but also modern scholarship quite independently, using austerely critical and rational approaches, has pronounced this collection the earliest and the most authentic evidence for all this. Christian tradition and modern scholarship converge on precisely that conclusion. In that respect this collection of writings that we call the New Testament is completely distinctive and indispensable; and it still performs this function of witness, whatever errors may be in it, because it remains the indispensable primary evidence.

To illustrate this collective kind of authority as the earliest evidence, I'd like to appeal to an analogy from the Arizona Desert. Somewhere near a place called Winslow, there is a famous crater, dear to the geological textbooks. It is believed to have been struck out by a meteorite. Geologists and geophysicists have examined that crater critically and closely. They've analysed its composition, they've looked at its contours. No doubt they've made allowance for all the layers of earth and detritus of rock that have been deposited since the impact. And by these techniques they are able to identify the various stages of development of that crater and distinguish the earlier from the later deposits. And the result is that they are able at least approximately to measure the original impact and to calculate the size and the composition of the meteorite.

Now, our early Christian documents – Epistles, Gospels, Acts, Revelation – bear witness to a vast impact. These writings would never have been written at all but for the existence of the Christian movement and the Christian community: to that at least they bear witness. But, more than that, the Christian movement and the Christian community are without plausible explanation unless Jesus did indeed show himself alive to his friends after his death, and unless this one whom they believe that they saw alive was such a one as he is found to be in the traditions preserved about him. So this evidence of an impact that we are examining bears witness to the launching of the Christian Church, it bears witness to something that caused that launching, which it is very difficult to explain away by any other means, and it shows that that cause was congruous with the traditions about Jesus that are also preserved among these writings.

All the variety of religious experiences represented in the New Testament documents – and they are diverse – converge on this common conviction – that the one whom the Christians believed that they knew alive and found present with them is the same Jesus who was crucified. It's the continuity between the Jesus who was a man of Nazareth and the Lord whose presence they know in worship and in work that is their common conviction. And without this conviction the rise of Christianity and the separation of Christians from the Jews is a total enigma.

And so I submit, that without presupposing anything about inerrancy or inspiration or the word of God, here is a body of ancient documents that examined critically by the ordinary methods of scholarship, turns out to be evidence – the primary evidence – of an impact, an unparalleled impact, in history, pointing to what has come to be summarized by the Christian confession – 'Jesus *is* one in being, or of one being, with God, and of one being with mankind. Jesus is Lord, Jesus is the Son of God; Christ has died, Christ is risen, Christ will come again!'

What does that say about the kind of authority carried by the New Testament? It says that the New Testament is, beyond all dispute, the authority for the Christian confession, and is such because it is the earliest body of evidence. You can subject it to the acids of criticism and treat it with the most rigorous rational investigation and it will still come up as the best evidence for the beginnings of Christianity. That doesn't mean that every verse in the New Testament carries gospel truth or is without error. Neither does it pretend to mean that value-judgements can be proved by any purely historical research. What it does mean is that when we treat this body of documents seriously and show it the elementary respect of examining it critically, it yields evidence for precisely 'what makes Christians tick'. It carries the authority of basic evidence, showing how the friends of Jesus were led through historical events to those momentous value-judgements that they made – 'Jesus is Lord'; and giving us data whereby we can judge for ourselves whether those value judgements were justified. That, I suggest, is the function of these documents.

So why should we not be glad and grateful to let the New Testament perform its proper function and use the critical work of commentators to help it to do so? Don't torture each verse into carrying a message direct from God to our present circumstances – that isn't its function. Use the critical skill of the commentators. Please use it critically, not following what they say just because they say it. We must do them too the honour of criticizing them; we must use our own critical acumen, of which we have plenty, on the critics. But why not listen respectfully to what they say and try to understand why they say it. And don't blame them for not writing our sermons for us, and see whether we aren't joyfully and grandly convinced, as I certainly am, that the New Testament as a whole points to that tremendous impact, that unprecedented force, without which the genesis of the Easter belief and the launching of the Church are totally inexplicable: a conclusion that alone I believe makes sense of the data that the New Testament offers us. Why not recognize witness to Christ Jesus as the function of the New Testament, as Luther did, and rejoice and glory in it? It isn't its function to be an oracle, it isn't meant to tell us the answers to our present predicament, it has no mandate at all to hand out guaranteed error-free statements. What has the Bible to say about genetic engineering? Or euthanasia or abortion? Nothing at all. But it can bring us to God through Jesus Christ and there by the Holy Spirit we may by the grace of God receive guidance into all truth. Its function is to point us and lead us to the knowledge of God in Jesus Christ, when we reverently and conscientiously apply our shrewd, critical senses to it, as we do to all else.

I am wont to present this in terms of a diagram and an epigram. Imagine in your mind's eye a triangle. Now, do not expect God's answers to your questions to come straight along the base of the triangle, from the New Testament ('A') to your predicament ('B'). Things from the Bible do sometimes leap out and hit us. But that is not its normal function. No! We have to let the New Testament lead us up another side of the triangle. We have to climb up with its help from the New Testament ('A') to the knowledge of God in Christ ('C') at the apex of the triangle. And it is from the encounter with God, through Christ, by the Holy Spirit, in the Christian fellowship, to which the New Testament may lead us – all that at 'C' – that, by the grace of God, we may find God's answer to our immediate need, coming down the third side of the triangle, from that apex, 'C', to our predicament, 'B'.

It is the proper function of the New Testament to show us Jesus Christ, so that in him we may find God and through him, by the Holy Spirit, in the Church, find and follow the will of God. I like to translate my triangular diagram into an epigram, by saying that the New Testament is not so much a compass or a chart by which we may find our own way through the shoals, as 'instructions for finding the Pilot'.

If we so understand the New Testament, our sermon preparation and our other uses of it may be no easier; but they will be free from those literalistic anxieties, that sense of guilt, that perplexity about the critical commentator, because we shall be taking as many of the relevant considerations as we can into account, and looking to its total, collective witness, the immensely impressive, awe-inspiring witness of this tremendous impact-mark – and endeavouring to share the thrilling vision, the revelation, to which it leads us, in fellowship with fellow seekers, through Christ, by the Spirit, in the Body of Christ: inspiration indeed, in the sense that the Holy Spirit is at work in the Church, but not in so vague a sense as simply saying, 'Scripture is the inspired word of God'.

## 28 Religion

The word 'religion' means 'binding', as does 'obligation'; and that is unfashionable. The cry today is for freedom: I must be free to choose for myself what seems to suit me – yoga, perhaps, for relaxation, transcendental meditation for peace of mind. I must be free to pick and choose. If that is what we say, it is nothing new. It was the Roman poet Lucretius, more than 2,000 years before Richard Dawkins, who exclaimed about the evil that *religio* (binding) could do. But there was another versifier, in the nineteenth century, who wrote:

Make me a captive, Lord,
And then I shall be free;
Force me to render up my sword,
And I shall conqueror be.

And when you come to think about it, was he not right? Paradoxically, if we take away the divine imperative, the *religion*, there is no freedom worthy of the name. Christian worship is a duty before it is a comfort, an obligation before a release. It is only if we accept that obligation, laid upon us not by a harsh decree but by the stupendous love of God, that we find real freedom, with consolation and joy.

When Moses drew near to investigate the burning bush, there came a voice: 'Take thy shoes from off thy feet, for the place whereon thou standest is holy ground.' We shall never be a whole and sound and happy society until we recover a sense of awe. It is only the *holiness* of the divine self-giving that can bring us *wholeness*.

> How shall I sing that Majesty
> Which angels do admire?
> Let dust in dust and silence lie;
> Sing, sing, ye heavenly choir.

# 4

# Sermons

## 1 The Sunday next before Advent. Yetminster, 1995

It sometimes seems as though this world of ours is full of exiles and refugees. One wonders whether ever before in all history there have been so many people battering on the doors of the immigration authorities, pleading to be let in and given a corner where they can settle: boat people from Vietnam, and other refugees from persecution or the horrors of war, in the Southern Sudan, in Rwanda – in Bosnia . . . you could extend the catalogue for ever! Our days could be called the age of the refugee.

And yet, when you come to think of it, seeking a home is no new tune: it is already a leading motif – a leitmotiv – in the Bible. The Hebrews of the Old Testament were never tired of telling the refugee story. Our fathers were slaves in Egypt, they said: but God brought them out of the iron furnace, out of the house of bondage, and promised them a good home, a land flowing with milk and honey – if only they, for their part, would keep the terms of the agreement that he made with them. It's often been said that the Hebrews defined their God that way. Who is God? He is the one who brought us out of slavery into a spacious land.

But the promise of a home never worked out permanently. As the story goes on, the Israelites prove unfaithful, and they are exiled from the promised land and deported to Mesopotamia: and evidently some are scattered further north, driven hither and thither over many alien countries.

So, in the Old Testament passage read today in place of an Epistle (Jeremiah 23), God is redefined: no longer the God who brought them out of Egypt under the leadership of Moses, now he is the God who is going to bring them out of all countries whither he had driven them, bring them back by the agency of a just ruler, a descendant of the royal line of David, and settle them once more in their own land. Within limits, that came true. And yet, even when they had got home, there was continued dis-ease and restlessness: too often they were under the heel of foreign powers. And even in the days of Jesus of Nazareth his fellow countrymen were bitterly conscious of still not being free. Although they were in their own land, it was dominated by the Roman army of occupation. It has been plausibly suggested that thinking Jews of our Lord's day felt as though the Babylonian captivity was still not over: still they sighed for emancipation. Perhaps it's not surprising, then, if some of them seem to have seen in Jesus the ideal emancipation, the new Moses – 'that Prophet that should come into the world', as today's Gospel puts it. His 'charisma' (as we might put it today) and his magnetic personality seemed to mark him out as the ideal leader: surely it was he who would at last lead them in a successful campaign, to kick out the Roman army and get their home back for them once and for all! It's easy to imagine in the light of current events in Israel. Wasn't Jesus going to be the ideal king, or, as they called it, the one appointed by God, the anointed leader, the Messiah, the Christ?

When Jesus came to that shocking death, the bottom dropped out of their hopes. Or did it? The extraordinary thing is that his movement was not extinguished. A group of his followers emerged, still calling him King (or Messiah, or Christ). They still called Jesus King; yet – even more surprisingly – they seem no longer to have had territorial aspirations. They were convinced that Jesus really was King of the Jews (and not the pretender he was crucified for being); yet they no longer looked for any tangible land. If in the early days they asked questions along those lines and still saw Jerusalem as the focus of their hopes, there seems to have been no question of trying to get the land back. Here was a royalist, monarchist, movement and national loyalty, yet without any talk of a visible realm.

I can think of no explanation for that, except that Jesus had himself reinterpreted kingship for them. It didn't sink in, during his lifetime; but eventually, swept to the heights by his resurrection, and by finding him alive and with them, they began to grasp the message: Jesus was King of Israel, but 'Israel' was to include everyone – Gentiles, too – and the realm included and transcended all territories: it was the kingdom of God.

But isn't that much too easy a way out of the difficulty? What would our Bosnian refugee say if we said, 'Don't worry: you have a home in heaven'? It's all very well to say that, after all, the failure to establish a home for Israel in a tangible bit of land was not a failure but a success, because 'home' was lifted up from earth to heaven. But isn't that exactly what Karl Marx complained about? Isn't it just a device to keep the rebellious quiet? Don't agitate, it seems to say, don't rock the boat, be submissive and wait for pie in the sky.

To see it like that is to see less than half the picture. If our citizenship is in heaven, if our baptism certificate is our real passport, that doesn't for a moment mean that we don't care what happens on earth. On the contrary, it's a conviction that stiffens us to be good citizens on earth. Many of the great social reformers have been Christians, working for better conditions on earth precisely in the name of heaven. Loyal citizens (after all) have a way of making the land of their exile as like as they can make it to their native land. You can tell the Asian quarter by the smell of curry; and you should be able to know a Christian settlement by its own fragrance. The true citizens of heaven live out their citizenship wherever they are on earth. That is the test of the reality of their claim, it is the stamp upon their passport. Are they the ones who keep going a human quality of life, with compassion for the disadvantaged, concern for children and the aged? Do they respect the dignity of a person? Are there gentle words, to meet anger and indignation with healing and forgiveness? Or again, do they have the courage to attack abuses in their area? Are they ready to suffer for their principles? Always, genuine citizenship in heaven will stand, on earth, for human values. The fact that Christ is king in heaven is reflected by his citizens on earth: he makes them a lifeline to fellow exiles. Such are the pledges that the age-long promise of a settled home is real. This is what stirs up the wills of God's faithful people to bring forth plenteously the fruit of good works. So, when the season of Advent starts, next Sunday, we shall cry out to God with firmer ground for hope than the Israelites. Like them, we shall cry out of bondage, longing for release from troubles and anguish, from sin and failure. But our cry 'O come, O come Emmanuel' is firmly based on the fact that God has come in Jesus Christ and, in him, has redefined for ever the hope of our liberation. We aren't promised instant relief from trouble. The Lord comes in many different ways and at many different times, and we can't choose or wholly understand. What we can be sure of, if we will trust in him, is that our citizenship in heaven will give us poise and pride enough to make us effective in the land of our adoption.

'Blessed be the God and Father of our Lord Jesus Christ (says 1 Peter), who, according to his abundant mercy hath begotten us again unto a lively hope by the resurrection of Jesus Christ from the dead, to an inheritance incorruptible, and undefiled, and that fadeth not away, reserved in heaven for us.'

## 2 Epiphany. Winchester, 1991

Recently I was speaking to a group of army chaplains. It was at a conference in Germany, and it fell to me to conduct daily Bible-studies for
them on doctrinal matters. They were eager for a doctrinal ingredient
in their spiritual diet.

It is, of course, to the doctrinal centre of our faith that Epiphany
leads us. Epiphany celebrates the way in which God lets us see his
eternal reality in the transitory world in which we live.

Epiphany tells how God expressed himself in Jesus – spoke his
Word, uttered himself, supremely and decisively (so Christians hold)
in the dimensions of a single, human life. God's clearest and closest
communication with us humans – so we believe – is in Jesus, a human individual who turned out to be completely one with God, and
through whom God introduces himself to us. That is the distinctly
Christian conviction; and what we think about at the Epiphany season is the way in which God leads us to Jesus, and shows himself to
us in him.

And what is this way? How are we led to find God in Jesus Christ?
We know the Bible stories; but can we receive such a revelation still?
How, if at all, may one be led by God in these traumatic, disillusioned
days to find the expression of God's very self in Jesus Christ?

The answer suggested by our favourite Epiphany stories in the Bible
is that it needs supernatural portents. But is that the only way? May it
not be that these familiar Bible stories have become the favourite stories that they are, not because they show the only way of epiphany (of
revelation), but because they are the earliest stories and also, of course,
because they have a poetry about them and can be represented in picture and song? One of the nicest greeting-cards I received this Christmas carried a photograph of that celebrated twelfth-century carving at
Autun in Burgundy. It shows three magi (tradition, not the Bible, makes
them three). They are in bed together, still uncomfortably wearing their
crowns (for tradition, again, insists that they were kings). All three are
huddled together under a single, rather inadequate blanket. One appears to be snoring – eyes closed, lips parted. One sleeps quietly, lips
and eyes both shut. The third is opening a sleepy eye, because his hand
is outside the coverlet, and an angel is gently touching it with one long,
elegant, angelic finger, and pointing to the star. 'Wake up and look!',
the angel seems to say.

It took a heavenly portent to start the wise men on their way; and so,
too, with the shepherds. But my question is, 'Are there no other ways

of starting?' – for, frankly, there are few of us who expect a heavenly portent today. Can we be led today to a point at which God shows himself to us, speaks his Word, in Jesus Christ, without a star or an angelic choir – though, to be sure, nothing could come much closer to an angelic choir than what we are blessed with here.

In a Christmas article in *The Times*, the Bishop of Oxford said that, for him, it began with reading Aldous Huxley. Huxley observed, from right outside any distinctively Christian tradition, that, at the heart of every religion, is the paradox that we find ourselves only by losing ourselves. If so, thought Bishop Richard Harries, that paradox must be at the heart of God's own nature; and what more sublime expression could there be of God's losing himself to find himself than the incarnation? In Jesus Christ, human, vulnerable, and mortal, God gives himself away, and, through that hazard, brings life to the world. That, said the Bishop, is how he came to a confrontation with God in his Word made flesh.

So may I, too, be allowed a moment of autobiography? It's impossible fully to know oneself; but I think that I can see two major epiphanies in my long life, as well as all the lesser ones that – thank God! – keep coming. Of the first there is not time now to speak. The second has come gradually, through years of the closest study of Christian origins. It has been my professional job to bring as critical and as sceptical an eye as possible to the examination of all the evidence I can find, in the New Testament and outside it, for the nature and origin of the Christian movement, and, above all, of the figure at its heart.

It has been my duty to ask, ruthlessly and with no holds barred, Is this true? Does that stand up to scrutiny? Where is the evidence for such and such a view? How much is legend, how much is history?

In the process, naturally, I have indeed had to jettison some of the beliefs with which I set out. But the central beliefs, I can truly say, have been reinforced; and, above all, the belief in the Word made flesh – the incarnation of God in Jesus, the heart of the Epiphany. This has been impressively deepened and confirmed for me by my sceptical studies.

It's a long story, but let me put it briefly like this. Begin with early Christian belief. There is no doubt that the earliest Christians believed that they experienced a divine, transcendent presence. (The earliest Christian documents, St Paul's letters, provide ample evidence about it.) It was a presence that brought a new quality of life. It broke down barriers of hatred. It released people from the prison of sin and vice. It was a presence, so they were convinced, that was nothing less than the very presence of God and this, in a new form; for, amazingly, they called it by the common Jewish name 'Jesus', the name of the man who, very recently, had been done to death.

That is extraordinary. How did it come about? Certainly not through the mere enthusiastic imagination of his followers. Deification is a familiar phenomenon – not least in the period of Christian beginnings. Elevating a human hero (like Heracles) by excited enthusiasm to the level of deity – that is a quite common thing. But mere deification comes nowhere near the richness that Christians found in the living presence of the risen Lord. It goes almost no way towards explaining the Christian experience of forgiveness, light, and life in Jesus Christ.

Try looking back, then, at the traditions in the Gospels about Jesus the man. Sift them critically, as the ancient historian must, and ask what sort of picture they yield. The extraordinary answer is that the undoubtedly human figure reflected in the traditions can't be divested of a certain devastating directness of contact with God. So disturbingly close to God that at last they could bear it no longer and did away with him, this human, historical person is as close to God, as direct in his contact with God, as that divine, transcendent presence of Christian experience. The two are continuous.

Thus, the notorious Christian paradox – Jesus the Christ, human and divine, truly man, truly God – is precisely that towards which we are steered by the hard experience, ruthlessly tested and sifted, as surely as the magi were by their star.

Critical scholarship has, for me, been part of my epiphany story, my chorus of angels, my star. It has guided me to a paradox that the evidence refuses to resolve in either direction. The evidence demands the paradox. It is not satisfied either with 'man but not God' or with 'God but not man'. As surely as by some supernatural portent, I find myself constantly led by historical investigation to the one who, as a man, was totally divine.

And before this presence, what can I do but fall on my knees and confess, 'My Lord, and my God!'? And what is adequate to hold us, in a global hurricane, if not this faith? It is like an anchor (as the Epistle to the Hebrews says) that will not snap or drag. Those army chaplains know it and we pray for them now, as they try to share their faith with others in this Iraq crisis of 1991. And we pray for ourselves and for Christians everywhere, that, through us, others may be led to God through Jesus Christ, and find in him their light, their purpose and their strength to whom, through this Jesus Christ, by the Holy Spirit, in the Church, be honour and glory for ever.

## 3 The Conversion of St Paul. Cambridge, 1998

*In the Church's Calendar 25 January is St Paul's Day – the festival of the Apostle's conversion.*

It is fashionable at present to disparage St Paul, both as a man and as a writer. He was a misogynist, they say; he was arrogant and opinionated; he was hopelessly obscure. But one cannot help noticing that a high proportion of these shafts of criticism are discharged by marksmen, and markswomen too for that matter, who simply do not know their target. A well-known public figure went on record recently, in a religious journal, to the effect that St Paul (I quote) 'was such a bigot that he was quite happy for those who disagreed with him to die'. But she did not give chapter and verse for this opinion; and since, in the preceding sentence, she had made two gross misquotations from a Gospel, it is not unfair to conclude that she was speaking quite literally without her book. And so it is with many of St Paul's critics.

That St Paul is a difficult writer, who could deny? The reason for this may be, in part at least, that he seems to think in Aramaic but dictate in rather erratic Greek – not the best recipe for a lucid style. There is certainly much that remains obscure and is endlessly debated. But what is clear enough is the reflection, in all his letters, of one remarkable fact.

Here is a man who, on his own admission, started as an ardent, ultra-observant Jew, an extremist, a 'fundamentalist', as we might call him today. In the name of his ancestral faith, he turned the whole force of a literally murderous fury against every follower of the recently executed Jesus of Nazareth.

Why was that? Jesus had been a hugely acclaimed teacher and healer. Yes; but his views were so radical and unorthodox that, to a Jew like Paul, the Jesus-cult that had sprung up must have seemed nothing less than a fatal canker at the heart of Judaism. So he sets out to exterminate it. But very soon (as his letters clearly show) he has done a complete U-turn no less. He is convinced, now, that, after all, Jesus represents the very heart of Judaism, the goal and climax of Israel's vocation and meaning. To belong to Jesus, to be incorporated in him, St Paul now believes, is to be incorporated in the people of God even if you are a Gentile.

When the needle on the dial spins so wildly, one naturally asks: Is this not some kind of religious fantasy, some manic disorder? Besides, what could it mean to speak of being *incorporated* in a contemporary individual, recently executed? According to the Acts of the Apostles, Paul was indeed accused of madness. When Paul was being given a hearing before King Herod Agrippa, the Roman governor Festus shouted out: 'Paul, you are mad.' 'I am not mad, your Excellency,' he calmly replies; 'I am speaking words of sober truth.' And this is exactly what his epistles are: not bigoted, not arrogant (even if sometimes difficult), but a sober confession of conviction. And what they say is this: the man, Jesus of Nazareth, who fell foul of authority and was put to death, is alive and present, in a transcendent dimension. He sums up in himself the people of God; and (more) his unseen but real presence brings the very presence of God Almighty.

It is a mind-boggling conviction – this continuity between the individual recently put to death, and the transcendent presence, here and now the 'Body' in which Christians are limbs; but this is what is reflected, soberly and consistently, in all the letters of St Paul.

What is the result? That a crucified man should be found as a transcendent presence doesn't solve the problem of evil and suffering. In a way, it only intensifies it. But what it does bring is the experience of a Creator who heals and renews and recreates, from within the suffering. Through Jesus Christ come the judgement and mercy of God himself, bringing repentance and forgiveness, a new life of creative activity, and the summons to work for him, with passionate adoration, among Gentiles as much as among Jews, and the capacity to use the whole of life both dark and light – purposefully and creatively for his glory.

Well, then not madness perhaps; but surely, at the very least, some exceptional, mystic experience, genuine (it may be) but not for the average person? On the contrary, it is a conviction reflected, not only by Paul but by practically all the other writers in the New Testament, each in his own idiom and manner, and by Christians of all sorts ever since. And to prove how universal it is, one only has to remember that, from the earliest days till now, Christians have always used the formula, 'through Jesus Christ our Lord'. (We have already used it in today's worship.) So easily they might have said 'because of Jesus': because of all that he taught us, because of the noble example he held up, we understand God better, we are enlightened. But that is not the formula we use. From the beginning until this very day, with St Paul and all the other pioneers, we have been saying 'through Jesus Christ', as a living, present Mediator, present now as he was 2,000 years ago.

This is the distinctive faith and experience of Christians everywhere and at every period astonishing, yet well attested: the divine mediator, through whom God draws near to us and we to God, wears a human face and bears a human individual's name – Jesus. He suffered under

Pontius Pilate, but is alive for ever more. Here is a word from God, far transcending all that we can ask or think, yet spelt out for human understanding.

Why, then, disparage his Apostle, as a crank or a psychopath? Should we not rather join in the ancient prayer for his day that we, having his wonderful conversion in remembrance, may show forth our thankfulness for the same by following the holy doctrine that he taught, through Jesus Christ our Lord?

## 4 The Third Sunday before Lent: Septuagesima. Pevensey, 2003

Today is the first of three Sundays that lead, like a flight of steps, to the threshold of Lent – Ash Wednesday. Lent is the season when we are bidden to search our conscience before God and seek to renew our faithfulness, and I want to suggest that the Gospel for today – however difficult it is to understand – may serve at least to trigger some thoughts about both justice and mercy; and this may serve already as a beginning to our self-searching, and lead to prayer for responsible attitudes towards justice and mercy, individually and in public life. What we think and do does matter.

Today's Gospel, in St Matthew 20, is the parable of the labourers in the vineyard. It is notoriously obscure. The story, you remember, shows us an eccentric employer who decides – quite arbitrarily, as it would seem – to give a full day's wage to everybody who works at all in his vineyard that day, regardless of how few hours he has put in. So those hired at the end of the day, who did just about a quarter of a day's work, got equal pay with the ones who had toiled from dawn to dusk.

'Very odd!' we say. '*Outrageous*', said the ones who had worked all day. But, says the introduction to the parable (surprisingly), that's what the kingdom of heaven is like. So, is the kingdom of heaven essentially something unfair? It would be rash to say we understood this strange story.

Meanwhile, however, perhaps it can at least trigger for us some important considerations about strict, numerical justice, as contrasted with other ways of meeting a situation – strict equity over against generosity, Portia's quality of mercy, contrasted with Shylock's pound of flesh. What is our attitude to such matters? Might this be something to search our hearts about?

As an aside, it so happens that, in today's Epistle, 1 Corinthians 9.24, St Paul has occasion to allude to one of the most strictly just and ruthlessly exact measurements in the world he knew – namely, a measurement used in the Olympic Games. Obviously in a sprint there can only be one winner; or, if there is a dead heat, the race will have to be run again. All-important is the exact and just count of time, down to a split second. Not that St Paul is there contrasting exact justice with anything else. He's only saying that, as a faithful evangelist, he has to be as purposeful and as determined and as self-disciplined as an Olympic athlete out to win, in these exacting conditions.

But that's by the way. Returning to our parable, let's be clear that even if the kingdom of heaven is somehow like that strange employer's ways, it doesn't follow that strict, numerical justice isn't important in the eyes of God. On the contrary, society would go to pieces without it. For a full day's labour, in the days of the parable, one coin, a *denarius*, is said to have been the usual pay (translated by the Authorized Version of the Bible rather comically to us, as 'a penny'); and, in all equity, the full denarius ought, therefore, to have been reserved for those who had worked right through the day.

On the other hand, there are situations where not justice but *generosity* is the only way forward. Think, for a moment, of today's Old Testament reading – part of the story of how God made a good world. We know only too well that the story is to go on – in next Sunday's reading – to show that human pride and avarice spoiled that world, so that Adam and Eve were expelled from the Garden. What can meet such a calamity? Nothing can regain paradise-lost now, except something much deeper than numerical justice. Divine *forgiveness* has got to come on the scene, and forgiveness is not numerically just.

Again, think of the 'Third-World' debt, as we call it, *where justice won't work*. No doubt it's a fact that countries do indeed owe astronomical sums to the affluent West – or North (however you look at it). But it may well be that the only way forward, in the circumstances, is simply to cancel the debt. That may be the only way of prising open the jaws of the trap, and setting a 'Third-World' economy on its feet. (Alas, it may also be true that the debt is only going to start growing again immediately, unless affluent countries *also* change their exploitative ways of trading.) But anyway, what I'm saying is that here's a concrete example of a situation where strict justice, by itself, is simply not constructive. It won't get you anywhere. Some measure of generous self-sacrifice may be necessary, in certain circumstances; indeed, one might plausibly imagine that the labourers in the vineyard who had still not been hired at the end of the day were there precisely because they were unemployable: nobody wanted them. Perhaps they will never stand on their own feet again without a little priming of the pump – some initial generosity such as that employer did offer.

Today's Collect begs for just such generosity from God for us: we who are justly punished for our offences, beg God *mercifully* to deliver us by his goodness. We ask God to abandon justice and instead show us pure mercy. We're paupers. We shall never stand up again unless he makes a concession.

And indeed, concession is of the nature of forgiveness everywhere. Forgiveness isn't strict numerical justice. The injured person gives up his *rights* and instead makes a concession, not demanding his pound of flesh, but letting the offender off *gratis*. So the kingdom of heaven *is* like the eccentric employer, in so far as he recognizes the constructive power of generosity.

But deep down (and this is my last point) – even when unmeasured generosity goes into action, there is a justice at work even there. If the offender is offered forgiveness and remission, and if he is going truly to accept it, it isn't a soft option, violating true justice: it *is* every bit as *demanding* as numerical justice, but its demands are on a different level – the personal, the psychological, the spiritual level: repentance is spiritually costly; costly, not in terms of cash or time, but in terms of personal response: the output of spiritual energy.

Think of criminal law. Society would go to pieces (we say it again) if there were no fixed penalties such as a fine or imprisonment. But such penalties are external and superficial, applied to what can be seen and touched and measured. What matters much more is the inward, the personal, the deep-down invisible attitude. An offender may pay the fine, but still not be penitent or forgiven. A victim may be compensated materially, but still not restored or rehabilitated or ready to forgive. Justice may and must be done on the tangible level. But if the victim is to be healed and the offender restored, what is needed is repentance, a change of heart, forgiveness, recovery of the 'self', reconciliation. All that's very costly, but not in a way that can be weighed and measured. It's a different, deeper justice.

And it follows that responsible legislation, on the tangible, measurable level, ought always to be aimed, not at retaliation or reprisals, but at restoration and reconstruction on that deep level; and I believe that ordinary citizens like ourselves have the power and the duty to influence thought and action in this direction.

Might we, perhaps, pray then, in the coming weeks, for wisdom and courage to support and promote justice, both between individuals, and nationally and internationally – and always such justice on the tangible level as *makes for* that deeper justice on the level of persons in relation?

Might we pray, too, for an open-handed and forgiving spirit – yet never as a soft option or an easy way out, but always with a view to the costly building up of penitence, forgiveness and reconciliation?

In a word, may we pray that, as the Psalmist says, mercy and truth may meet together, righteousness and peace may kiss each other? May the cross of Christ and his painful reconciliation be at the heart of all our dealings, public and private. In us and in our area, may mercy and truth be enabled to meet each other, may righteousness and peace kiss each other: it can happen, by the power of the Holy Spirit and to the glory of God.

Amen!

So be it!


## 5 Palm Sunday. Chetnole, 2000

In an age of opinion-polls we can imagine ourselves as reporters, carrying our microphones back 2,000 years, and collecting opinions among the pilgrim crowds that streamed towards Jerusalem for the Passover festival, on that spring day long ago, which we now call Palm Sunday. The place is a-buzz with excitement: there's expectation in the air: there's a feeling that we're on the verge of some tremendous event.

Let's hold out the microphone to this tough, fierce-looking young man. 'Sir – what d'you think's going to happen? What d'you think *ought* to happen?' 'Oh, I'd like to see us get together and push out that hateful Roman army of occupation that's holding us down – push them into the Mediterranean! It could happen, you know. It might happen this Passover. We have the weapons, and there's a natural leader among us – a strong young man named Jesus, from the north of the country: he could unite us in one big effort. God be praised!' 'Thank you, Sir.'

But here comes a very different type – a respectable, well-dressed, city man. We put the question to him. 'Oh,' he says, 'I haven't a doubt that we're in great peril, every Passover season, from the hot-heads. We Jews can't possibly defeat the Romans, you know. They've got the whole empire behind them. It would be lunacy to try. Diplomacy's the only way. Keep on the right side of the governor, and then we can keep the Temple safe, keep it from being defiled by pagans, keep the Temple system going. God save us from the hot-heads!'

So, we've collected two completely opposite opinions. But over there, there's a little separate crowd forming round a man riding a donkey. They say it's that Jesus whom the fighter named. Let's see if we can get a word from him. But no, we can't get near him: his excited supporters are shoulder to shoulder.

But wait! I think we may be in luck after all. He's just reached the bend in the road from which the city of Jerusalem begins to come into view; and he seems to be weeping. There's a startled hush among his followers, and now we can hear his words from where we stand. Jesus wept over the city (St Luke's Gospel tells us): He said, 'If only you had known what belongs to peace – you, Jerusalem, whose name sounds like "peace"! If only you, the City of Peace, had known! But now your chance has come and gone, and you're on the way to ruin!'

Why? What does Jesus mean? Everyone knows he's a great patriot, proud to be a Jew, a passionate lover of the city. He undoubtedly believes in the high destiny of Israel. Yes! But evidently he understands the destiny of Israel very differently from the hot-heads, very differently from the cheering crowds who throng him.

We've managed to struggle near to the donkey, even if we can't reach his rider. Why not put the microphone to the donkey? After all, Balaam's ass, in the Old Testament story, was given a human voice. What can this little animal tell us? I think what he's saying is something like this: 'If a great conqueror intends to use brute force, he'll ride a war-horse. To be mounted on a donkey, like the peaceful conqueror in the Old Testament book of Zechariah, may be a signal that his chosen way is not the way of violence. I'm a signal, says the donkey, a warning signal, to the hot-heads.' Well, if so, these crowds seem to have ignored the signal.

But we know that equally the opposite faction are ignoring what Jesus is doing and saying. The Temple establishment, represented by the second person we interrogated, is hanging on to the ideal of keeping the Temple ritually pure and exclusive. They are looking for the glory of Israel in keeping the traditions correct and uncontaminated. They must hang on to the Temple at all costs.

Jesus, by contrast, sees the glory of Israel to lie in bringing the compassion of God to bear on all alike – specially the outsider, the poor, the disadvantaged. He sees that true purity lies precisely in getting one's hands dirty in service.

So the way of Jesus is neither with the hot-heads who want to use brute force to assert the claims of Israel, nor with the exclusive conservatives who simply want to keep the Temple-system of Judaism going. The third way of Jesus falls foul of both. And because he was absolutely consistent and absolutely dedicated to this third way, it brought him to the cross. He collided fatally with both parties and the Roman army. Like the dedicated servant in the book of Isaiah, he faithfully submitted to ridicule and hostility rather than alter his course. Like the glorious divine figure in today's Epistle (from Philippians 2), he knew that to be like God means giving, not getting: it meant emptying oneself out for the sake of others, not grasping at one's own advantage.

So, Jesus held steadily to his course, against both those other streams; and it brought him to death – the terrible death of the cross.

But Easter follows on the heels of Palm Sunday and Good Friday. What does that say to us? It says that the way that Christ went is the way God himself goes (for Christ is one with God). When Christ gives himself away in service to others, that is God's way. Christ's devoted care for others *is* itself God's glory. Easter doesn't *reverse* Good Friday: it shows us what Good Friday really means – we are shown God's way.

But how difficult it is to *go* his way with him! How can we find the moral sinews – the courage, the endurance? Let's hold out the microphone, finally, to someone who has actually done it, for instance that heroic old Chinese Roman Catholic bishop, Bishop Kung, who died recently. Because he refused to renounce his faith, when Communist China persecuted him, he spent 30 years of his life in prison. *But he held firm.* If we had asked him how, I'm sure he would have answered that the stamina came, not from *within* him, but from the God whom he trusted, *through Jesus Christ.* Christ reaches out his hand to us, and says 'Come with me!'

And those who *start* on the way of duty, trusting not themselves but the Holy Son of God, Christ Jesus, will find him as good as his word.

Thanks be to God!

## 6 'Songs of Praise'. Chetnole, 1996

Long my imprisoned spirit lay
Fast bound in sin and nature's night;
Thine eye diffused a quickening ray,
I woke, the dungeon flamed with light;
My chains fell off, my heart was free,
I rose, went forth, and followed Thee.

First, a little about the language of the Christian faith in general.

When we Christians try to talk about our faith about the Good News, the gospel – we find ourselves lost for words. Not that we don't use far too many words; we often do. A novelist once called it 'poor little talkative Christianity'. But however garrulous we are, the words can never be adequate – we're lost for the *right* words; they can never be *big* enough.

What are we trying to talk about? In ordinary life, an amazing amount of goodness comes our way (in among all the evil and violence of the world). We meet unexpected kindnesses, considerateness, even heroism; on our own small scale we find the power to *forgive* wrongs and the humility to *repent* of wrongs and *receive* forgiveness; we find the power to heal estrangements. Now, where does this power come from, and how do we gain access to it? The Christian good news is that it is in Jesus Christ that God has brought this creative power to its climax in human history, and that it is through Jesus Christ, in the fellowship of the Church, that we gain access to the volcanic power of his death and resurrection, and find healing and life and new hope.

But this world-shaking, life-imparting reality is so tremendous, so awe-inspiring, that we can't hope to express it properly. Look at what a lot of words I've used already, and how far they are from the glorious reality. We know it's good news, but it is *literally unspeakably* good. And yet, we've sometimes got to say something, when we're trying to share our faith. (Often example is more eloquent than words, but sometimes words are needed.) So we resort to the only means in our power; we use *picture*-language. We say: What God has done for us in Jesus Christ is far too big for words; but it's something like this, or something like that. We use pictures as a crutch to help us to move along, however clumsily. Our Lord himself did that, when he used his brilliantly chosen analogies – we call them his parables: 'the Kingdom of God is like a householder . . .' and so on. The Bible is full of picture-language; and in their turn the greatest hymns (and at last we've come to today's service) are full of the Bible. When everyone was brought up on the Bible, it was easy to recognize the allusions in the hymns to the picture-language of the Bible. Sometimes every other line fairly sang with overtones, and those who knew their Bibles caught them instantly. Now that the Bible is, for many, less familiar, the allusions may need to be spelt out.

We've just sung one of Charles Wesley's innumerable hymns, 'And can it be?', and Charles Wesley's hymns are always particularly rich in allusions to the Bible. I'm going to invite you to consider what lies behind just one verse of this remarkable hymn. But before we concentrate on verse 4, perhaps we should pause a moment on the strange picture-language of the first verse, because it may seem quaint or even crude. The Bible freely makes use of the picture-language of *blood*.

In those days, remember, the Jews were still, even at the beginning of the Christian era, offering animal sacrifices in the Temple, and blood flowed freely in symbolic rituals. It was not unnatural, therefore, that, in the language of the Christian Church, there are allusions to *the blood of Christ*. It was shorthand or picture-language for the overwhelming, indescribable generosity of God in Jesus, when, with his unswerving dedication, he went through with the violent death to which his love for us and his outspokenness led him; he literally spilled his blood for us and for all humankind.

So Charles Wesley starts his hymn with the language of blood; and he uses it in what may seem a crudely commercial way: 'Can it really be', he asks, 'that I should *gain an interest* in the Saviour's blood?' I take it that this is the language of the stockmarket; trusting in what the death of Christ has achieved is like some profitable investment, from which the believer receives dividends. Well, in a way, so he does; but we might feel this is sadly impersonal, mercenary language for such awe-inspiring, deeply personal love. And in verse 4 we do have a better picture. What God has done (says verse 4) in loving us supremely in Jesus Christ is like a great act of emancipation – it is like letting prisoners go free. Now, *there's* a vivid picture, and one more worthy of the mighty reality. But does it apply to *us*? Isn't the language of throwing open prison-gates over-sensational for those who are quiet, regular worshippers? Aren't we free already?

Well, perhaps we are more like prisoners than we care to think. Isn't it a fact that even the best of us still do need release from some sort of imprisonment? *You* will know, in your heart of hearts, whether this is so for you; and I will know, about myself, more than you can see. For instance, it might be that we're imprisoned in the fear of death. The Epistle to the Hebrews speaks of those who, through fear of death, have all their lifetime been subject to bondage, prisoners of fear. There are times when I know, myself, what that feels like, especially at my advanced age. Or perhaps the prison is something that prevents us from responding fully to the love of God and the love of our friends – some mistrust or underestimation of ourselves, possibly. Aren't we sometimes prisoners of *diffidence*? Or, for that matter, it might be the very opposite of diffidence – *over*-estimation of ourselves, which also can be very hampering. Or are we shackled by some *bad habit*? Or are we chained down by an unreadiness to forgive a wrong? *That's* a tragically common type of imprisonment. As a young curate in Rugby, I used to visit a picturesque old Irish lady, who used to reminisce about her stormy loves and the romances of her youth. And she always ended by saying: 'I can never forgive him, no never!' To her dying day, alas, I never managed to bring her to a better mind; she remained a prisoner. And so one might go on.

There are all sorts of circumstances from which the ardent love of God in Christ is yearning to release us if we can only believe the good news. When St Peter was in prison, in the story we heard just now (and yesterday, as it happens, was St Peter's Day), he couldn't at first believe it was true that he was being let out. He thought it was a dream. In the words from the letter to the Ephesians that were read just after that – words that might themselves possibly be a fragment of an early Christian hymn – the Christian believer is exhorted to wake up and respond to the light of Christ's presence: 'Awake, sleeper, rise from the dead, and Christ will shine upon you.'

The story in the Acts and the fragment of hymnody (if that's what it is) go hand in hand (it may be mere chance, but it's interesting that the Greek word for 'arise', in both passages, is a rather rare form of the word, which, in the whole New Testament, occurs only in those two places) and Charles Wesley's fourth verse has superbly caught the spiritual meaning of the Acts story, and turned it into an allegory in his hymn: 'Long my imprisoned spirit lay . . .'.

Perhaps here and now, perhaps some time soon when we can be quiet, we may ask God to show us if there is some prison in our lives from which we are being offered release. Does it sound too good to be true? Is it only a dream? It's true. It's an offer from God who, in Jesus Christ, has come to seek us out (as verse 3 affirms – another verse ringing with ideas from the Bible). He has come, he has searched for us, he has laid down his life for our release. Forgiveness, freedom from self, freedom from fear – all this can be ours, in Jesus Christ. Can we respond? Shall we have cause to thank him for showing us a picture of ourselves?

> My chains fell off, my heart was free,
> I rose, went forth, and followed Thee.

## 7  St Jude. Clare College, 2004

Today is the Festival of St Simon and St Jude. Of Simon, virtually nothing is known except that he had perhaps once been a 'freedom fighter', before becoming one of the Twelve. The name of Jude – apparently a brother of the Lord – is attached to one of the smallest and most obscure of the books of the New Testament. (Was it, do you think, only by chance that Thomas Hardy's obscure character was named Jude?)

The Epistle of Jude consists largely of a stern warning against immoral deviants who had infiltrated the Church; but the details are so obscure that they can hardly say very much to us. However, the Epistle closes, as we heard, with an ascription of glory to God which is of unsurpassable majesty:

> Now to the One who can keep you from falling and set you in the presence of his glory, jubilant and above reproach, to the only God our Saviour, be glory and majesty, might and authority, before all time, now, and for evermore. (neb)

Today is also a day of retrospect for us all. As we look back, how much of Jude's affirmation may we claim for ourselves? Kept from falling? Above reproach? Before we come to grips with such a question, let me say two things. First, how deeply grateful I am, and touched almost to tears, for the generosity of those who have devised this occasion, and how sorry I am not to be able to share it with you in person.

But, second, there is no denying that I am also embarrassed by it. Apart from the inestimable value of any Christian Eucharist, celebrated together by a gathering of friends, what in particular is this one but the celebration of a survival? And survival is something that a good many other Fellows of Clare have been rather good at, as well as being much more distinguished than this one. And besides, we all know Ben Jonson's observation: 'It is not growing like a tree / In bulk, doth make Man better be.' Bulk, in itself, is nothing to boast of.

Myself, being now almost 100 per cent sedentary, I am rather frightened at increasing bulk. Obviously, it's the quality of a life that matters, not its length or breadth. Indeed, a poignant part of retrospect is the loving remembrance of splendid friends who had comparatively short lives and who have gone before us. However, being generously offered the chance, of course I am eager to give thanks to God and to countless friends for the happiness that these years have brought, and the lessons they may teach, whether or not St Jude's exultant words apply. What an unbelievable privilege for a Christian minister to be pastor to a small, compact, accessible community! When I was made a Fellow there were – can you believe it? – only 20 of us. There were, I suppose, about 300 undergraduates and a comparatively small number of postgraduate students, and a moderate-sized domestic staff, and (I may add), at weekends, a handful of boisterous little boys, outrageously pirated by us from city parishes, without a by-your-leave to the incumbents, to provide trebles for the chapel choir, in the days before it became famous. What would not a parish priest today, struggling with six or seven whole parishes, give for so compact a community?

In addition to the pastoral privilege and inseparably entwined with it, there was also the lively interest of the academic life, continued and intensified after I ceased to be Dean but was still graciously accorded a Fellowship. Specially rewarding was the close friendship with a number of research students from all over the world, as we worked together for three or four years on some New Testament problem. The joy and pride of seeing them rise to positions of eminence and influence have been very great.

In addition, of course, there was the challenging privilege of living in the company of world experts in many different areas of learning (myself sometimes foolishly trying to conceal my own ignorance). There was also the aesthetic delight of living in lovely quarters (if, at times, a little austere), and in buildings of rare beauty, close to a garden second only to the Garden of Eden. Of course there were times of student unrest, and of anxiety, dissent and anger in the community; but who in the world could ask for a more privileged life? Such is my retrospect, and so it must be, *mutatis mutandis*, with many of you.

But what, then, of Jude's doxology? 'Without falling'? 'Above reproach'? For my part, nothing of the sort! I am only too conscious of lost opportunities, disgraceful self-love, and the many ugly deformities of sin. Perhaps you, too, must harbour some regrets for time past. I wonder, indeed, whether Jude's words (or perhaps the bit of liturgy he borrowed?) may have been meant to apply, not to a lifetime's expectations, but rather to the immediate crisis he was addressing. It may well be that the faithful could resist the particular temptation constituted by those heretics, and in that limited sense could stand firm and without reproach. That, however splendid, would be a different matter from claims for a lifetime of impeccable conduct.

What gives us hope for the outcome of our lives and makes room for ultimate confidence and exultation cannot be our own achievement but the sheer, unmerited love of God in Jesus Christ. He unites us as limbs in the Body of Christ, and from that we draw strength when our own stamina fails. He calls us to share the stability of being part of the Temple of God (as the Collect reminds us). He lifts us up again and again after every fall, and restores us to the family. There is a hint of all this in Jude's own 'keep yourselves in the love of God'; and the joy above all joys is that we need not – we must not – wait for Jude's doxology to be fully realized. It is on the love of God alone that we rely.

In Christ, God accepts us now, just as we are. We place ourselves (to echo the language of a famous prayer) rough-hewn into the hands of the Master Craftsman, and we ask him to wield well his tools, cost what it may. In a brief or a long life, early or – like St Augustine – 'too late, Lord', we place ourselves into his strong and gentle hands. If we will let him, he can shape us, rough-hewn though we still may be, into such a form as may stand before him at last, jubilant and without re-proach. For as often as we eat this bread and drink this cup, we declare the Lord's redeeming death, till he comes.

Thanks be to God!

*A sermon sent to be preached in Clare College Chapel at the commem-oration of his 60 years as a Fellow of the College, 28 October 2004.*

# Epilogue: Salute to the White Doves

O sweet White Doves! Mine is not the privilege of overlooking your mansion, but I do look out on one of your favourite stamping grounds, the lawn and the gravel. 'Stamping'? Say rather 'pattering' of little pink feet. You come in squads of ten or twelve to work the territory for tit-bits; but what you seem to like best is the underside of the mud-guards of the cars parked there. You stretch your delicate necks to peck at them. I have seen you even climb up on top of a tyre, to have a close encounter with its covering. Can it be that the tyres pick up tiny slugs and insects from the roads and carry them there? Often, your party includes a male, with his distinctively drooped wings and puffed-out breast, comically bowing and scraping and making a perfect nuisance of himself to the ladies – until he spies a specially luscious bit of food, when he will leave off courting and scratch it for himself from beneath your very beaks. I fear chivalry is not his job. Your morals are not impeccable (peckable?). There is one of you who dresses for all the world just like a wood pigeon, and another who sports one tell-tale dab of dark on her white. Do you know that we humans use the White Dove as a symbol of peace? When Noah sent a dove from the ark – whether white or not, who knows – she brought him an olive-twig, showing that the war was over and the drowning waters were receding. (Read Genesis 8.10, 11). Actually, however, I guess you are decidedly hawkish at heart (however much a peregrine falcon may despise you). Certainly your aerobatic displays are fierce and breathtaking, dashing and diving at top speed, seemingly for the sheer devilry of it. Encore! For entertainment value, Red Arrows aren't in it.

So, I salute you respectfully, and I salute those who look after you, as I salute the kind friends who patiently look after me.

*Charlie's room at the Old Vicarage had been the Vicar's study; it looked out over the main entrance and the big lawn and garden in front of the house, where he could see all the comings and goings and the antics of the White Doves, who lived in a cote behind the house. – PM*

CPSIA information can be obtained
at www.ICGtesting.com
Printed in the USA
BVHW03s0305100518
515823BV00003B/22/P